Love

Vol. 2

by

andi watson

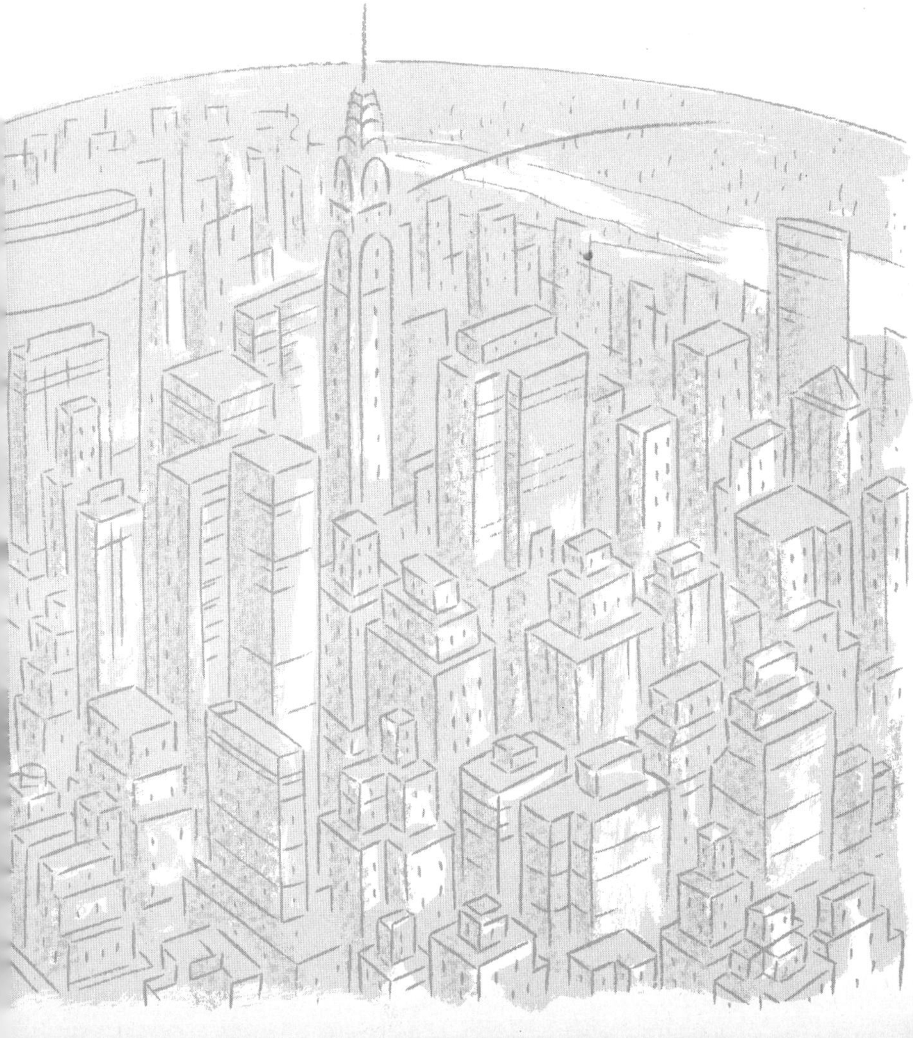

afterword by **Johanna Draper Carlson**

book design by **Keith Wood**
series edited by **Jamie S. Rich**
collection edited by **James Lucas Jones**

Woodercaps Font designed by **Woodrow Phoenix**

This book collects issues 7-12 of the Oni Press
comic book series *Love Fights*.

Published by Oni Press, Inc.
Joe Nozemack, publisher
James Lucas Jones, editor in chief
Randal Jarrell, managing editor

ONI PRESS, INC.
6336 SE Milwaukie Avenue, PMB30
Portland, OR 97202
USA

www.onipress.com
www.andiwatson.com

First edition: December 2004
ISBN 1-929998-87-2

1 3 5 7 9 10 8 6 4 2
PRINTED IN CANADA

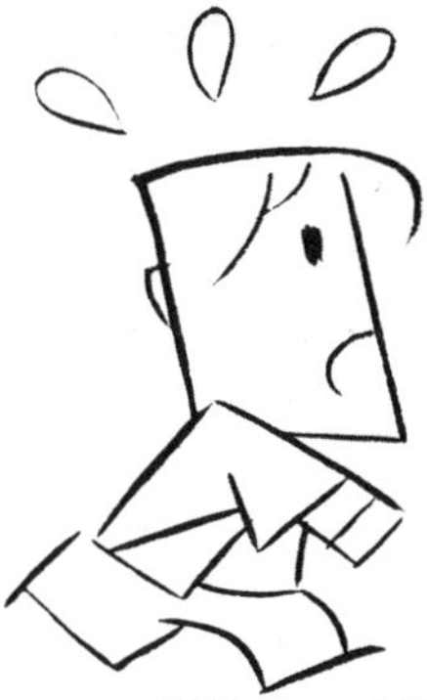

love

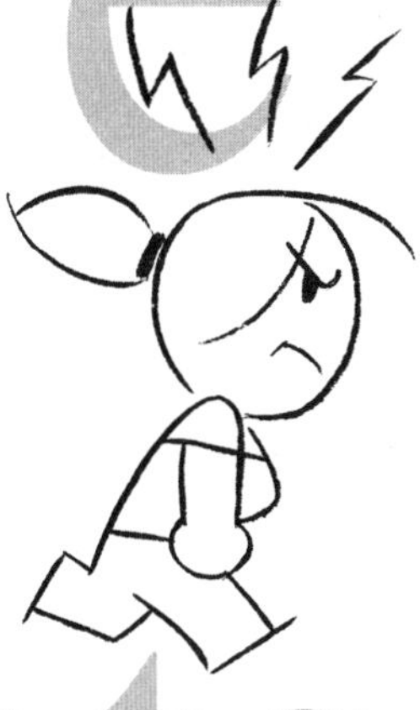

fights

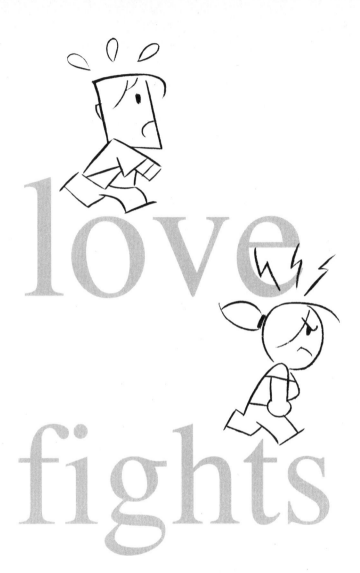

Love Fights ™
#7

andi watson

ONI PRESS
$2.99 U.S., $4.60 CAN.

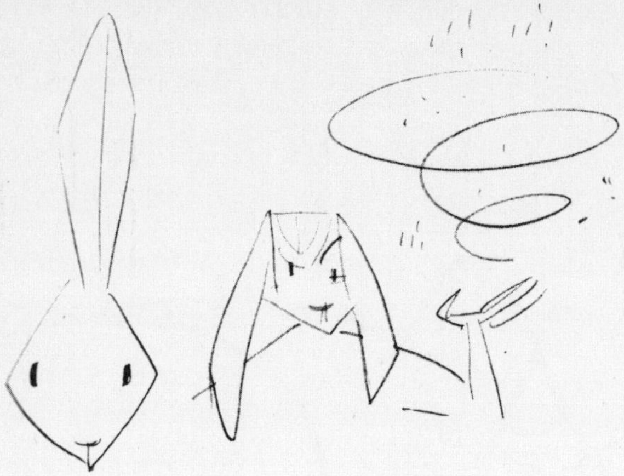

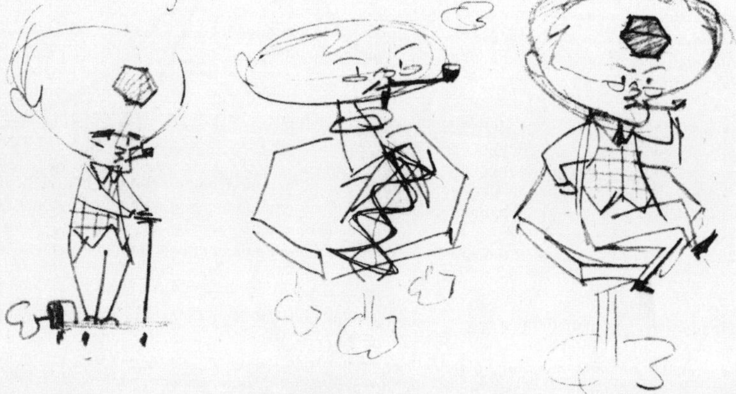
Dr. Hexagon

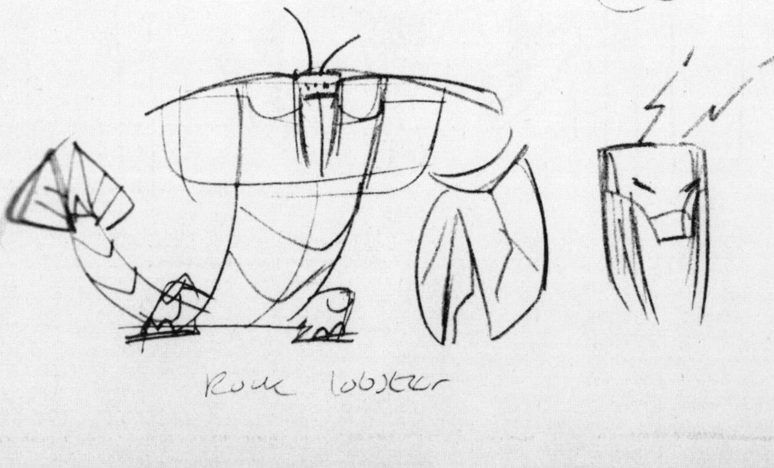
Rock lobster

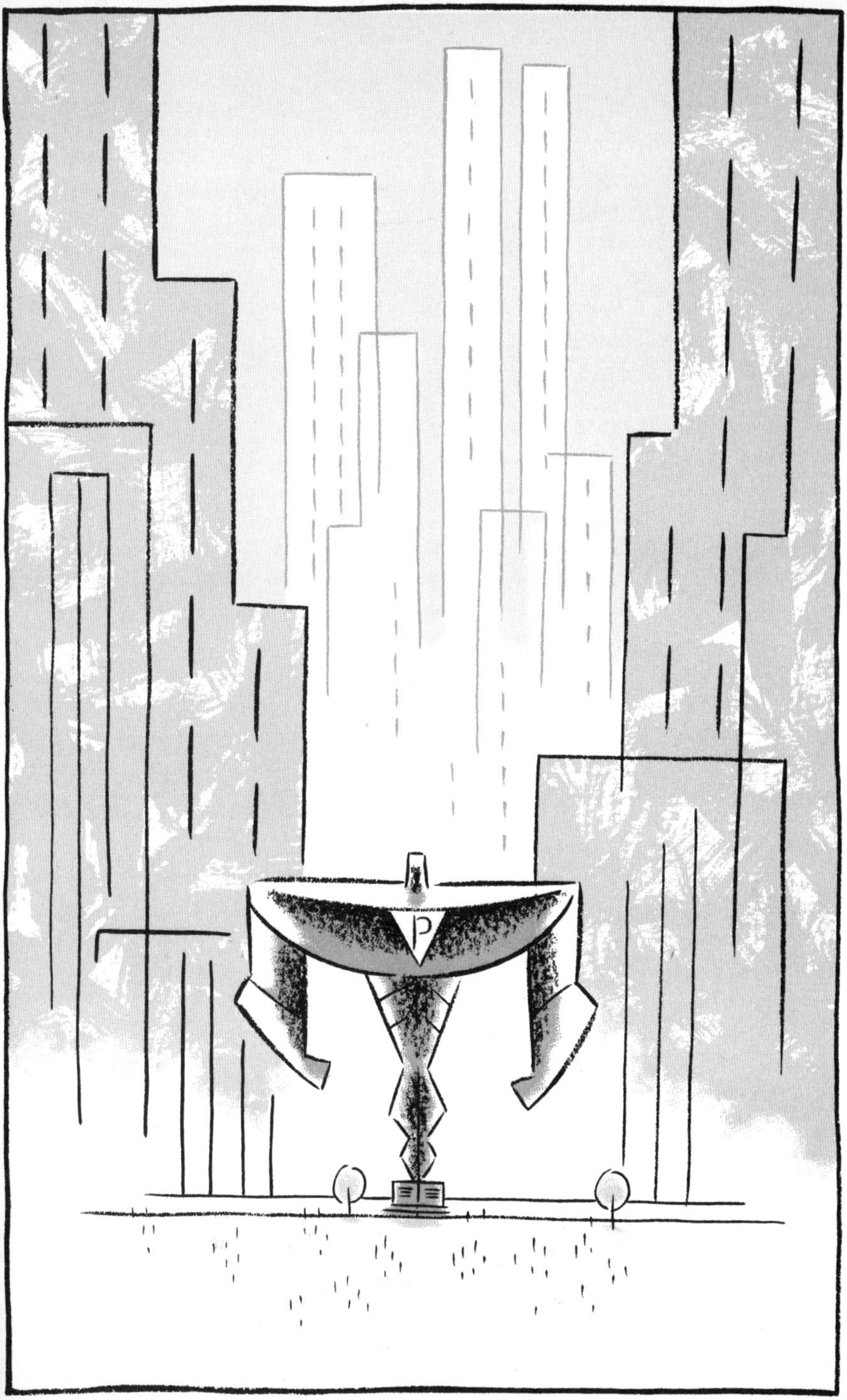

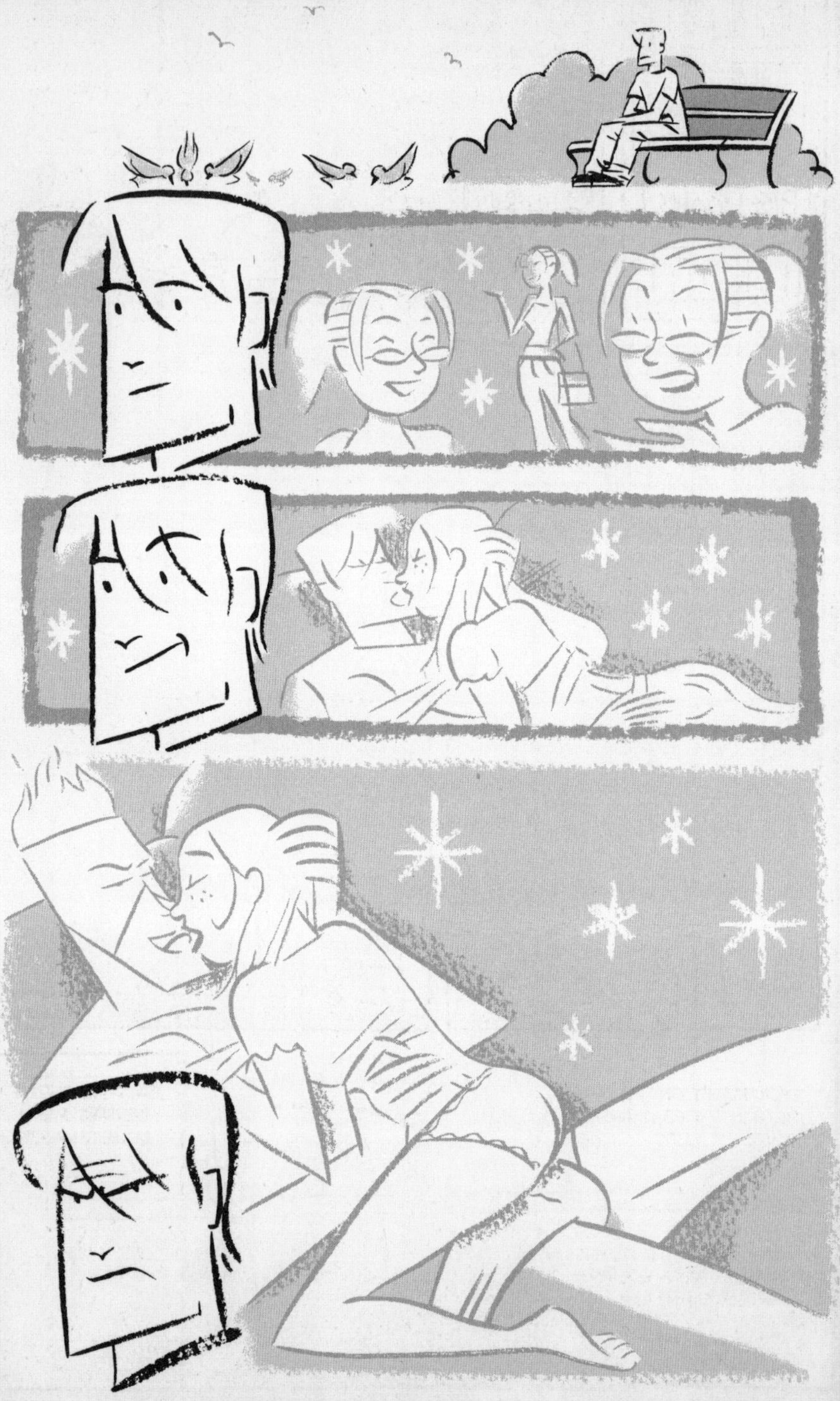

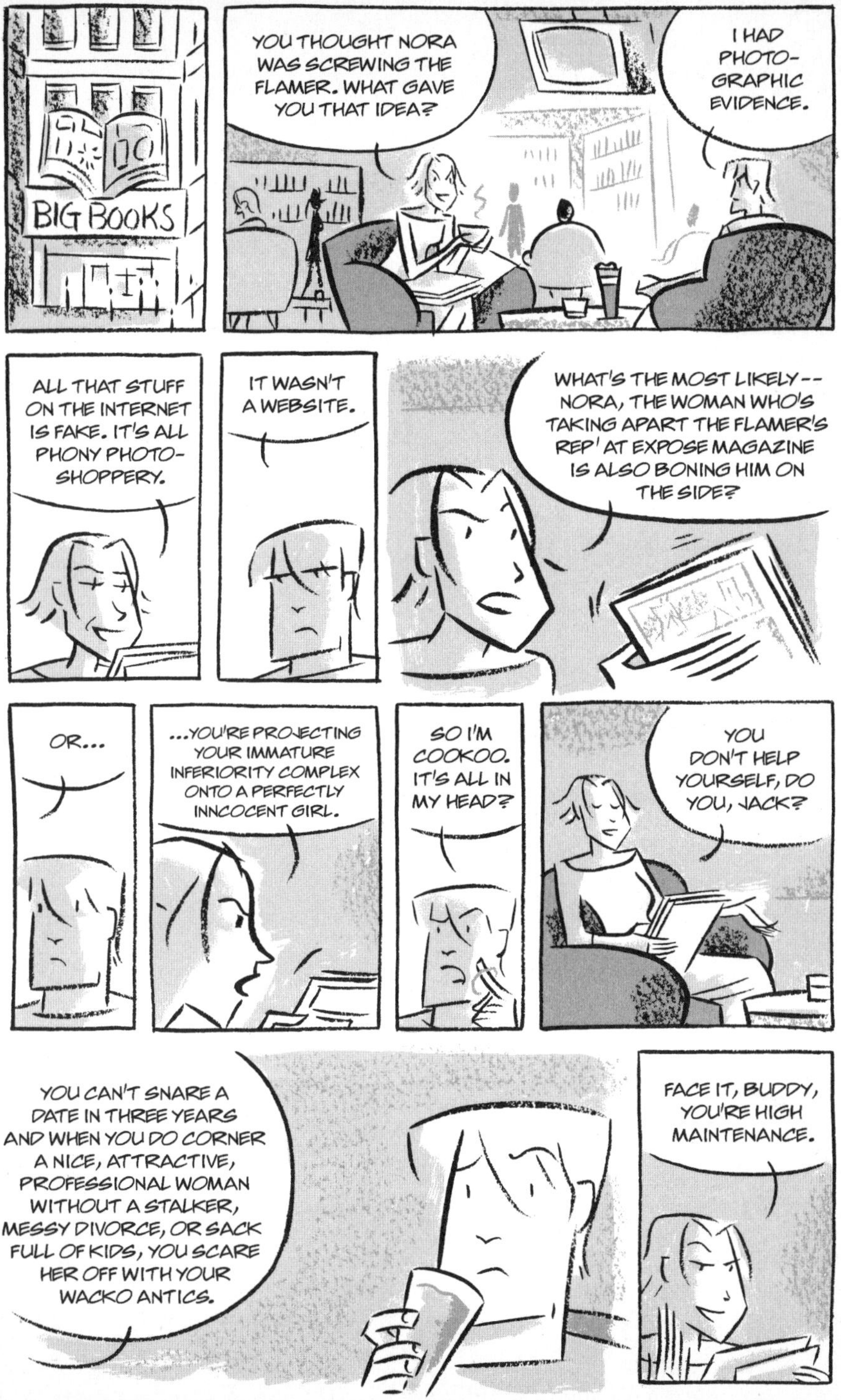
BIG BOOKS
YOU THOUGHT NORA WAS SCREWING THE FLAMER. WHAT GAVE YOU THAT IDEA?
I HAD PHOTO-GRAPHIC EVIDENCE.
ALL THAT STUFF ON THE INTERNET IS FAKE. IT'S ALL PHONY PHOTO-SHOPPERY.
IT WASN'T A WEBSITE.
WHAT'S THE MOST LIKELY-- NORA, THE WOMAN WHO'S TAKING APART THE FLAMER'S REP' AT EXPOSE MAGAZINE IS ALSO BONING HIM ON THE SIDE?
OR...
...YOU'RE PROJECTING YOUR IMMATURE INFERIORITY COMPLEX ONTO A PERFECTLY INNCOCENT GIRL.
SO I'M COOKOO. IT'S ALL IN MY HEAD?
YOU DON'T HELP YOURSELF, DO YOU, JACK?
YOU CAN'T SNARE A DATE IN THREE YEARS AND WHEN YOU DO CORNER A NICE, ATTRACTIVE, PROFESSIONAL WOMAN WITHOUT A STALKER, MESSY DIVORCE, OR SACK FULL OF KIDS, YOU SCARE HER OFF WITH YOUR WACKO ANTICS.
FACE IT, BUDDY, YOU'RE HIGH MAINTENANCE.

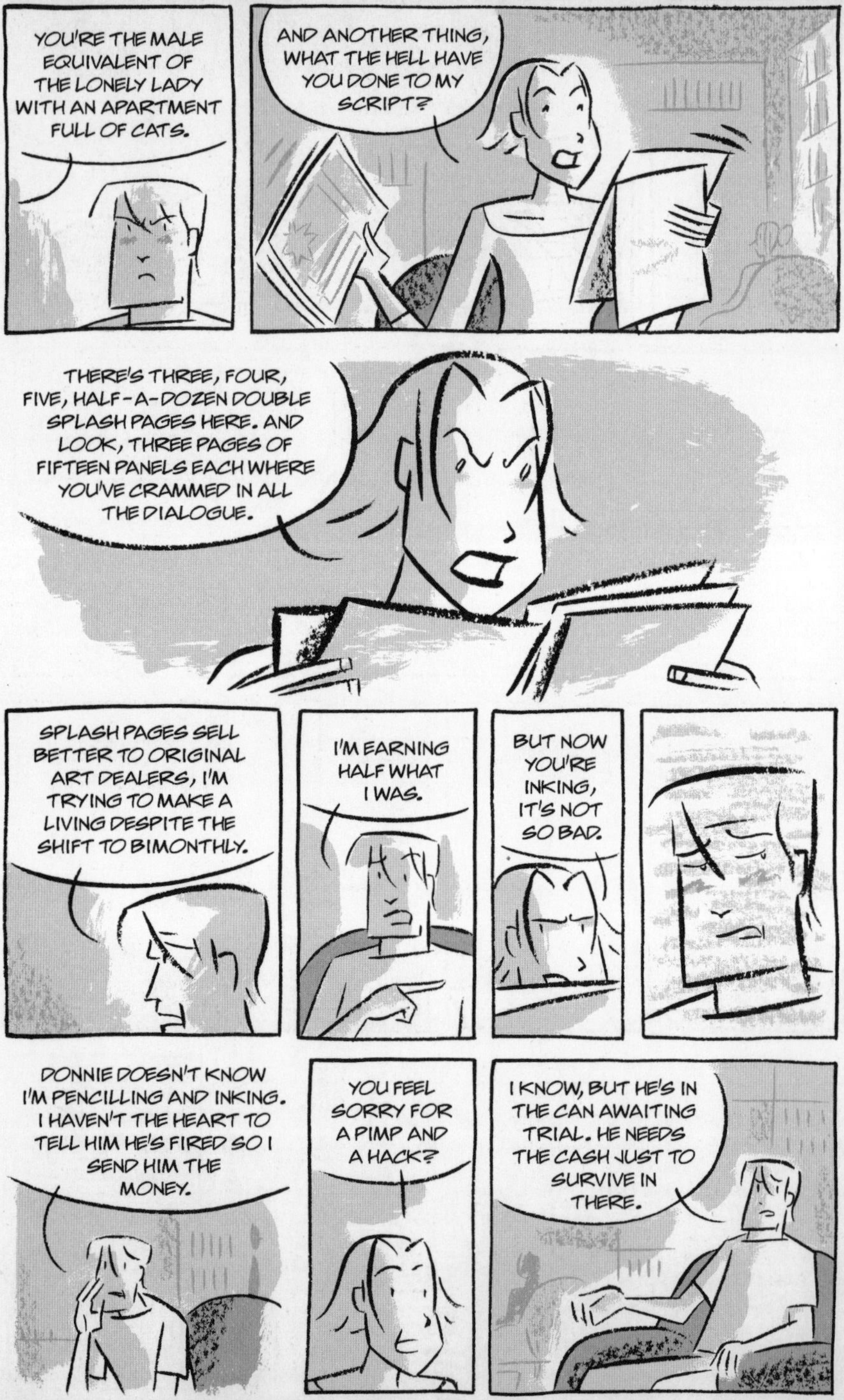
YOU'RE THE MALE EQUIVALENT OF THE LONELY LADY WITH AN APARTMENT FULL OF CATS.
AND ANOTHER THING, WHAT THE HELL HAVE YOU DONE TO MY SCRIPT?
THERE'S THREE, FOUR, FIVE, HALF-A-DOZEN DOUBLE SPLASH PAGES HERE. AND LOOK, THREE PAGES OF FIFTEEN PANELS EACH WHERE YOU'VE CRAMMED IN ALL THE DIALOGUE.
SPLASH PAGES SELL BETTER TO ORIGINAL ART DEALERS, I'M TRYING TO MAKE A LIVING DESPITE THE SHIFT TO BIMONTHLY.
I'M EARNING HALF WHAT I WAS.
BUT NOW YOU'RE INKING, IT'S NOT SO BAD.
DONNIE DOESN'T KNOW I'M PENCILLING AND INKING. I HAVEN'T THE HEART TO TELL HIM HE'S FIRED SO I SEND HIM THE MONEY.
YOU FEEL SORRY FOR A PIMP AND A HACK?
I KNOW, BUT HE'S IN THE CAN AWAITING TRIAL. HE NEEDS THE CASH JUST TO SURVIVE IN THERE.

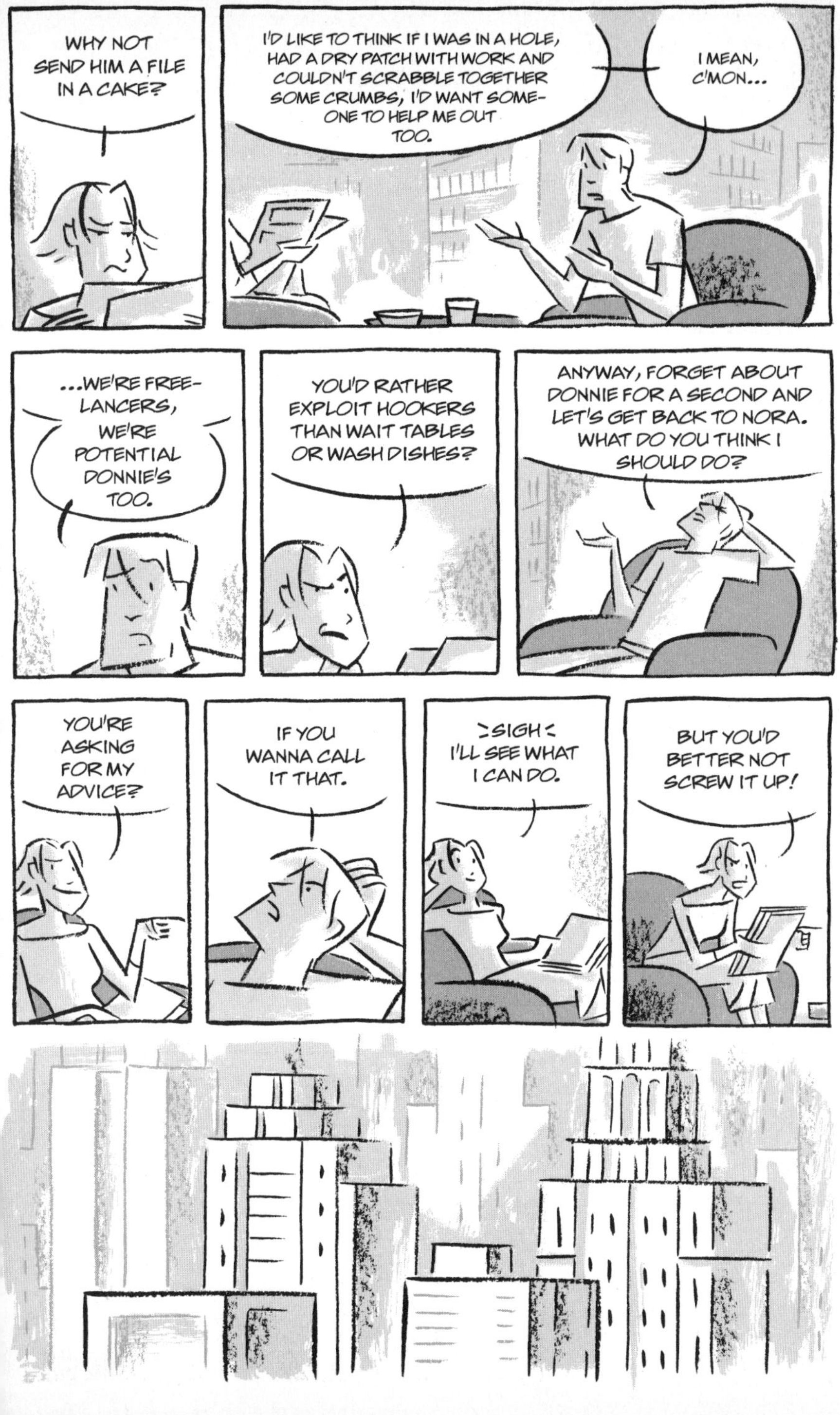
WHY NOT SEND HIM A FILE IN A CAKE?
I'D LIKE TO THINK IF I WAS IN A HOLE, HAD A DRY PATCH WITH WORK AND COULDN'T SCRABBLE TOGETHER SOME CRUMBS, I'D WANT SOME-ONE TO HELP ME OUT TOO.
I MEAN, C'MON...
...WE'RE FREE-LANCERS, WE'RE POTENTIAL DONNIE'S TOO.
YOU'D RATHER EXPLOIT HOOKERS THAN WAIT TABLES OR WASH DISHES?
ANYWAY, FORGET ABOUT DONNIE FOR A SECOND AND LET'S GET BACK TO NORA. WHAT DO YOU THINK I SHOULD DO?
YOU'RE ASKING FOR MY ADVICE?
IF YOU WANNA CALL IT THAT.
>SIGH< I'LL SEE WHAT I CAN DO.
BUT YOU'D BETTER NOT SCREW IT UP!

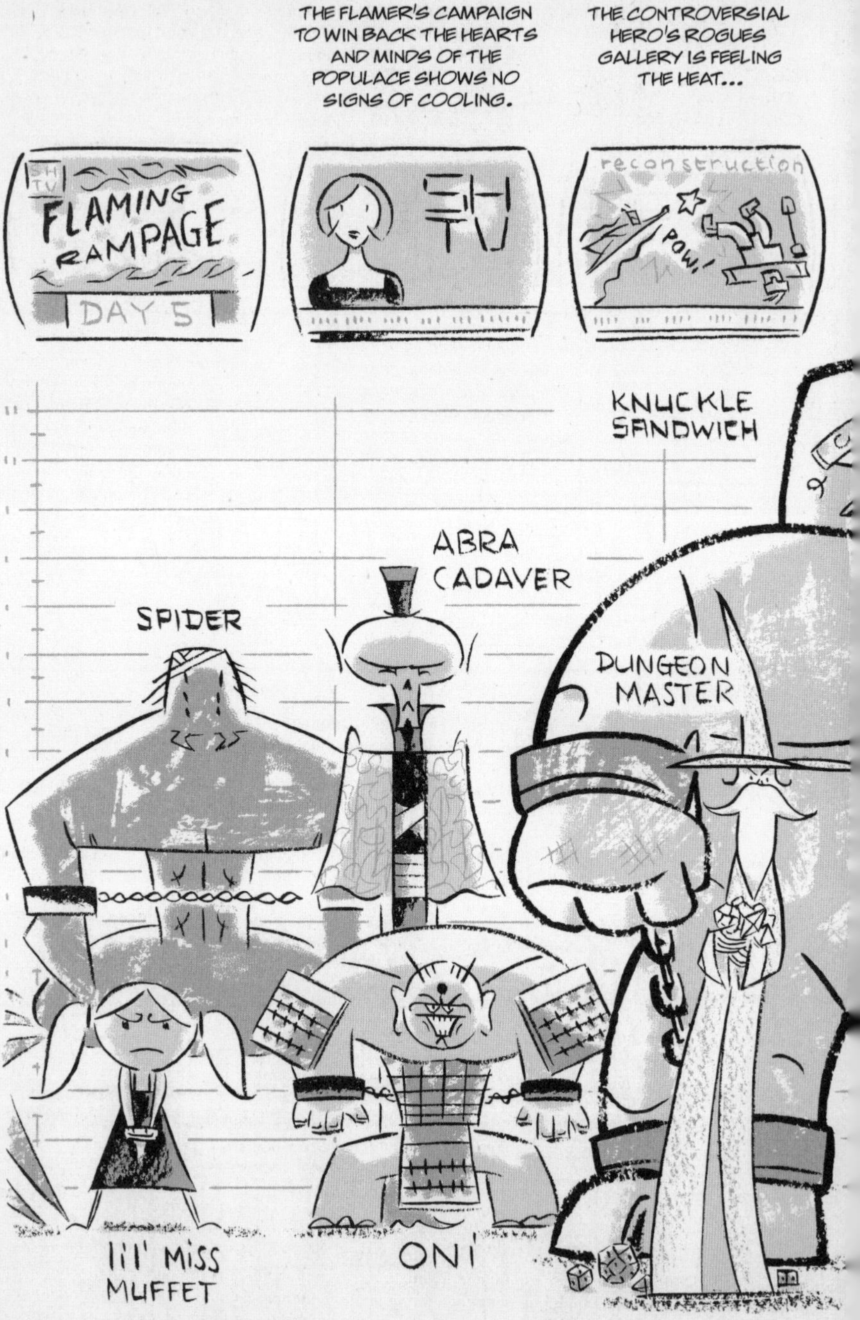
THE FLAMER'S CAMPAIGN TO WIN BACK THE HEARTS AND MINDS OF THE POPULACE SHOWS NO SIGNS OF COOLING.
THE CONTROVERSIAL HERO'S ROGUES GALLERY IS FEELING THE HEAT...
SH TV
FLAMING RAMPAGE
DAY 5
SH TV
reconstruction
POW!
KNUCKLE SANDWICH
ABRA CADAVER
SPIDER
DUNGEON MASTER
lil' MISS MUFFET
ONI

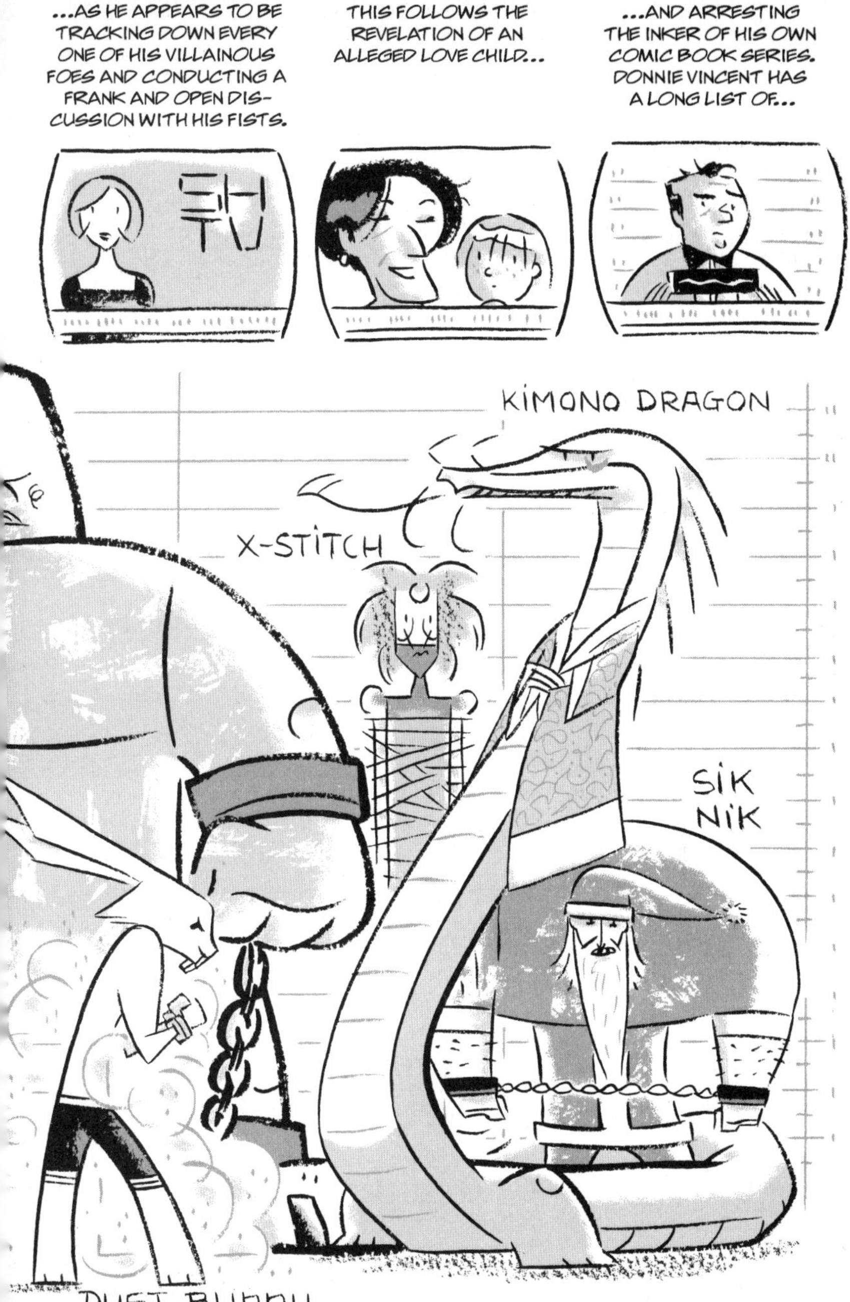
...AS HE APPEARS TO BE TRACKING DOWN EVERY ONE OF HIS VILLAINOUS FOES AND CONDUCTING A FRANK AND OPEN DISCUSSION WITH HIS FISTS.
THIS FOLLOWS THE REVELATION OF AN ALLEGED LOVE CHILD...
...AND ARRESTING THE INKER OF HIS OWN COMIC BOOK SERIES. DONNIE VINCENT HAS A LONG LIST OF...
KIMONO DRAGON
X-STITCH
SIK NIK...
DUST BUNNY

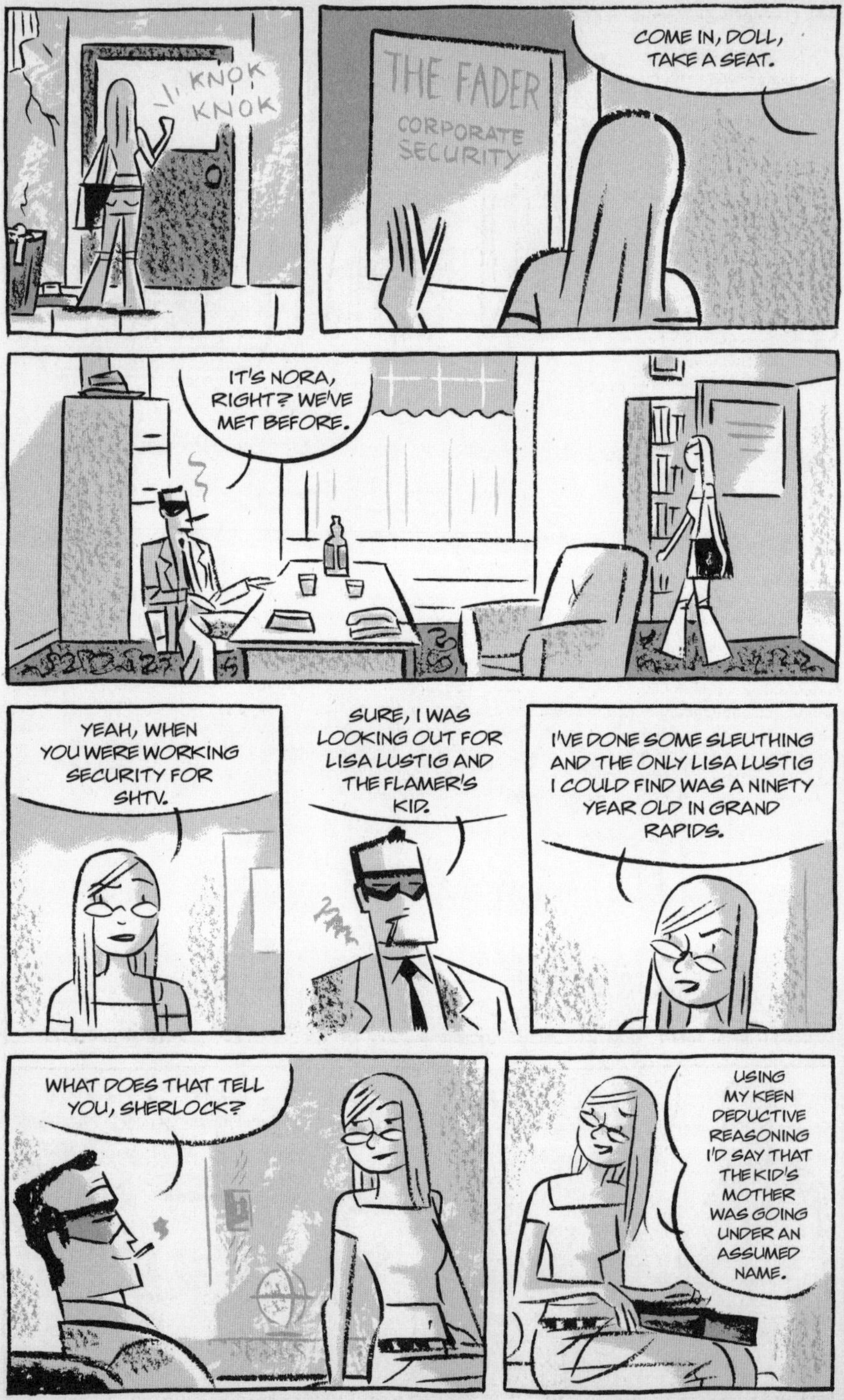
KNOK KNOK
THE FADER CORPORATE SECURITY
COME IN, DOLL, TAKE A SEAT.
IT'S NORA, RIGHT? WE'VE MET BEFORE.
YEAH, WHEN YOU WERE WORKING SECURITY FOR SHTV.
SURE, I WAS LOOKING OUT FOR LISA LUSTIG AND THE FLAMER'S KID.
I'VE DONE SOME SLEUTHING AND THE ONLY LISA LUSTIG I COULD FIND WAS A NINETY YEAR OLD IN GRAND RAPIDS.
WHAT DOES THAT TELL YOU, SHERLOCK?
USING MY KEEN DEDUCTIVE REASONING I'D SAY THAT THE KID'S MOTHER WAS GOING UNDER AN ASSUMED NAME.

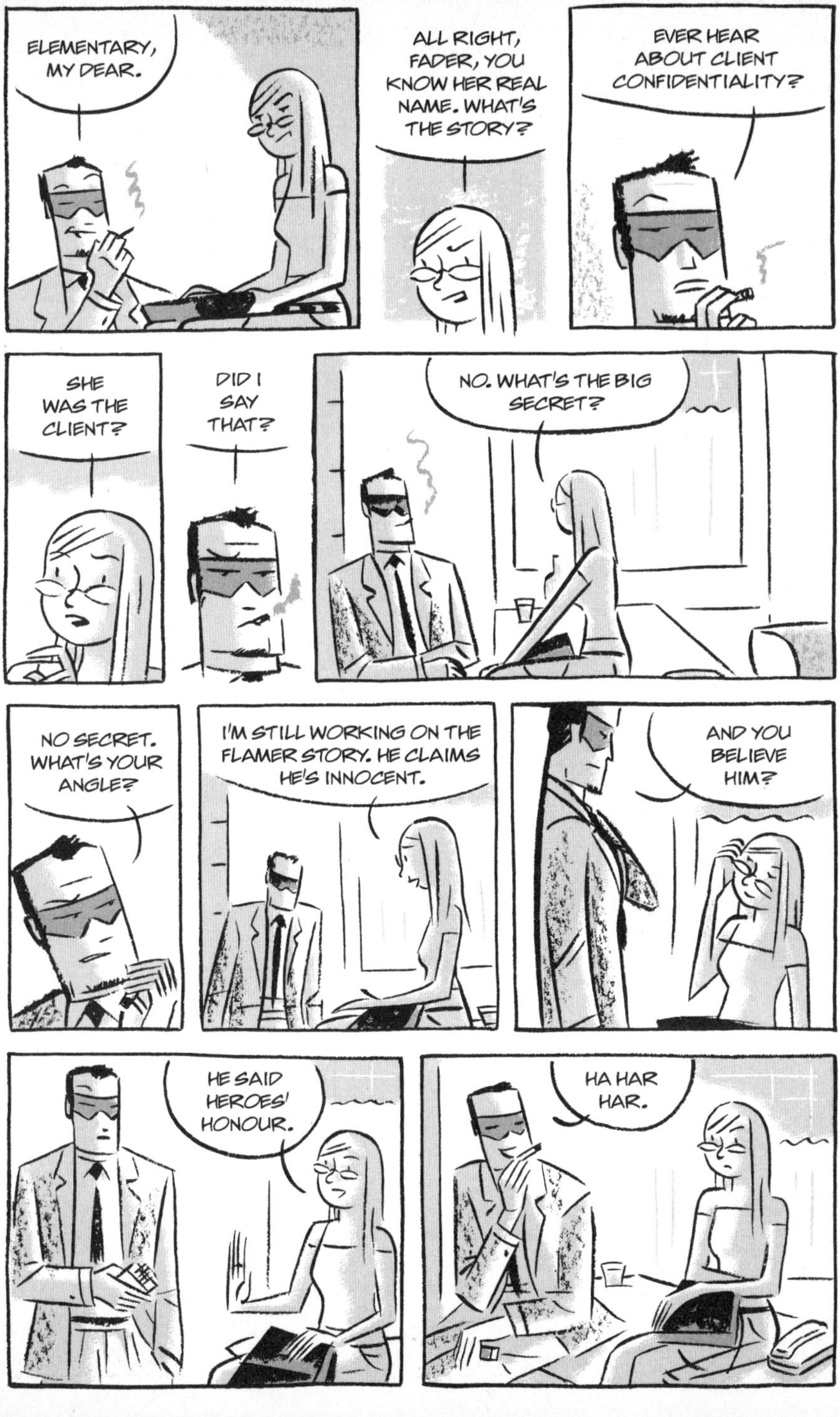
ELEMENTARY, MY DEAR.
ALL RIGHT, FADER, YOU KNOW HER REAL NAME. WHAT'S THE STORY?
EVER HEAR ABOUT CLIENT CONFIDENTIALITY?
SHE WAS THE CLIENT?
DID I SAY THAT?
NO. WHAT'S THE BIG SECRET?
NO SECRET. WHAT'S YOUR ANGLE?
I'M STILL WORKING ON THE FLAMER STORY. HE CLAIMS HE'S INNOCENT.
AND YOU BELIEVE HIM?
HE SAID HEROES' HONOUR.
HA HAR HAR.

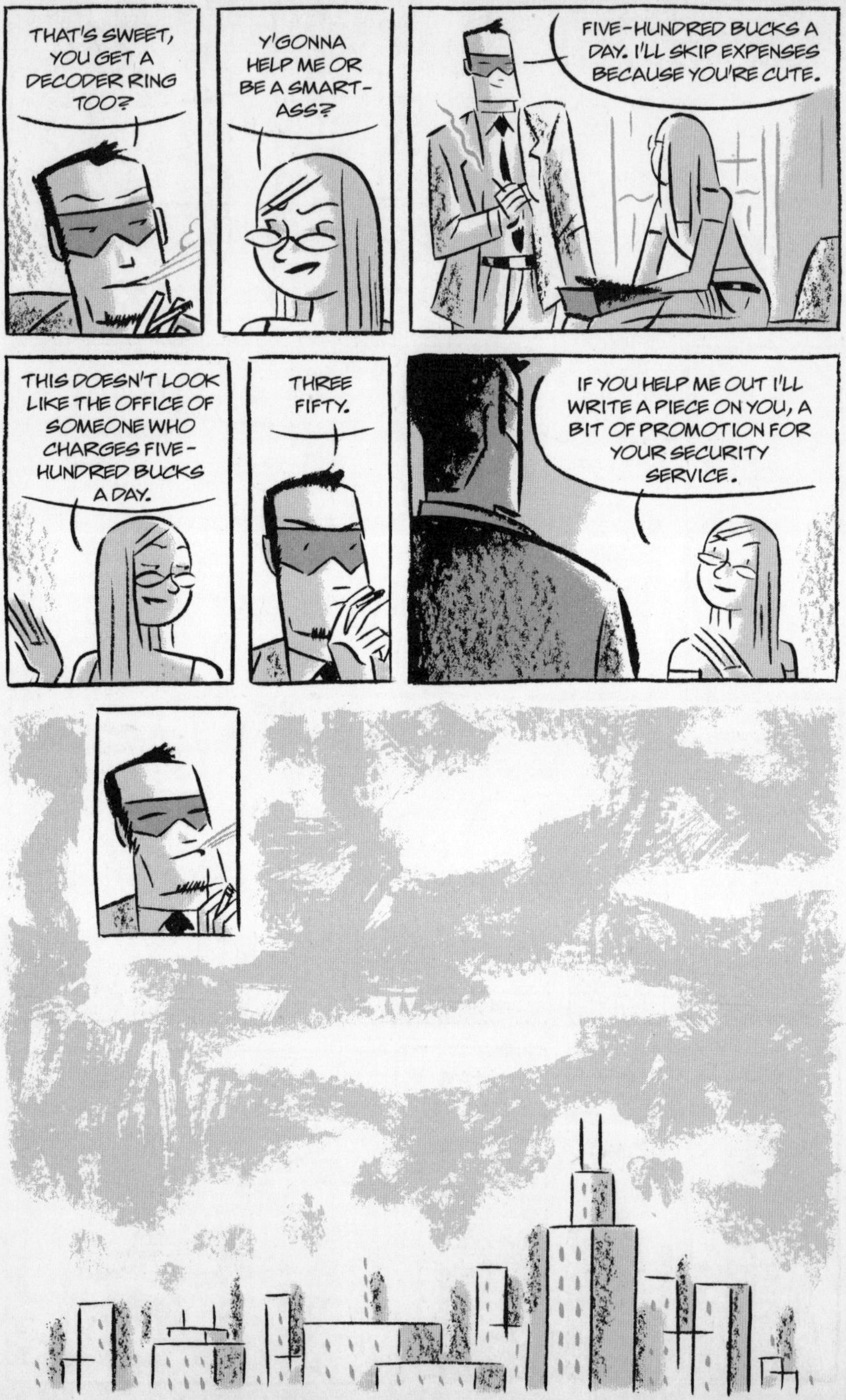
THAT'S SWEET, YOU GET A DECODER RING TOO?
Y'GONNA HELP ME OR BE A SMART-ASS?
FIVE-HUNDRED BUCKS A DAY. I'LL SKIP EXPENSES BECAUSE YOU'RE CUTE.
THIS DOESN'T LOOK LIKE THE OFFICE OF SOMEONE WHO CHARGES FIVE-HUNDRED BUCKS A DAY.
THREE FIFTY.
IF YOU HELP ME OUT I'LL WRITE A PIECE ON YOU, A BIT OF PROMOTION FOR YOUR SECURITY SERVICE.

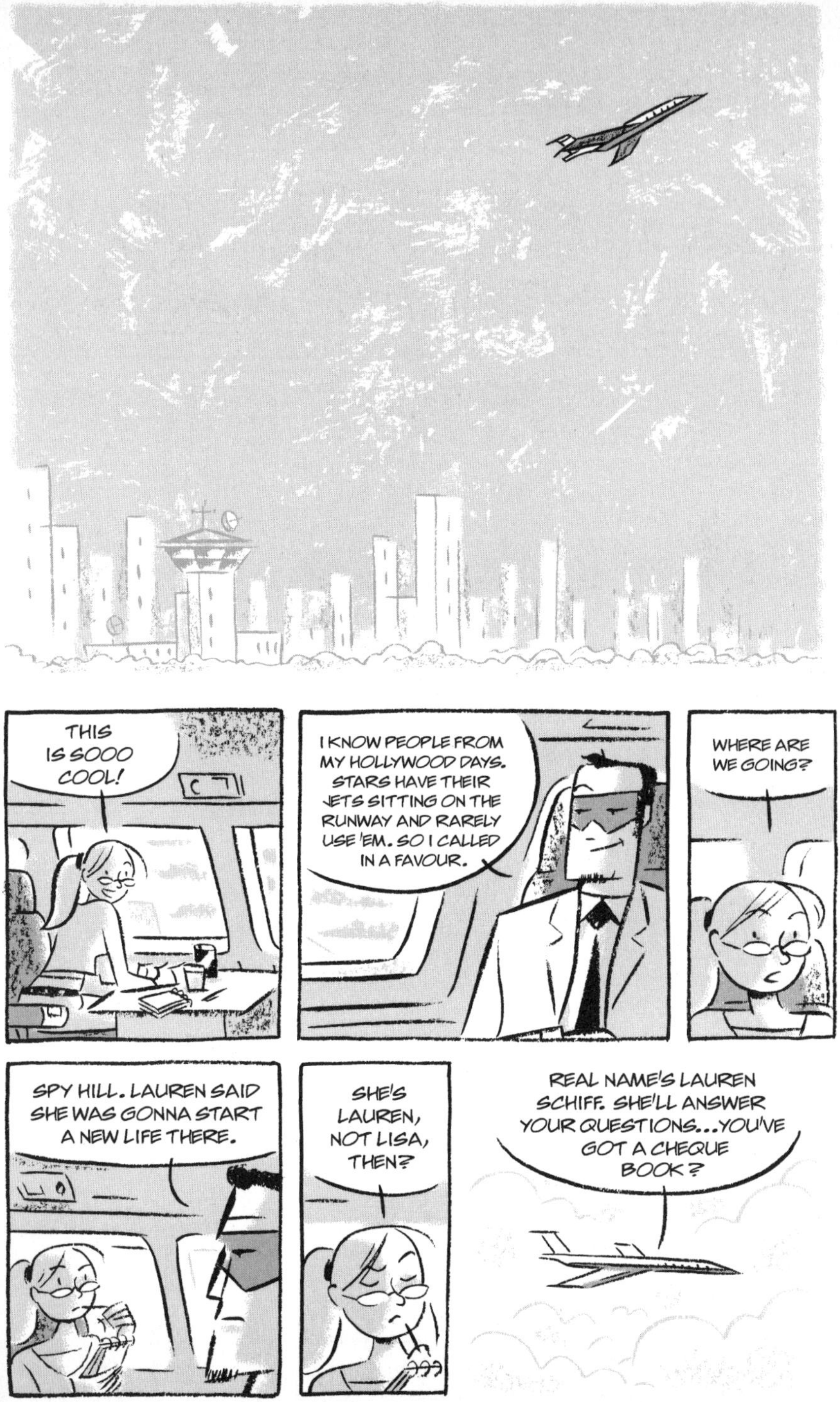
THIS IS SOOO COOL!
I KNOW PEOPLE FROM MY HOLLYWOOD DAYS. STARS HAVE THEIR JETS SITTING ON THE RUNWAY AND RARELY USE 'EM. SO I CALLED IN A FAVOUR.
WHERE ARE WE GOING?
SPY HILL. LAUREN SAID SHE WAS GONNA START A NEW LIFE THERE.
SHE'S LAUREN, NOT LISA, THEN?
REAL NAME'S LAUREN SCHIFF. SHE'LL ANSWER YOUR QUESTIONS...YOU'VE GOT A CHEQUE BOOK?

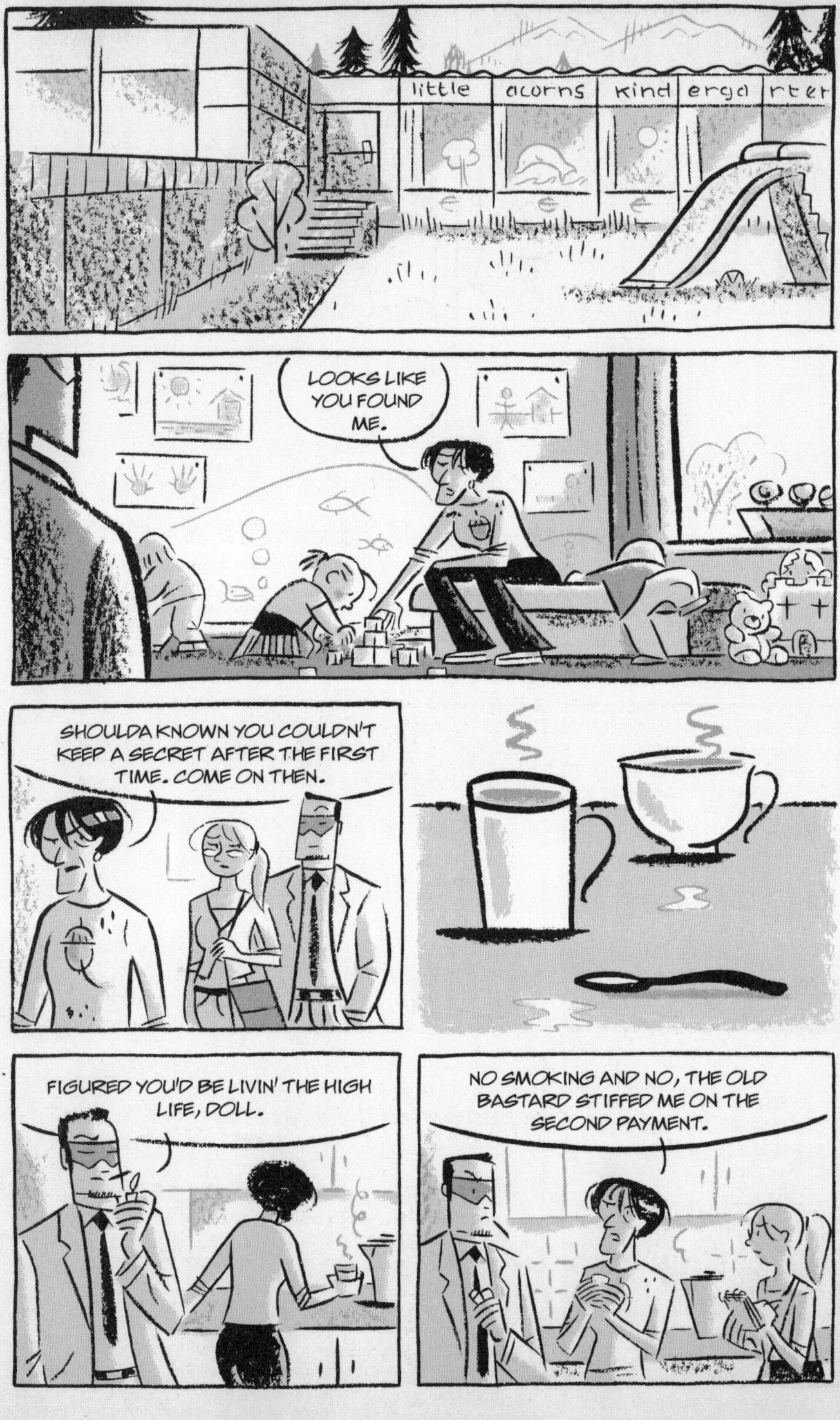
little acorns kindergarter
LOOKS LIKE YOU FOUND ME.
SHOULDA KNOWN YOU COULDN'T KEEP A SECRET AFTER THE FIRST TIME. COME ON THEN.
FIGURED YOU'D BE LIVIN' THE HIGH LIFE, DOLL.
NO SMOKING AND NO, THE OLD BASTARD STIFFED ME ON THE SECOND PAYMENT.

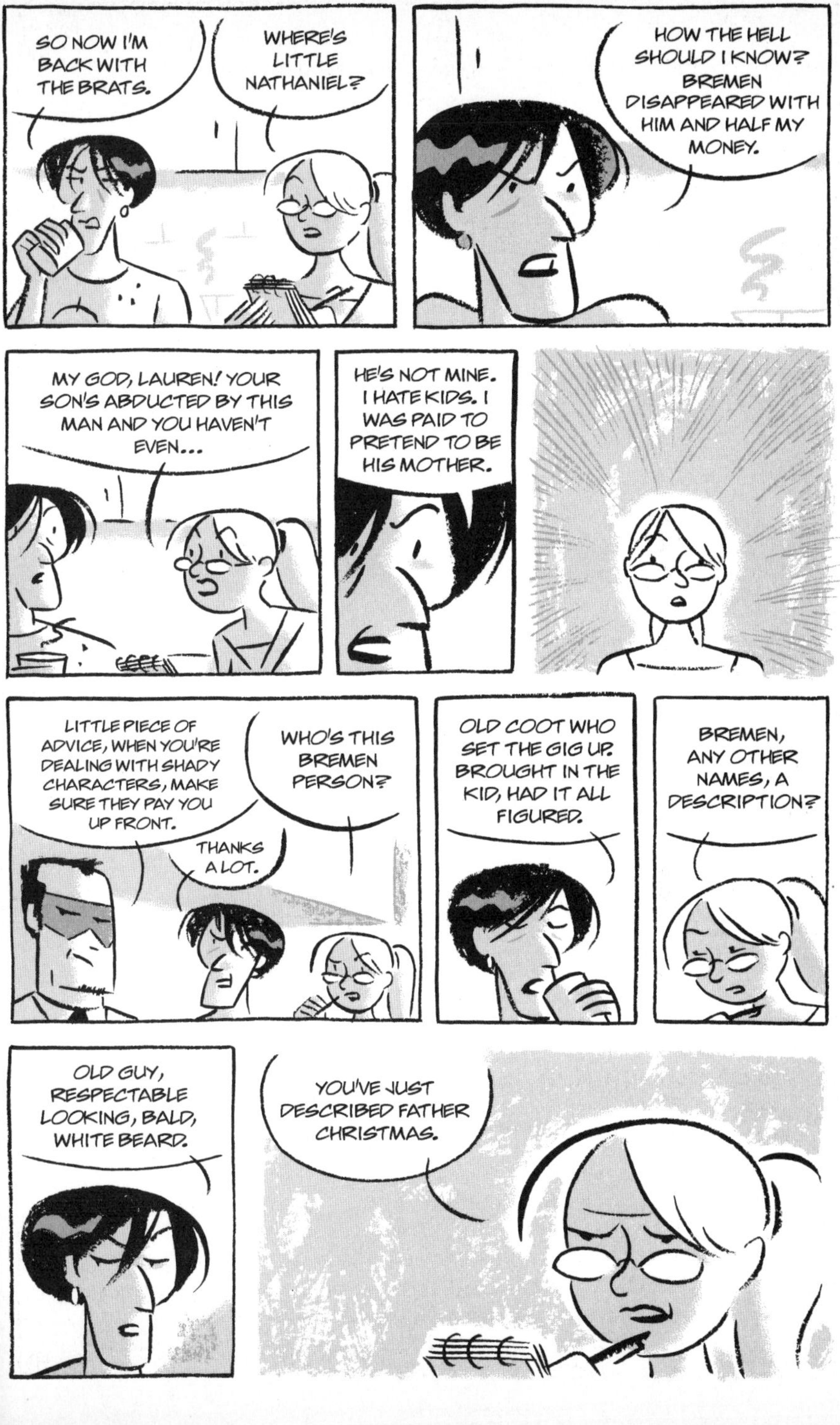
SO NOW I'M BACK WITH THE BRATS.
WHERE'S LITTLE NATHANIEL?
HOW THE HELL SHOULD I KNOW? BREMEN DISAPPEARED WITH HIM AND HALF MY MONEY.
MY GOD, LAUREN! YOUR SON'S ABDUCTED BY THIS MAN AND YOU HAVEN'T EVEN...
HE'S NOT MINE. I HATE KIDS. I WAS PAID TO PRETEND TO BE HIS MOTHER.
LITTLE PIECE OF ADVICE, WHEN YOU'RE DEALING WITH SHADY CHARACTERS, MAKE SURE THEY PAY YOU UP FRONT.
THANKS A LOT.
WHO'S THIS BREMEN PERSON?
OLD COOT WHO SET THE GIG UP. BROUGHT IN THE KID, HAD IT ALL FIGURED.
BREMEN, ANY OTHER NAMES, A DESCRIPTION?
OLD GUY, RESPECTABLE LOOKING, BALD, WHITE BEARD.
YOU'VE JUST DESCRIBED FATHER CHRISTMAS.

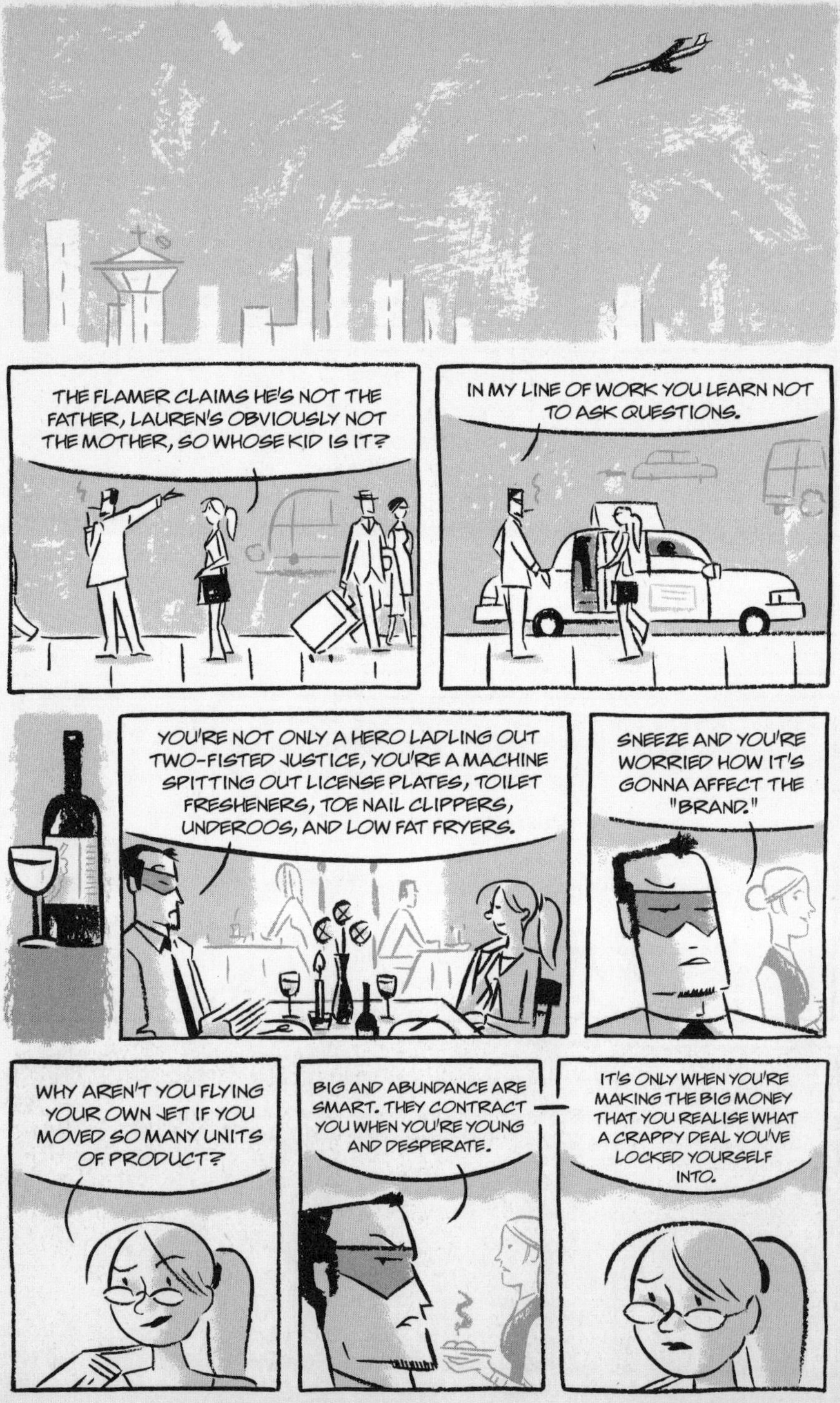
THE FLAMER CLAIMS HE'S NOT THE FATHER, LAUREN'S OBVIOUSLY NOT THE MOTHER, SO WHOSE KID IS IT?
IN MY LINE OF WORK YOU LEARN NOT TO ASK QUESTIONS.
YOU'RE NOT ONLY A HERO LADLING OUT TWO-FISTED JUSTICE, YOU'RE A MACHINE SPITTING OUT LICENSE PLATES, TOILET FRESHENERS, TOE NAIL CLIPPERS, UNDEROOS, AND LOW FAT FRYERS.
SNEEZE AND YOU'RE WORRIED HOW IT'S GONNA AFFECT THE "BRAND."
WHY AREN'T YOU FLYING YOUR OWN JET IF YOU MOVED SO MANY UNITS OF PRODUCT?
BIG AND ABUNDANCE ARE SMART. THEY CONTRACT YOU WHEN YOU'RE YOUNG AND DESPERATE.
IT'S ONLY WHEN YOU'RE MAKING THE BIG MONEY THAT YOU REALISE WHAT A CRAPPY DEAL YOU'VE LOCKED YOURSELF INTO.

SO YOU DECIDED TO GO FREELANCE?

COULDN'T AFFORD TO BUY OUT MY CONTRACT SO I BROKE IT AND GOT WORKED OVER BY THE LAWYERS.

WHAT ABOUT YOU, GOT A SQUEEZE?

I WAS SEEING THIS GUY.

TURNS OUT HE HAS ISSUES.

TOO BAD.

SHALL I ORDER ANOTHER BOTTLE?

SURE, WHY NOT.

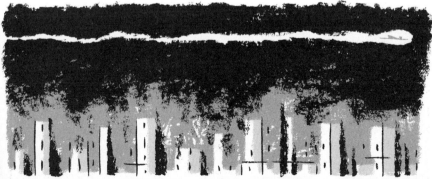

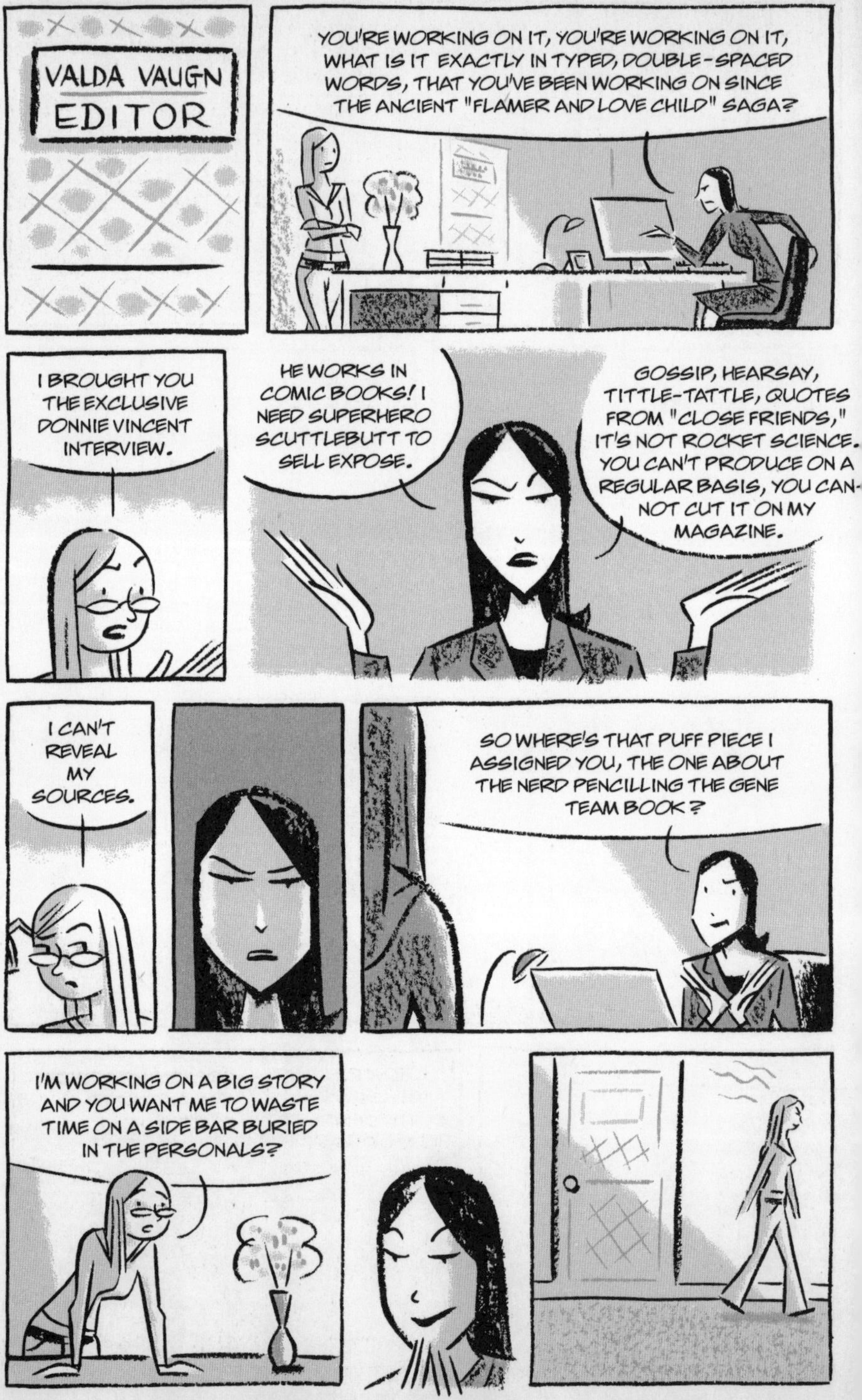
VALDA VAUGN
EDITOR
YOU'RE WORKING ON IT, YOU'RE WORKING ON IT, WHAT IS IT EXACTLY IN TYPED, DOUBLE-SPACED WORDS, THAT YOU'VE BEEN WORKING ON SINCE THE ANCIENT "FLAMER AND LOVE CHILD" SAGA?
I BROUGHT YOU THE EXCLUSIVE DONNIE VINCENT INTERVIEW.
HE WORKS IN COMIC BOOKS! I NEED SUPERHERO SCUTTLEBUTT TO SELL EXPOSE.
GOSSIP, HEARSAY, TITTLE-TATTLE, QUOTES FROM "CLOSE FRIENDS," IT'S NOT ROCKET SCIENCE. YOU CAN'T PRODUCE ON A REGULAR BASIS, YOU CANNOT CUT IT ON MY MAGAZINE.
I CAN'T REVEAL MY SOURCES.
SO WHERE'S THAT PUFF PIECE I ASSIGNED YOU, THE ONE ABOUT THE NERD PENCILLING THE GENE TEAM BOOK?
I'M WORKING ON A BIG STORY AND YOU WANT ME TO WASTE TIME ON A SIDE BAR BURIED IN THE PERSONALS?

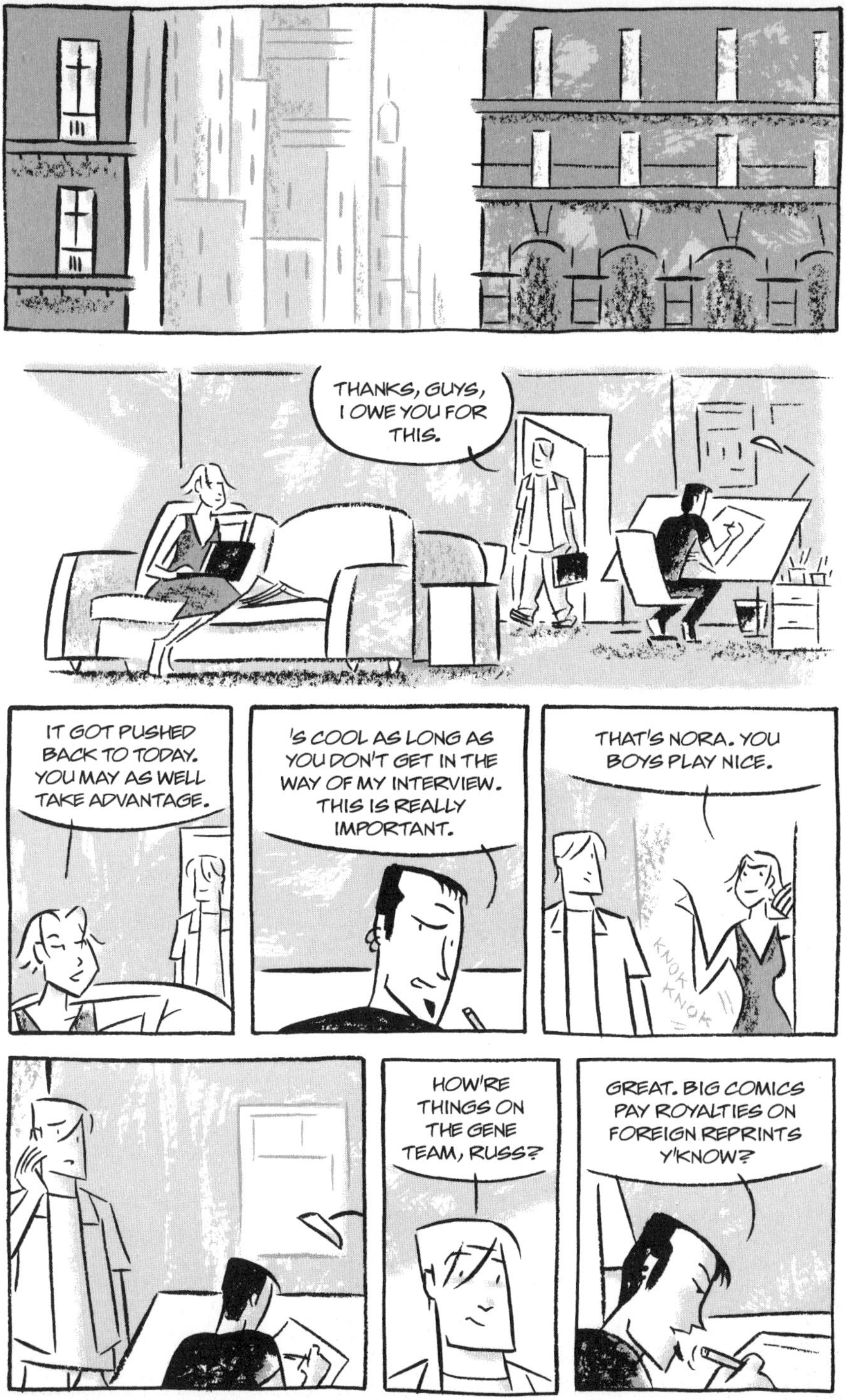
THANKS, GUYS, I OWE YOU FOR THIS.
IT GOT PUSHED BACK TO TODAY. YOU MAY AS WELL TAKE ADVANTAGE.
'S COOL AS LONG AS YOU DON'T GET IN THE WAY OF MY INTERVIEW. THIS IS REALLY IMPORTANT.
THAT'S NORA. YOU BOYS PLAY NICE.
KNOK KNOK
HOW'RE THINGS ON THE GENE TEAM, RUSS?
GREAT. BIG COMICS PAY ROYALTIES ON FOREIGN REPRINTS Y'KNOW?

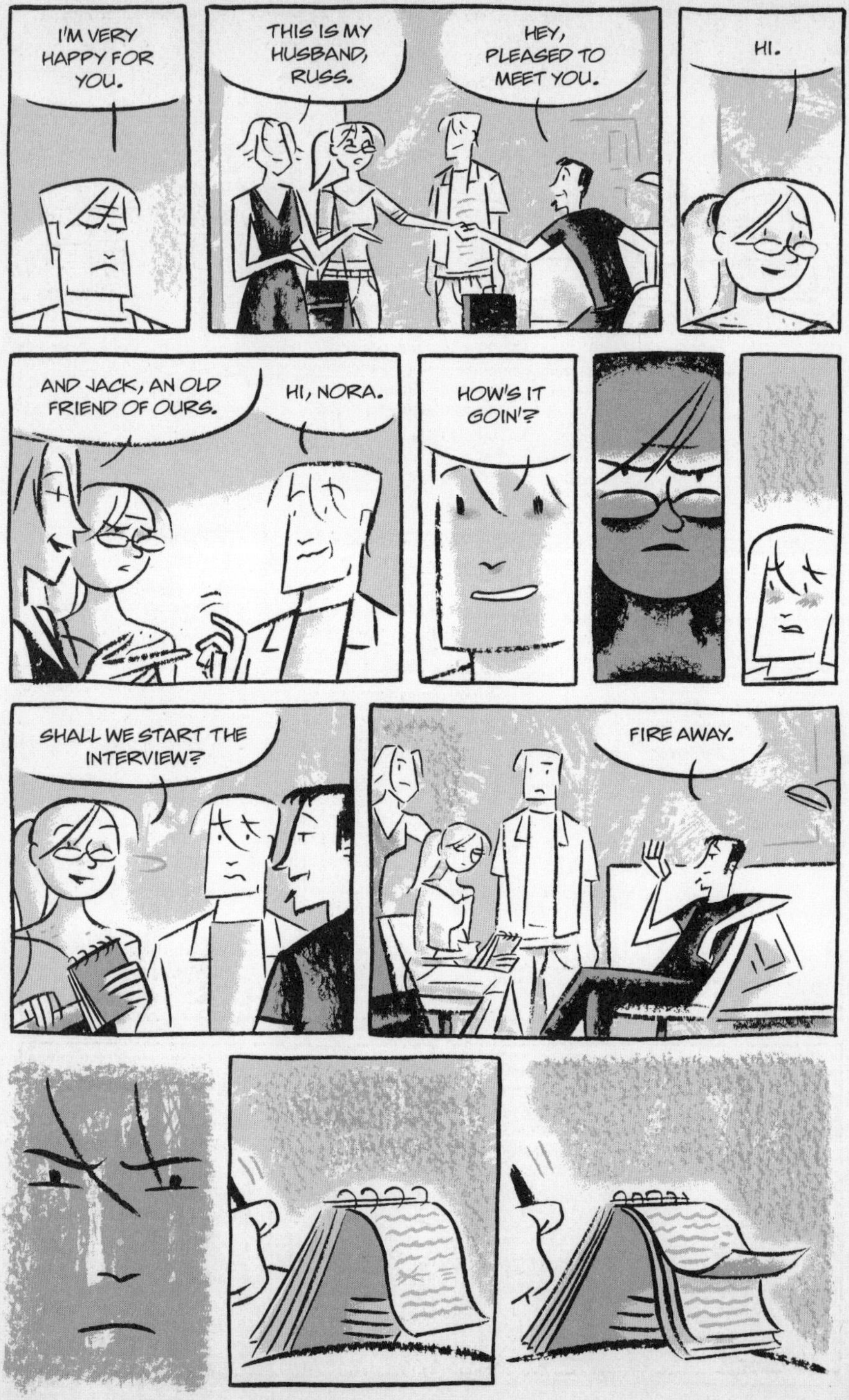
I'M VERY HAPPY FOR YOU.
THIS IS MY HUSBAND, RUSS.
HEY, PLEASED TO MEET YOU.
HI.
AND JACK, AN OLD FRIEND OF OURS.
HI, NORA.
HOW'S IT GOIN'?
SHALL WE START THE INTERVIEW?
FIRE AWAY.

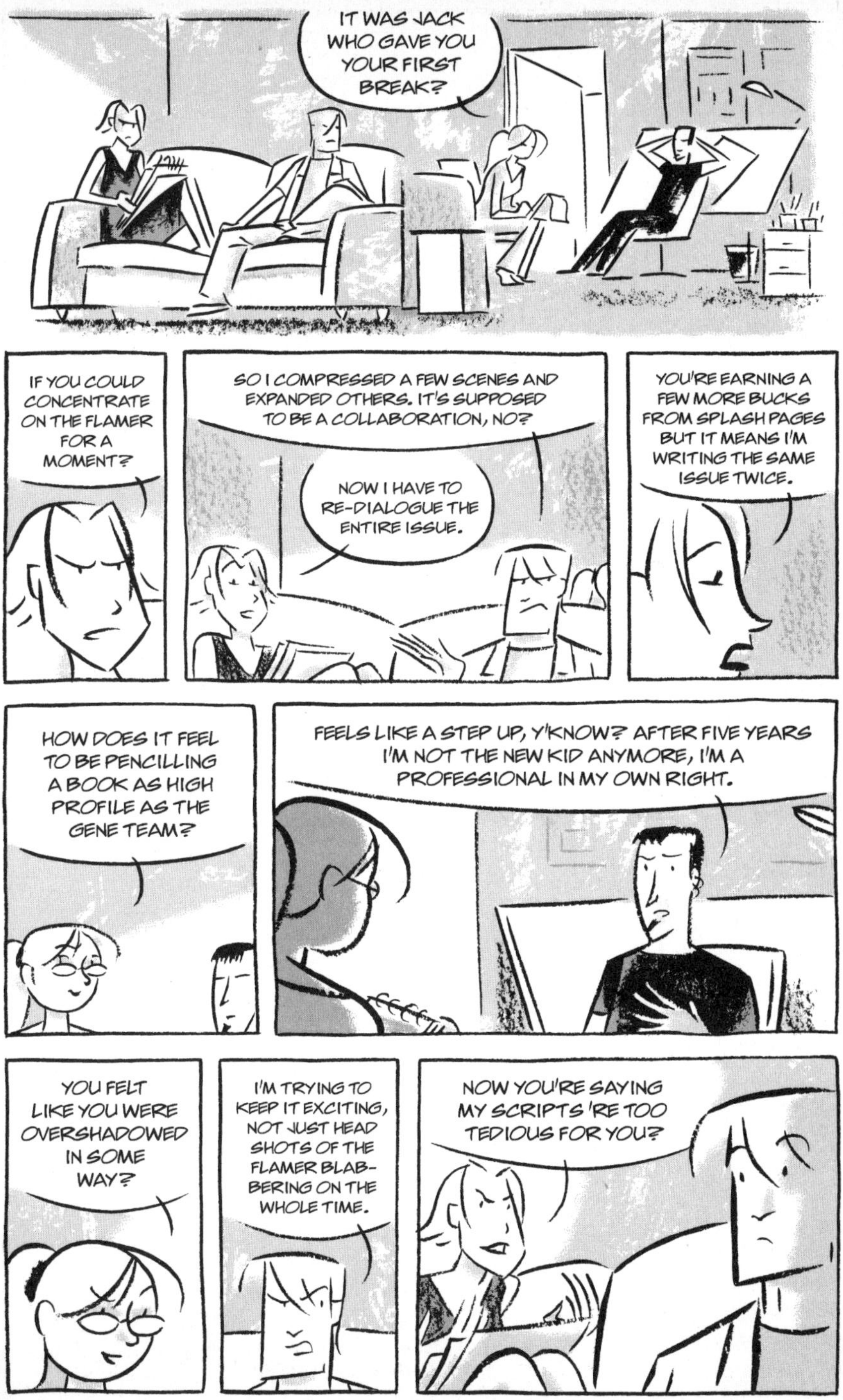
IT WAS JACK WHO GAVE YOU YOUR FIRST BREAK?
IF YOU COULD CONCENTRATE ON THE FLAMER FOR A MOMENT?
SO I COMPRESSED A FEW SCENES AND EXPANDED OTHERS. IT'S SUPPOSED TO BE A COLLABORATION, NO?
NOW I HAVE TO RE-DIALOGUE THE ENTIRE ISSUE.
YOU'RE EARNING A FEW MORE BUCKS FROM SPLASH PAGES BUT IT MEANS I'M WRITING THE SAME ISSUE TWICE.
HOW DOES IT FEEL TO BE PENCILLING A BOOK AS HIGH PROFILE AS THE GENE TEAM?
FEELS LIKE A STEP UP, Y'KNOW? AFTER FIVE YEARS I'M NOT THE NEW KID ANYMORE, I'M A PROFESSIONAL IN MY OWN RIGHT.
YOU FELT LIKE YOU WERE OVERSHADOWED IN SOME WAY?
I'M TRYING TO KEEP IT EXCITING, NOT JUST HEAD SHOTS OF THE FLAMER BLAB-BERING ON THE WHOLE TIME.
NOW YOU'RE SAYING MY SCRIPTS 'RE TOO TEDIOUS FOR YOU?

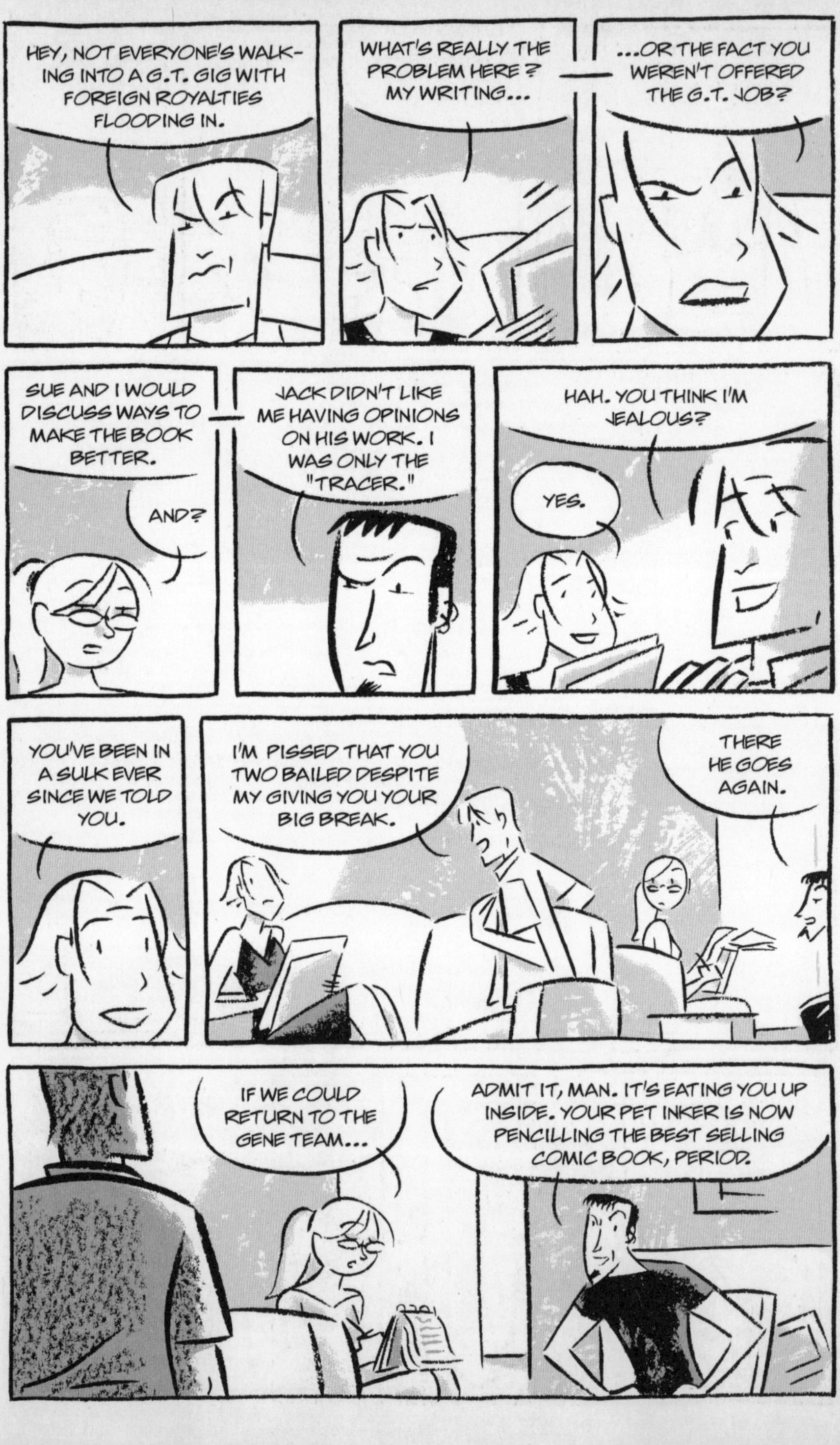
HEY, NOT EVERYONE'S WALKING INTO A G.T. GIG WITH FOREIGN ROYALTIES FLOODING IN.
WHAT'S REALLY THE PROBLEM HERE? MY WRITING...
...OR THE FACT YOU WEREN'T OFFERED THE G.T. JOB?
SUE AND I WOULD DISCUSS WAYS TO MAKE THE BOOK BETTER.
AND?
JACK DIDN'T LIKE ME HAVING OPINIONS ON HIS WORK. I WAS ONLY THE "TRACER."
HAH. YOU THINK I'M JEALOUS?
YES.
YOU'VE BEEN IN A SULK EVER SINCE WE TOLD YOU.
I'M PISSED THAT YOU TWO BAILED DESPITE MY GIVING YOU YOUR BIG BREAK.
THERE HE GOES AGAIN.
IF WE COULD RETURN TO THE GENE TEAM...
ADMIT IT, MAN. IT'S EATING YOU UP INSIDE. YOUR PET INKER IS NOW PENCILLING THE BEST SELLING COMIC BOOK, PERIOD.

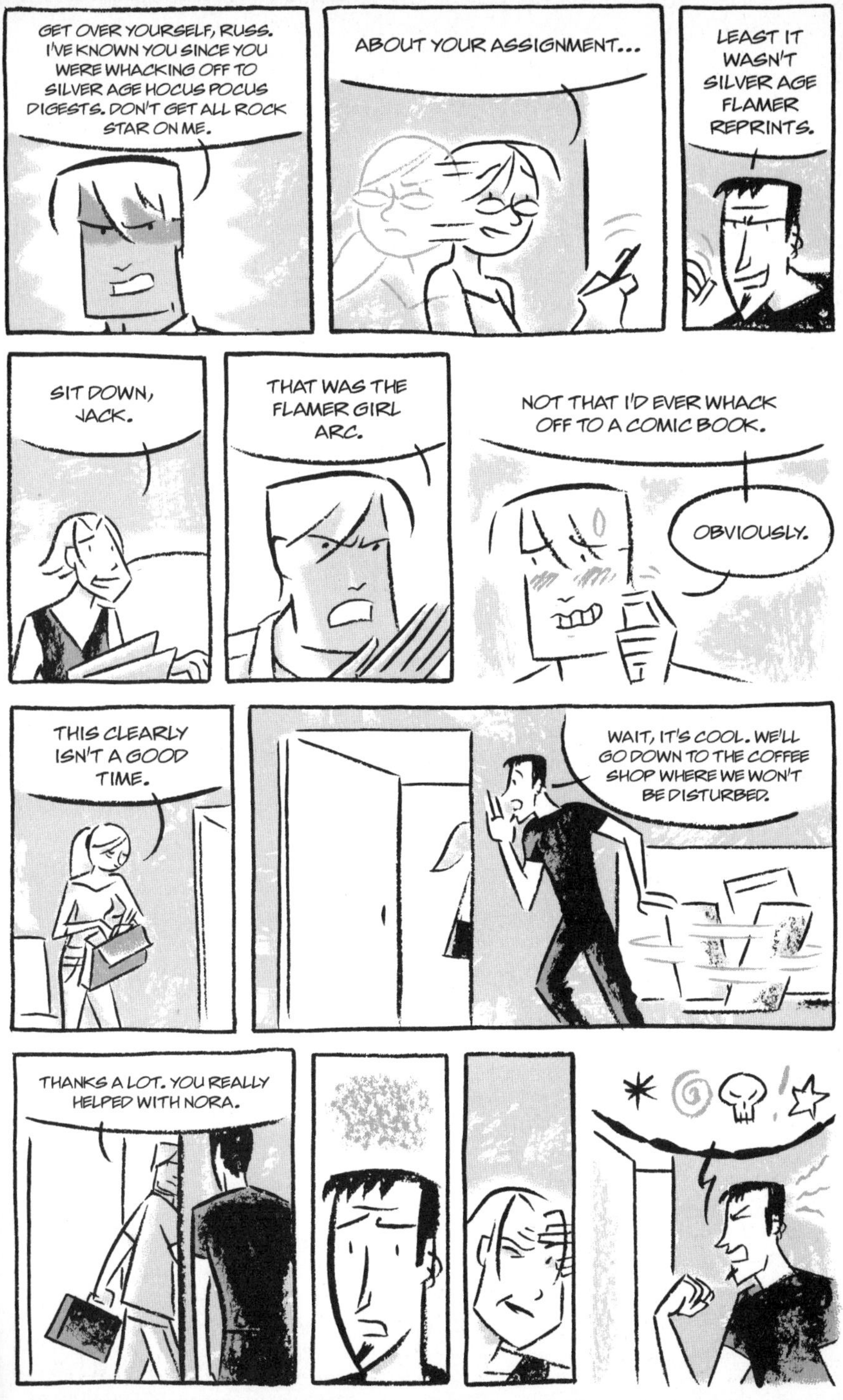

GET OVER YOURSELF, RUSS. I'VE KNOWN YOU SINCE YOU WERE WHACKING OFF TO SILVER AGE HOCUS POCUS DIGESTS. DON'T GET ALL ROCK STAR ON ME.
ABOUT YOUR ASSIGNMENT...
LEAST IT WASN'T SILVER AGE FLAMER REPRINTS.
SIT DOWN, JACK.
THAT WAS THE FLAMER GIRL ARC.
NOT THAT I'D EVER WHACK OFF TO A COMIC BOOK.
OBVIOUSLY.
THIS CLEARLY ISN'T A GOOD TIME.
WAIT, IT'S COOL. WE'LL GO DOWN TO THE COFFEE SHOP WHERE WE WON'T BE DISTURBED.
THANKS A LOT. YOU REALLY HELPED WITH NORA.

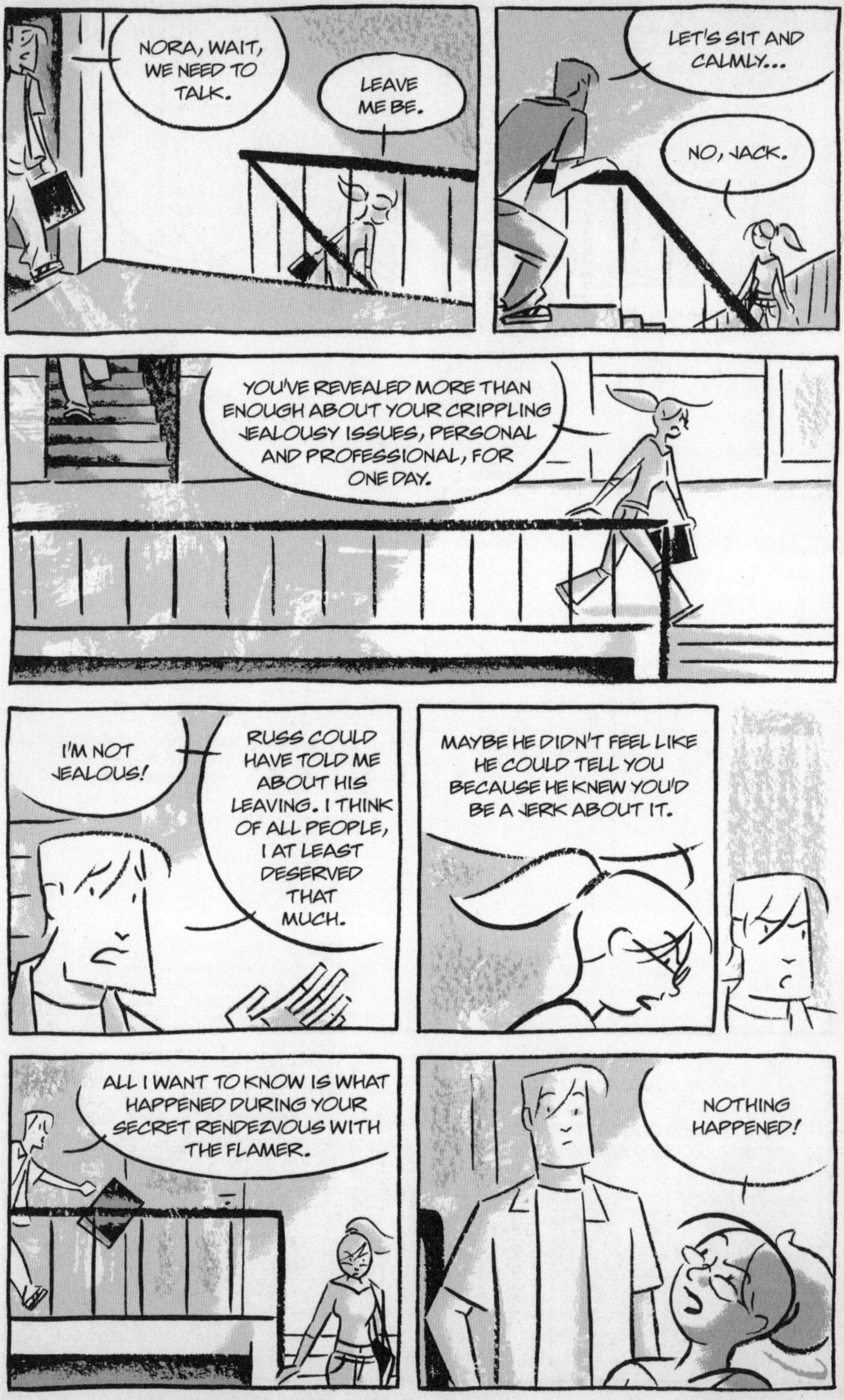
NORA, WAIT, WE NEED TO TALK.
LEAVE ME BE.
LET'S SIT AND CALMLY...
NO, JACK.
YOU'VE REVEALED MORE THAN ENOUGH ABOUT YOUR CRIPPLING JEALOUSY ISSUES, PERSONAL AND PROFESSIONAL, FOR ONE DAY.
I'M NOT JEALOUS!
RUSS COULD HAVE TOLD ME ABOUT HIS LEAVING. I THINK OF ALL PEOPLE, I AT LEAST DESERVED THAT MUCH.
MAYBE HE DIDN'T FEEL LIKE HE COULD TELL YOU BECAUSE HE KNEW YOU'D BE A JERK ABOUT IT.
ALL I WANT TO KNOW IS WHAT HAPPENED DURING YOUR SECRET RENDEZVOUS WITH THE FLAMER.
NOTHING HAPPENED!

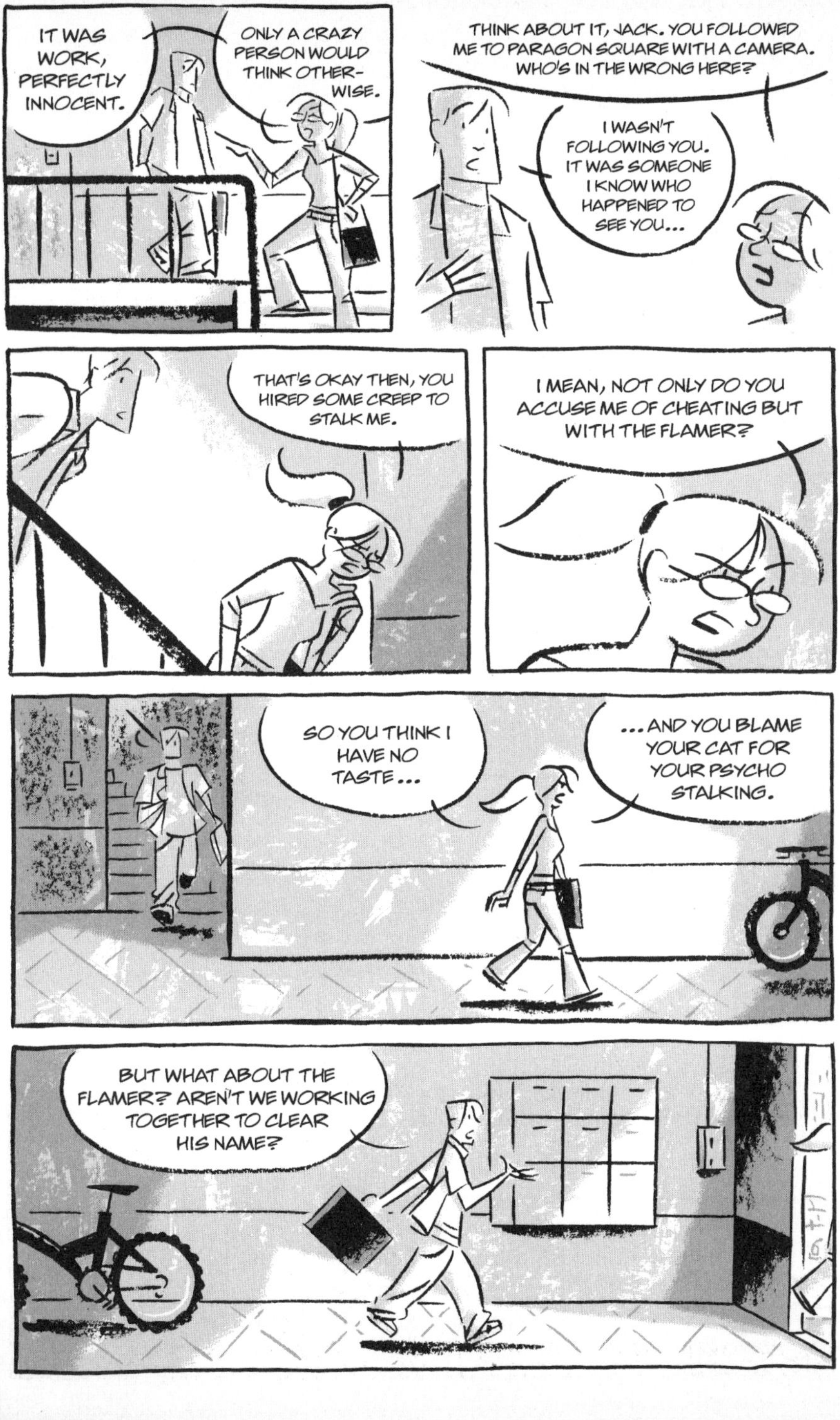
IT WAS WORK, PERFECTLY INNOCENT.
ONLY A CRAZY PERSON WOULD THINK OTHER-WISE.
THINK ABOUT IT, JACK. YOU FOLLOWED ME TO PARAGON SQUARE WITH A CAMERA. WHO'S IN THE WRONG HERE?
I WASN'T FOLLOWING YOU. IT WAS SOMEONE I KNOW WHO HAPPENED TO SEE YOU...
THAT'S OKAY THEN, YOU HIRED SOME CREEP TO STALK ME.
I MEAN, NOT ONLY DO YOU ACCUSE ME OF CHEATING BUT WITH THE FLAMER?
SO YOU THINK I HAVE NO TASTE...
...AND YOU BLAME YOUR CAT FOR YOUR PSYCHO STALKING.
BUT WHAT ABOUT THE FLAMER? AREN'T WE WORKING TOGETHER TO CLEAR HIS NAME?

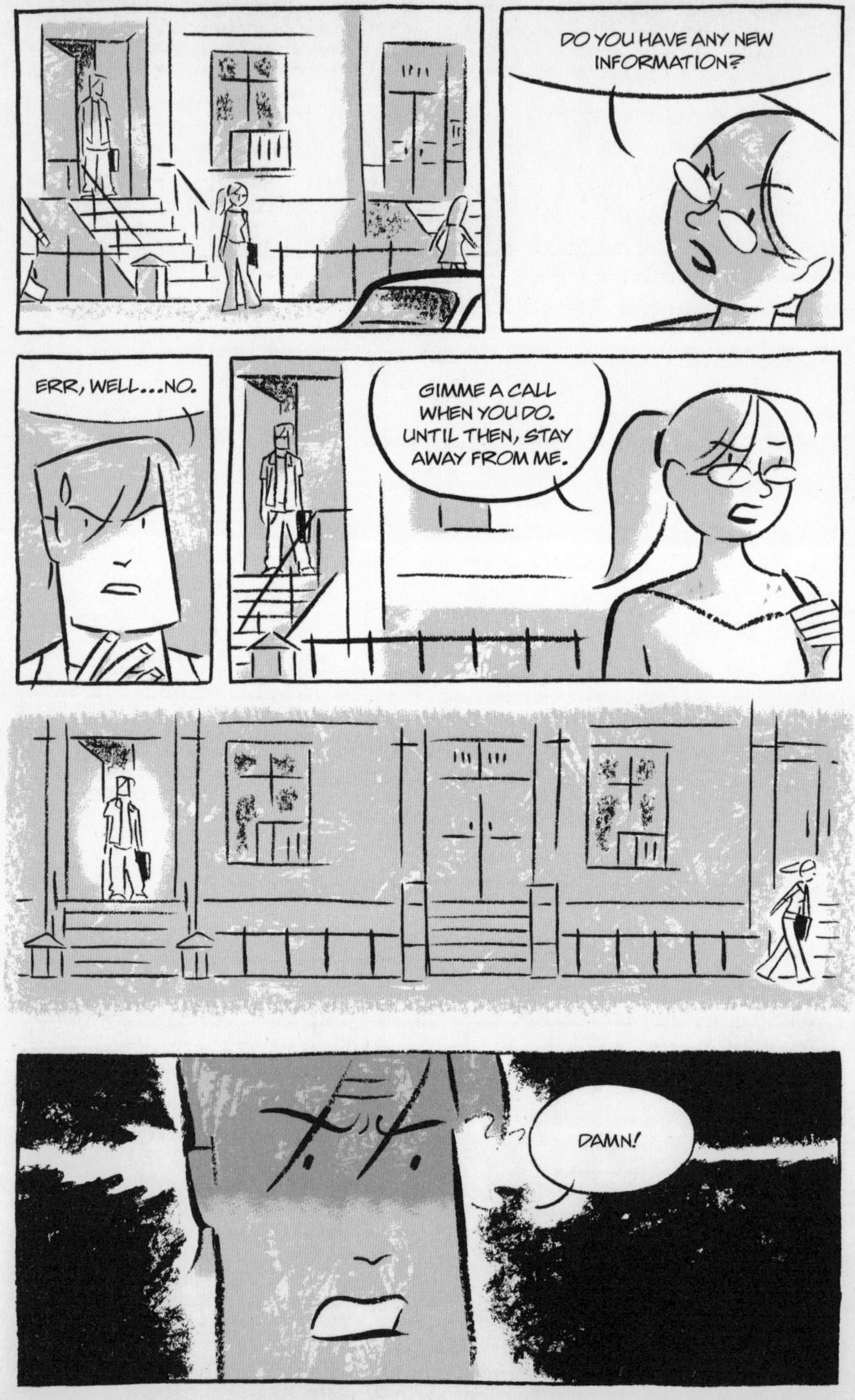
DO YOU HAVE ANY NEW INFORMATION?
ERR, WELL...NO.
GIMME A CALL WHEN YOU DO. UNTIL THEN, STAY AWAY FROM ME.
DAMN!

Love Fights™   #8

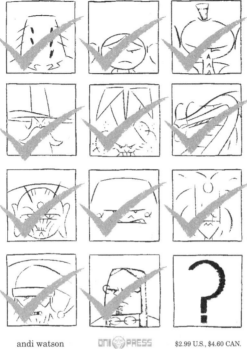

andi watson   ONI PRESS $2.99 U.S., $4.60 CAN.

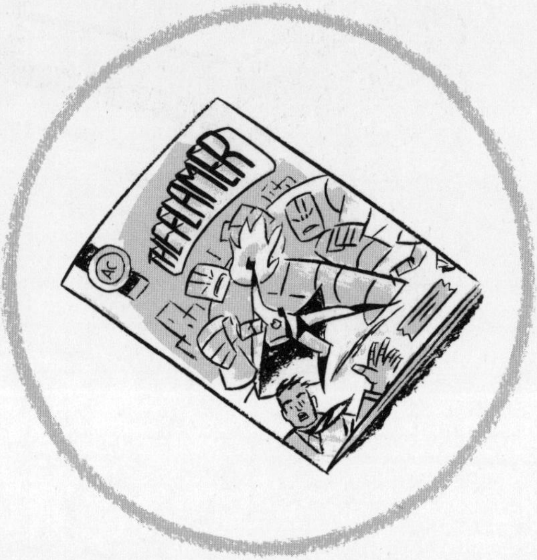
THE FLAMER

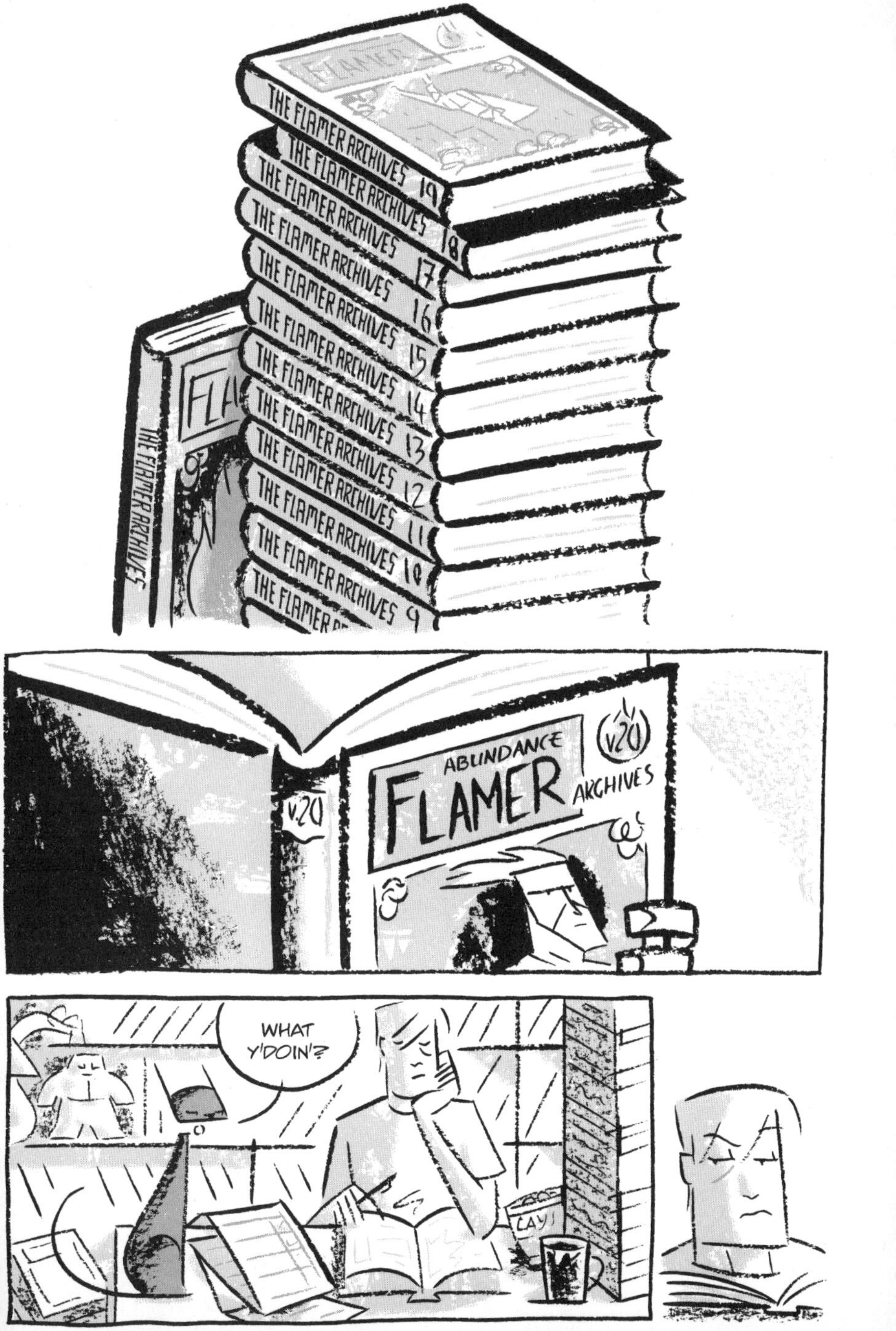
THE FLAMER ARCHIVES 19
THE FLAMER ARCHIVES 18
THE FLAMER ARCHIVES 17
THE FLAMER ARCHIVES 16
THE FLAMER ARCHIVES 15
THE FLAMER ARCHIVES 14
THE FLAMER ARCHIVES 13
THE FLAMER ARCHIVES 12
THE FLAMER ARCHIVES 11
THE FLAMER ARCHIVES 10
THE FLAMER ARCHIVES 9
THE FLAMER ARCHIVES
v.20
ABUNDANCE
FLAMER
ARCHIVES
v.20
WHAT Y'DOIN'?

STITCH

lil' MISS MUFFET

KNUCKLE SANDWICH

I'M READING ALL MY FLAMER BOOKS AND MAKING A LIST OF EVERY SINGLE BADDIE HE'S EVER FACED.

THEN I'M TICKING OFF EACH BADDIE THAT THE FLAMER'S TRACKED DOWN AND QUESTIONED ABOUT THE SCANDAL. WHO-EVER'S LEFT WHO HASN'T BEEN QUES-TIONED MIGHT BE THE ONE RES-PONSIBLE.

CHAIN MALE

LET ME SEE THAT.

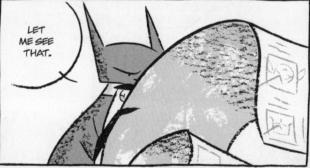

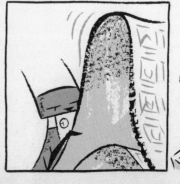

ALL RIGHT, CARRY ON.

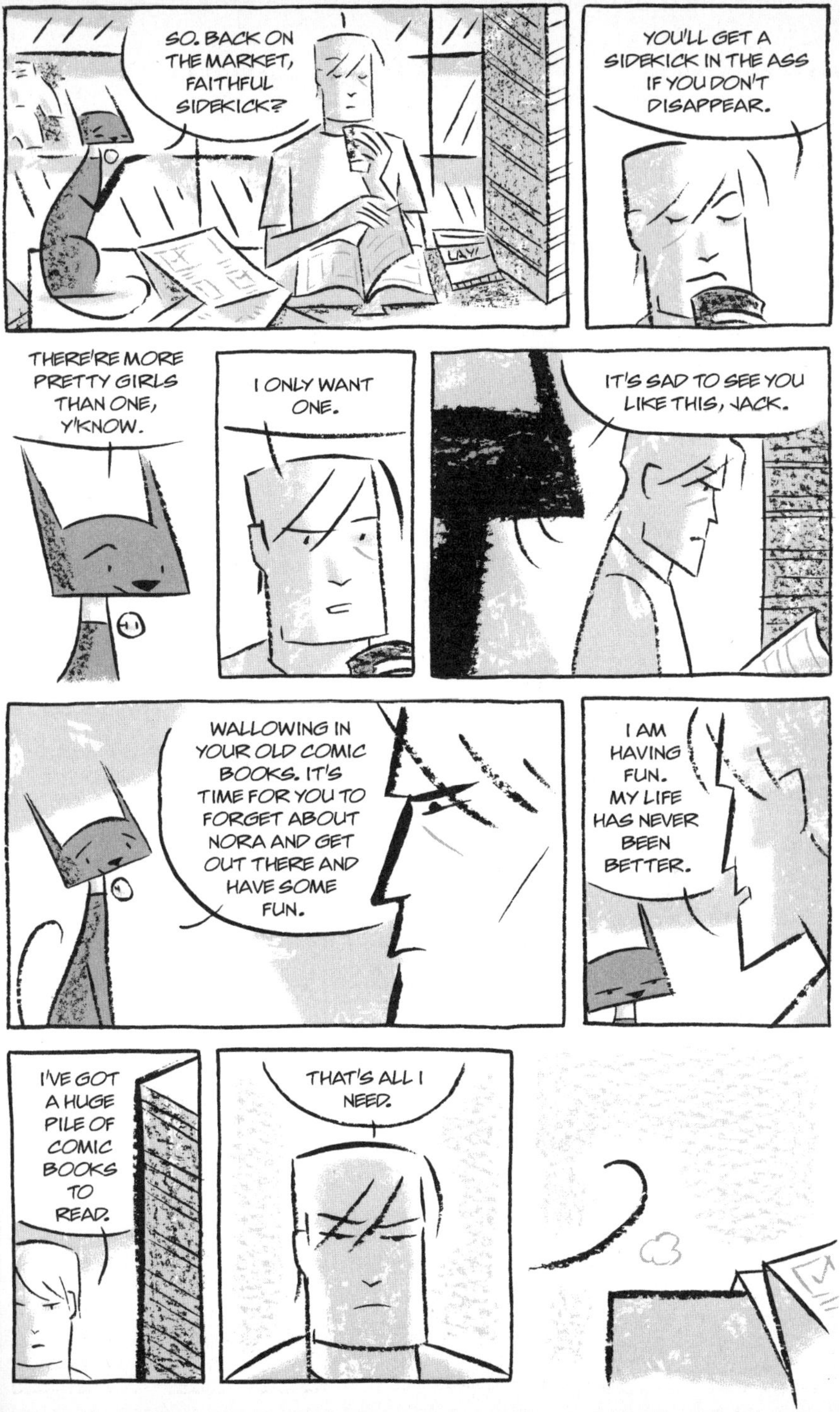
SO. BACK ON THE MARKET, FAITHFUL SIDEKICK?
YOU'LL GET A SIDEKICK IN THE ASS IF YOU DON'T DISAPPEAR.
THERE'RE MORE PRETTY GIRLS THAN ONE, Y'KNOW.
I ONLY WANT ONE.
IT'S SAD TO SEE YOU LIKE THIS, JACK.
WALLOWING IN YOUR OLD COMIC BOOKS. IT'S TIME FOR YOU TO FORGET ABOUT NORA AND GET OUT THERE AND HAVE SOME FUN.
I AM HAVING FUN. MY LIFE HAS NEVER BEEN BETTER.
I'VE GOT A HUGE PILE OF COMIC BOOKS TO READ.
THAT'S ALL I NEED.

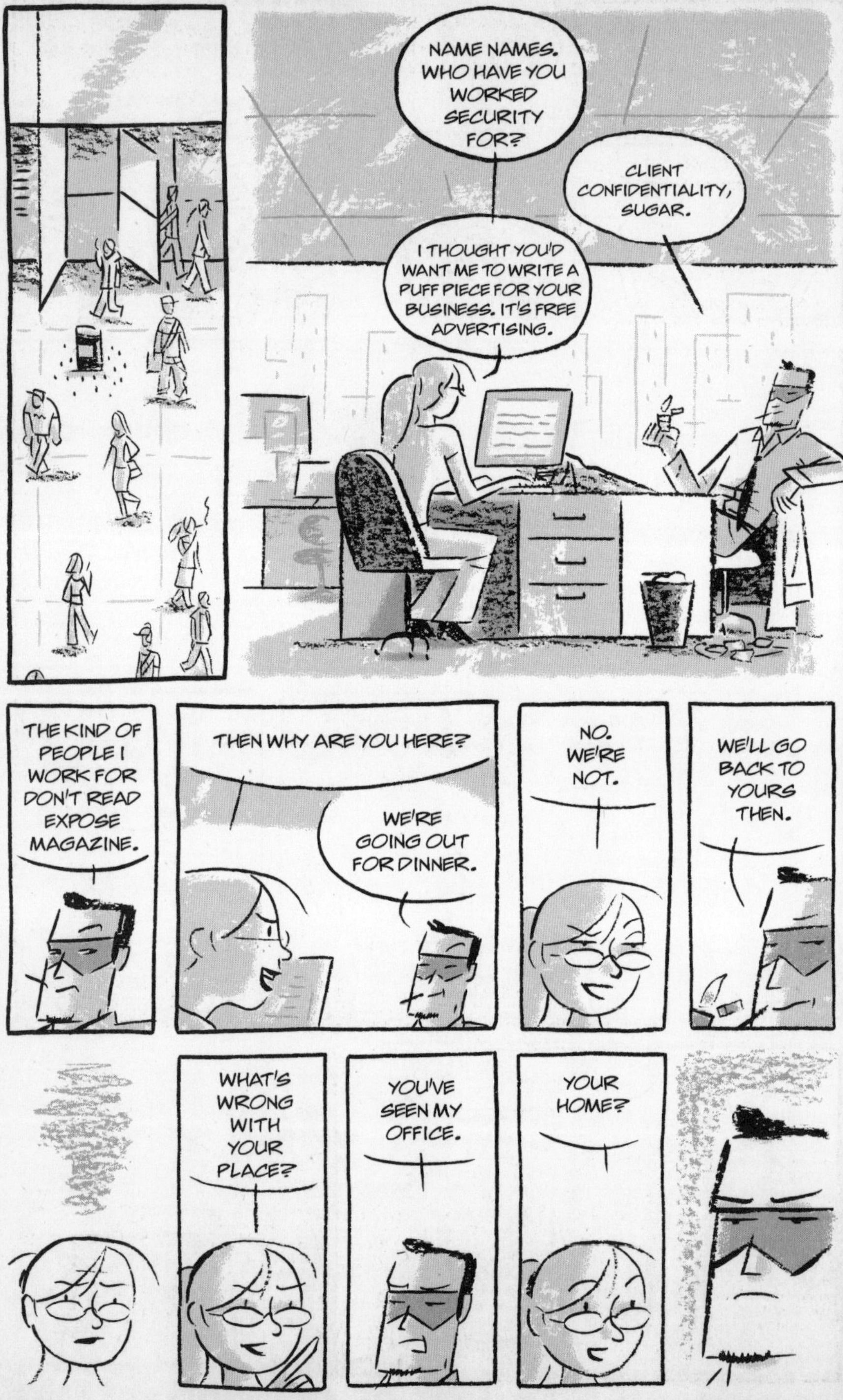
NAME NAMES. WHO HAVE YOU WORKED SECURITY FOR?
I THOUGHT YOU'D WANT ME TO WRITE A PUFF PIECE FOR YOUR BUSINESS. IT'S FREE ADVERTISING.
CLIENT CONFIDENTIALITY, SUGAR.
THE KIND OF PEOPLE I WORK FOR DON'T READ EXPOSE MAGAZINE.
THEN WHY ARE YOU HERE?
WE'RE GOING OUT FOR DINNER.
NO. WE'RE NOT.
WE'LL GO BACK TO YOURS THEN.
WHAT'S WRONG WITH YOUR PLACE?
YOU'VE SEEN MY OFFICE.
YOUR HOME?

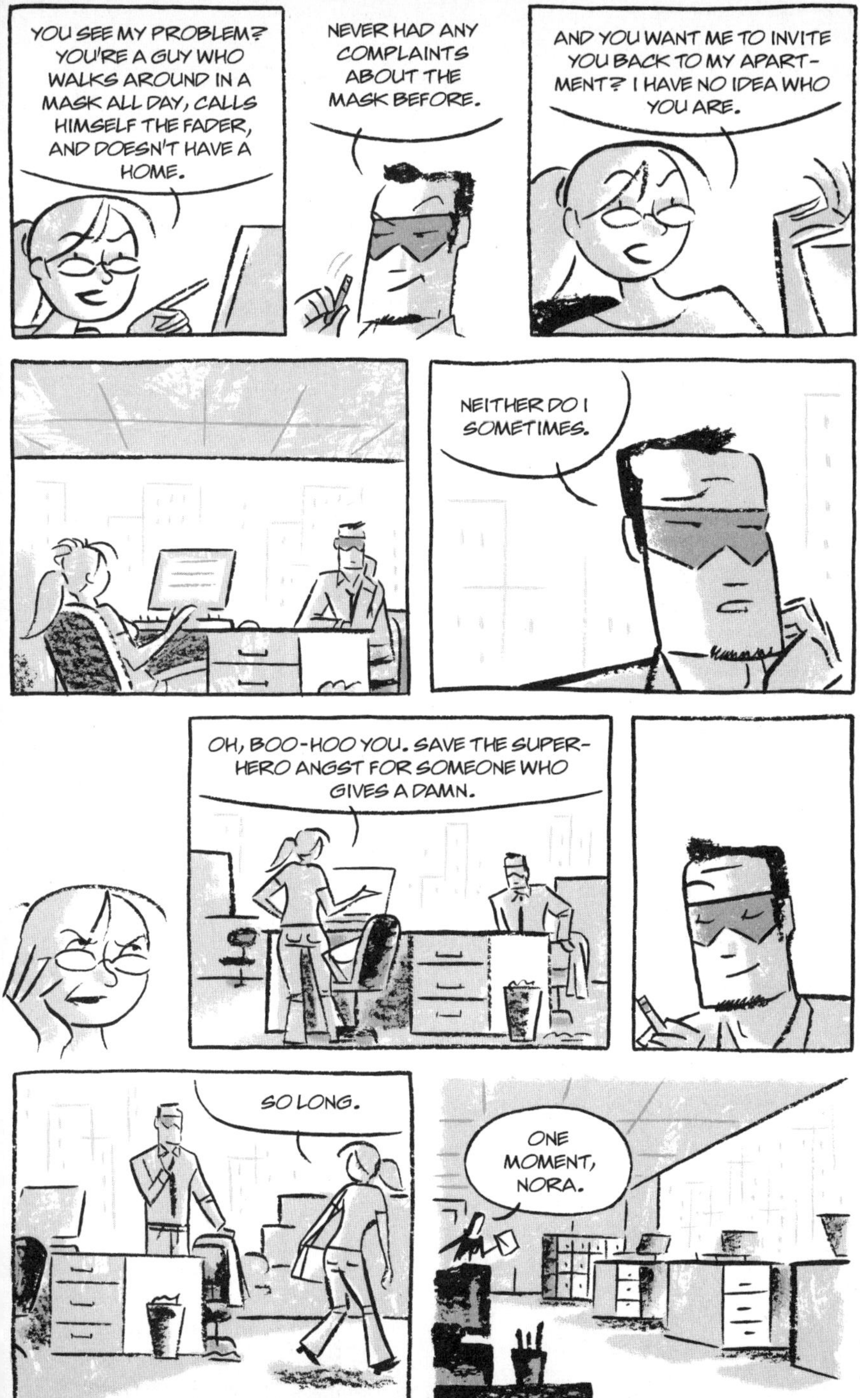
YOU SEE MY PROBLEM? YOU'RE A GUY WHO WALKS AROUND IN A MASK ALL DAY, CALLS HIMSELF THE FADER, AND DOESN'T HAVE A HOME.
NEVER HAD ANY COMPLAINTS ABOUT THE MASK BEFORE.
AND YOU WANT ME TO INVITE YOU BACK TO MY APARTMENT? I HAVE NO IDEA WHO YOU ARE.
NEITHER DO I SOMETIMES.
OH, BOO-HOO YOU. SAVE THE SUPERHERO ANGST FOR SOMEONE WHO GIVES A DAMN.
SO LONG.
ONE MOMENT, NORA.

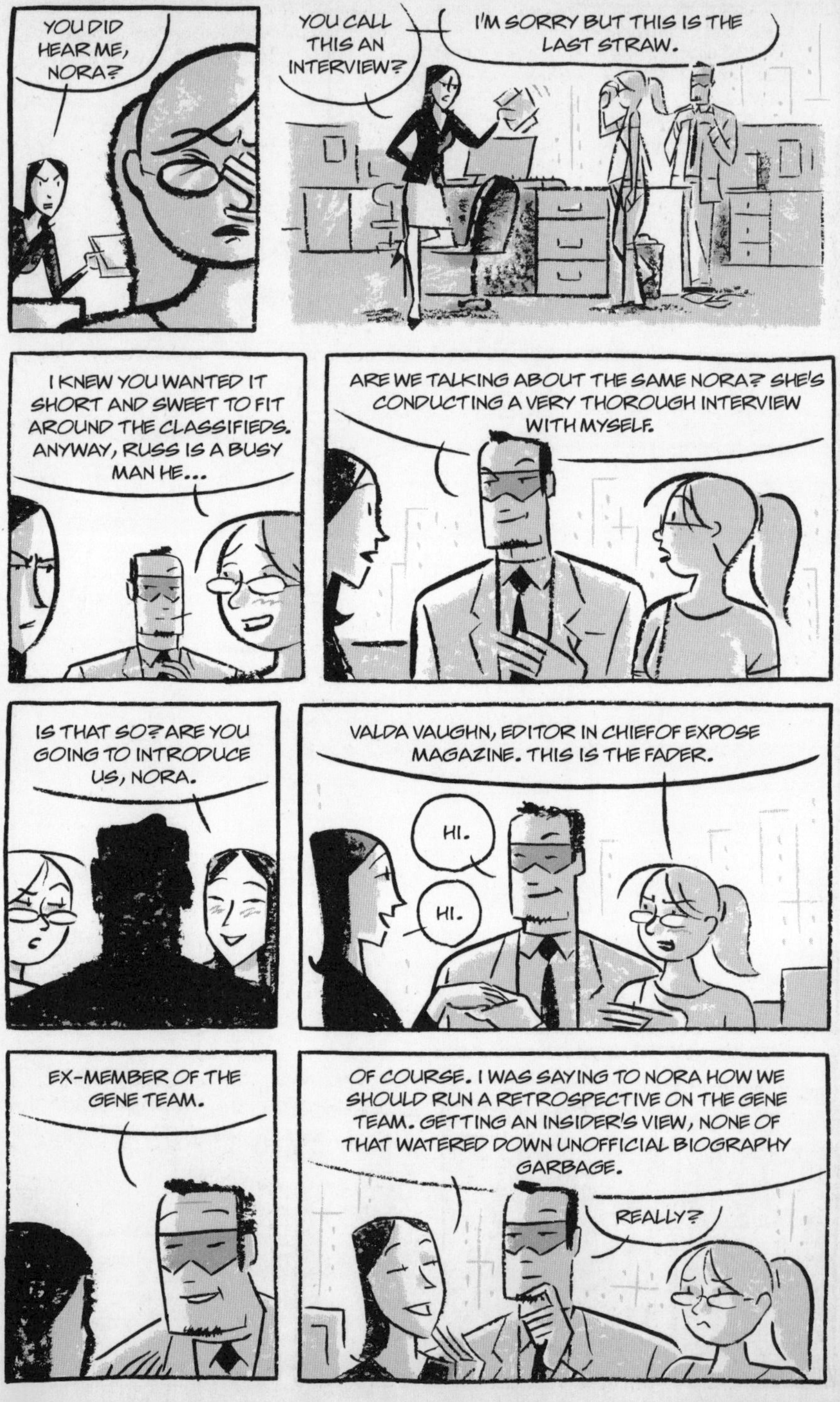
YOU DID HEAR ME, NORA?
YOU CALL THIS AN INTERVIEW?
I'M SORRY BUT THIS IS THE LAST STRAW.
I KNEW YOU WANTED IT SHORT AND SWEET TO FIT AROUND THE CLASSIFIEDS. ANYWAY, RUSS IS A BUSY MAN HE...
ARE WE TALKING ABOUT THE SAME NORA? SHE'S CONDUCTING A VERY THOROUGH INTERVIEW WITH MYSELF.
IS THAT SO? ARE YOU GOING TO INTRODUCE US, NORA.
VALDA VAUGHN, EDITOR IN CHIEFOF EXPOSE MAGAZINE. THIS IS THE FADER.
HI.
HI.
EX-MEMBER OF THE GENE TEAM.
OF COURSE. I WAS SAYING TO NORA HOW WE SHOULD RUN A RETROSPECTIVE ON THE GENE TEAM. GETTING AN INSIDER'S VIEW, NONE OF THAT WATERED DOWN UNOFFICIAL BIOGRAPHY GARBAGE.
REALLY?

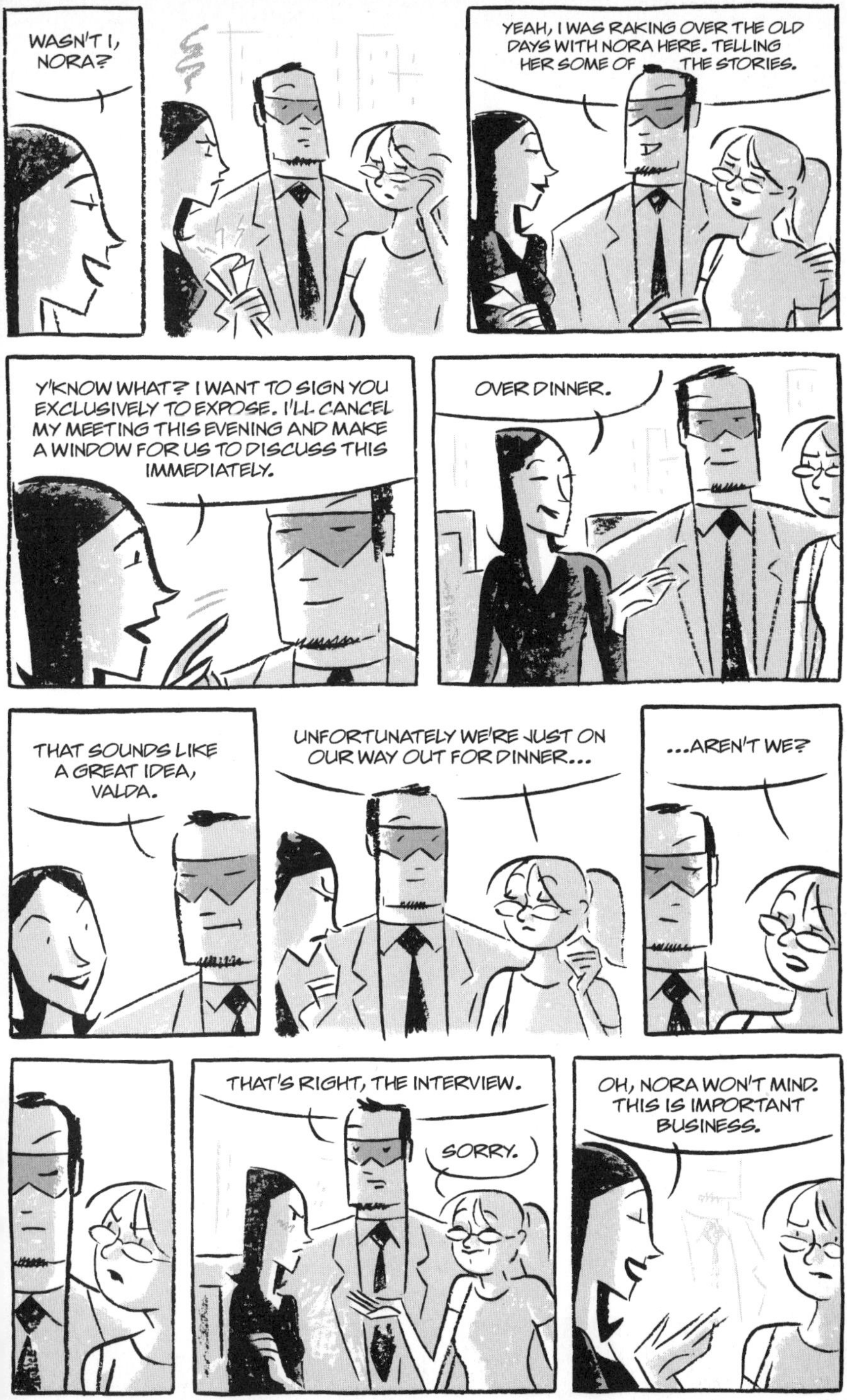
WASN'T I, NORA?
YEAH, I WAS RAKING OVER THE OLD DAYS WITH NORA HERE. TELLING HER SOME OF THE STORIES.
Y'KNOW WHAT? I WANT TO SIGN YOU EXCLUSIVELY TO EXPOSE. I'LL CANCEL MY MEETING THIS EVENING AND MAKE A WINDOW FOR US TO DISCUSS THIS IMMEDIATELY.
OVER DINNER.
THAT SOUNDS LIKE A GREAT IDEA, VALDA.
UNFORTUNATELY WE'RE JUST ON OUR WAY OUT FOR DINNER...
...AREN'T WE?
THAT'S RIGHT, THE INTERVIEW.
SORRY.
OH, NORA WON'T MIND. THIS IS IMPORTANT BUSINESS.

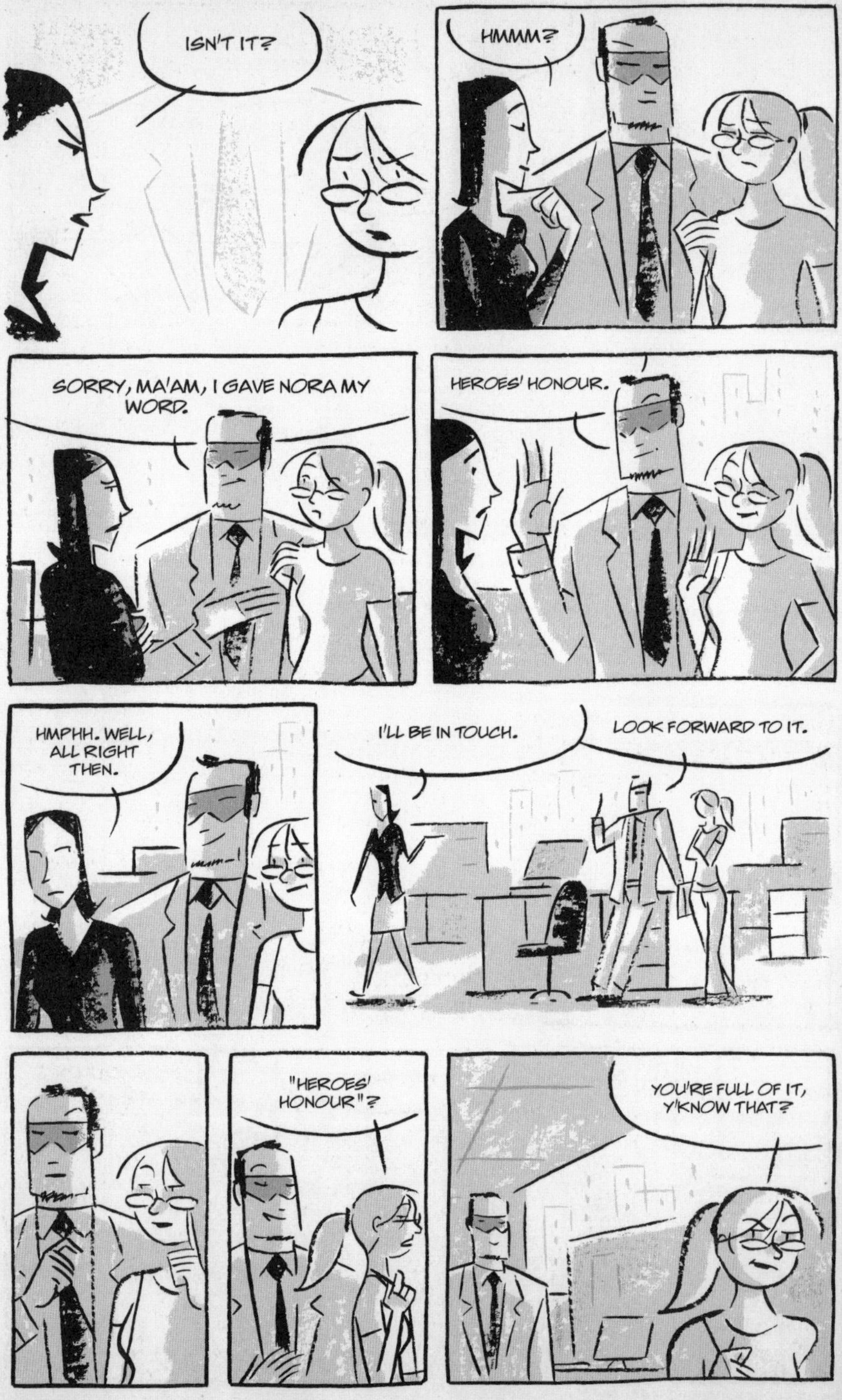
ISN'T IT?
HMMM?
SORRY, MA'AM, I GAVE NORA MY WORD.
HEROES' HONOUR.
HMPHH. WELL, ALL RIGHT THEN.
I'LL BE IN TOUCH.
LOOK FORWARD TO IT.
"HEROES' HONOUR"?
YOU'RE FULL OF IT, Y'KNOW THAT?

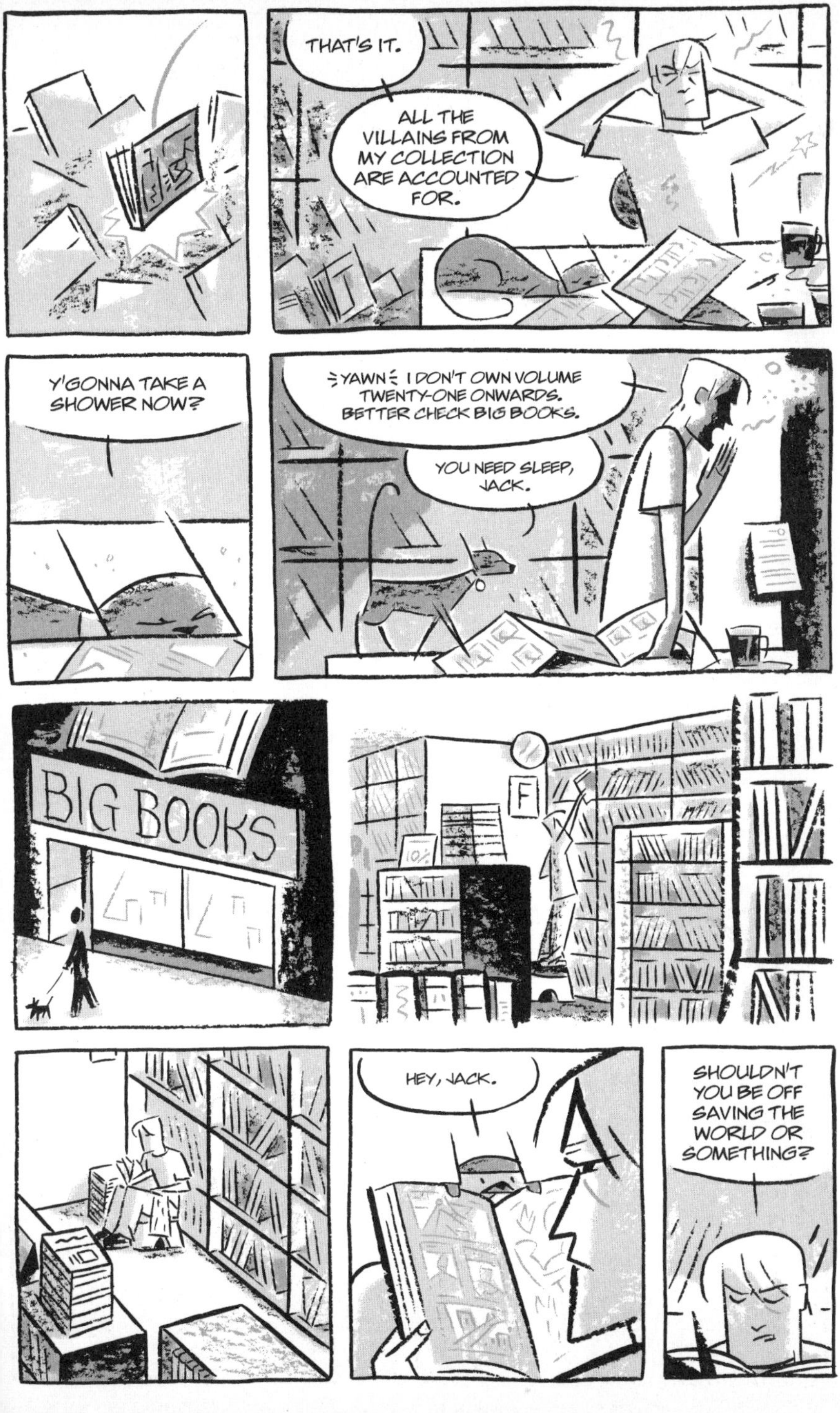
THAT'S IT.
ALL THE VILLAINS FROM MY COLLECTION ARE ACCOUNTED FOR.
Y'GONNA TAKE A SHOWER NOW?
≡YAWN≡ I DON'T OWN VOLUME TWENTY-ONE ONWARDS. BETTER CHECK BIG BOOKS.
YOU NEED SLEEP, JACK.
BIG BOOKS
F
HEY, JACK.
SHOULDN'T YOU BE OFF SAVING THE WORLD OR SOMETHING?

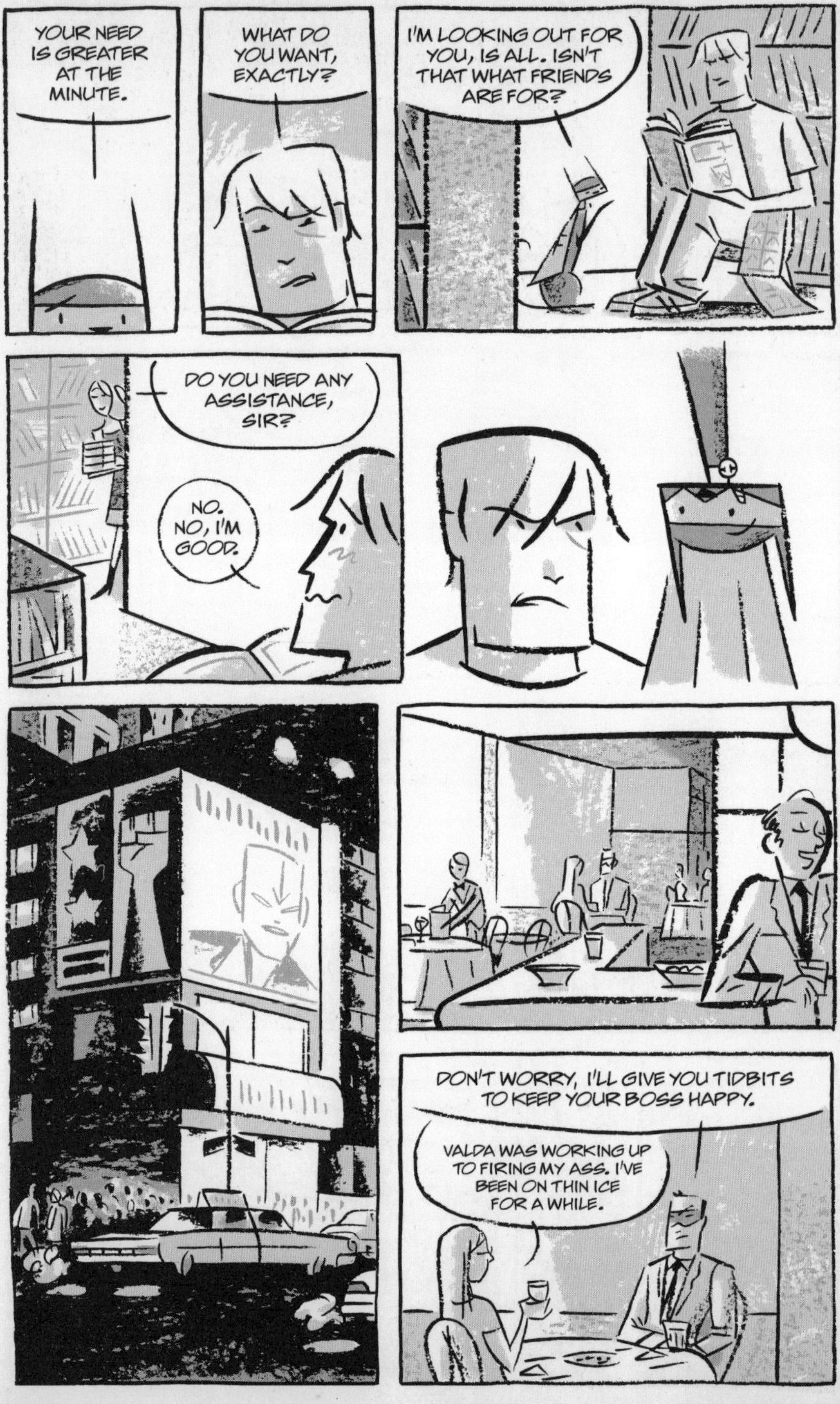

YOUR NEED IS GREATER AT THE MINUTE.
WHAT DO YOU WANT, EXACTLY?
I'M LOOKING OUT FOR YOU, IS ALL. ISN'T THAT WHAT FRIENDS ARE FOR?
DO YOU NEED ANY ASSISTANCE, SIR?
NO. NO, I'M GOOD.
DON'T WORRY, I'LL GIVE YOU TIDBITS TO KEEP YOUR BOSS HAPPY.
VALDA WAS WORKING UP TO FIRING MY ASS. I'VE BEEN ON THIN ICE FOR A WHILE.

SHE'S A GUTTER RAT.

COMING FROM A FREE-LANCE MERCENARY THAT'S QUITE SOMETHING.

YOU CAN DO BETTER. GO WORK SOMEWHERE ELSE.

I'M RAISING THE TONE. THE FLAMER STORY IS SERIOUS INVESTIGATIVE JOURNALISM.

YOU'RE OUT OF LEADS.

YOU'RE NO HELP.

I KNOW NOTHING.

YOU KNEW THERE WAS SOMETHING MORE TO THIS BREMEN GUY?

I KNEW THAT WASN'T HIS REAL NAME BUT THEN THAT'S NOTHING NEW. DID I THINK LAUREN WAS THE MOTHER OF THE FLAMER'S KID? UNLIKELY, BUT I DIDN'T KNOW FOR SURE.

UNTIL WE BECAME BETTER ACQUAINTED.

"BETTER ACQUAINTED"? THAT'S A EUPHEMISM FOR WHAT?

YOU'VE GOT A REPUTATION, FADER. IF YOU THINK I'M GONNA TAKE YOU HOME AND BECOME ANOTHER STAIN ON YOUR SPANDEX CAPE, FORGET ABOUT IT!

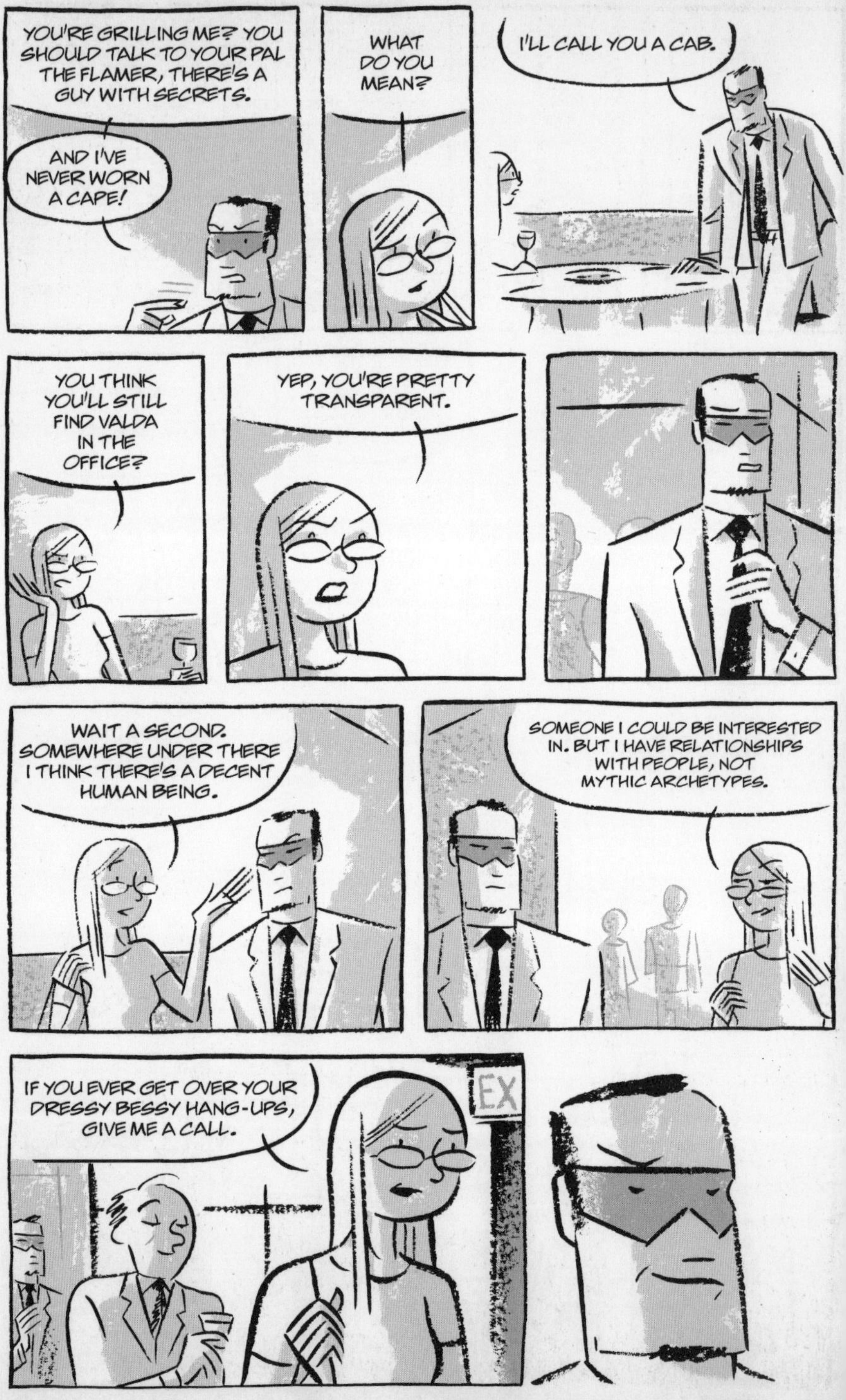
YOU'RE GRILLING ME? YOU SHOULD TALK TO YOUR PAL THE FLAMER, THERE'S A GUY WITH SECRETS.
AND I'VE NEVER WORN A CAPE!
WHAT DO YOU MEAN?
I'LL CALL YOU A CAB.
YOU THINK YOU'LL STILL FIND VALDA IN THE OFFICE?
YEP, YOU'RE PRETTY TRANSPARENT.
WAIT A SECOND. SOMEWHERE UNDER THERE I THINK THERE'S A DECENT HUMAN BEING.
SOMEONE I COULD BE INTERESTED IN. BUT I HAVE RELATIONSHIPS WITH PEOPLE, NOT MYTHIC ARCHETYPES.
IF YOU EVER GET OVER YOUR DRESSY BESSY HANG-UPS, GIVE ME A CALL.
EX

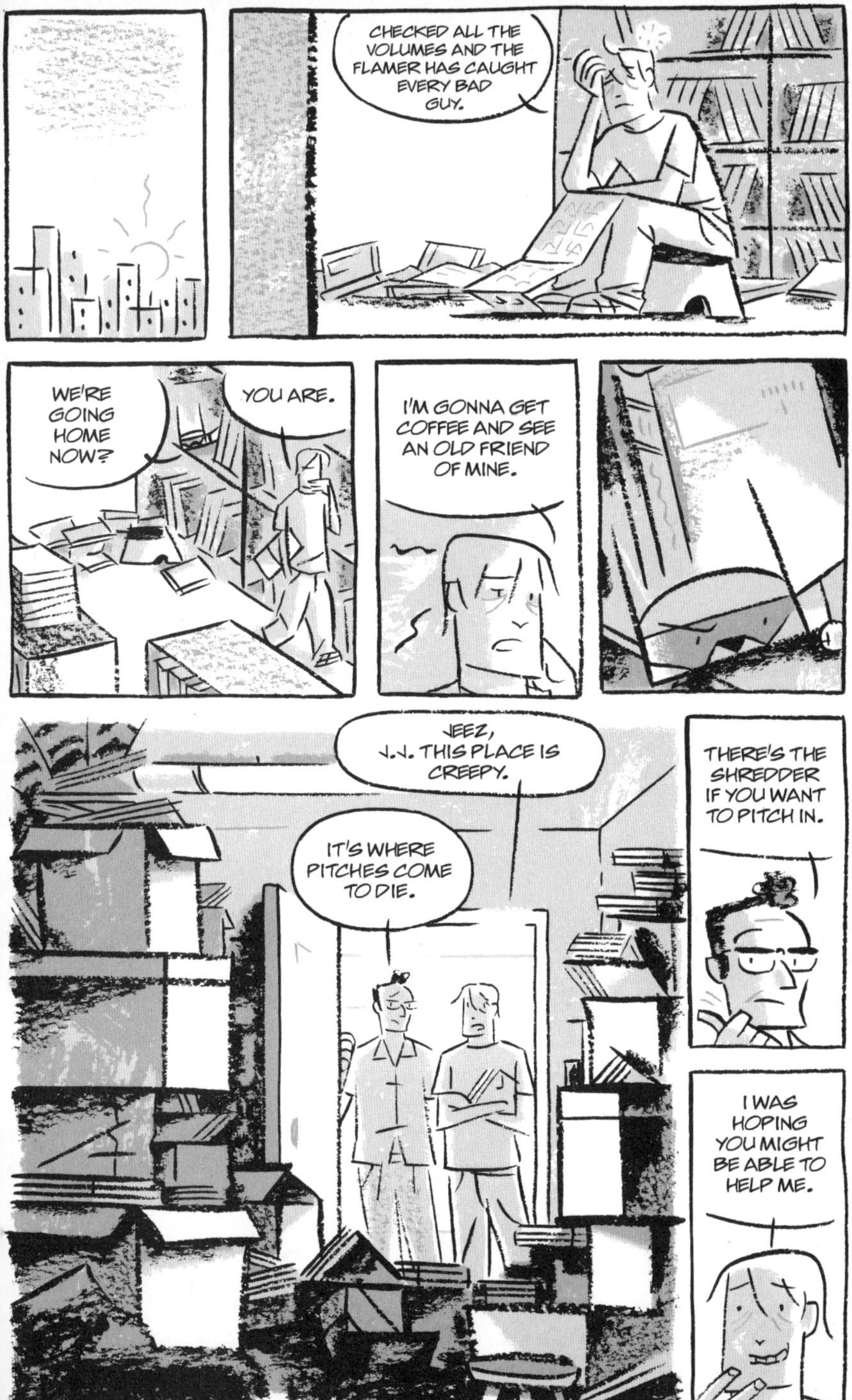
CHECKED ALL THE VOLUMES AND THE FLAMER HAS CAUGHT EVERY BAD GUY.
WE'RE GOING HOME NOW?
YOU ARE.
I'M GONNA GET COFFEE AND SEE AN OLD FRIEND OF MINE.
JEEZ, J.J. THIS PLACE IS CREEPY.
IT'S WHERE PITCHES COME TO DIE.
THERE'S THE SHREDDER IF YOU WANT TO PITCH IN.
I WAS HOPING YOU MIGHT BE ABLE TO HELP ME.

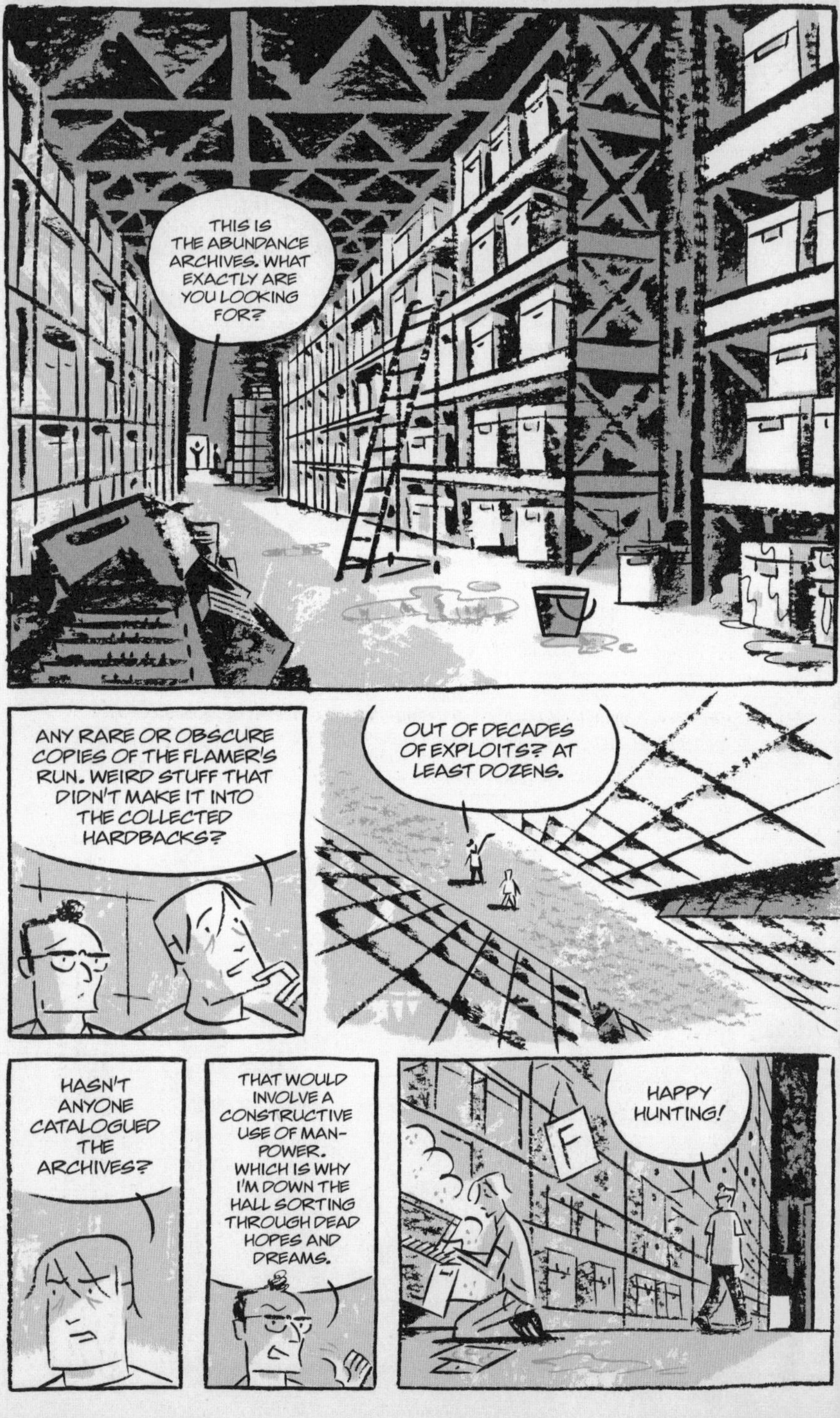
THIS IS THE ABUNDANCE ARCHIVES. WHAT EXACTLY ARE YOU LOOKING FOR?
ANY RARE OR OBSCURE COPIES OF THE FLAMER'S RUN. WEIRD STUFF THAT DIDN'T MAKE IT INTO THE COLLECTED HARDBACKS?
OUT OF DECADES OF EXPLOITS? AT LEAST DOZENS.
HASN'T ANYONE CATALOGUED THE ARCHIVES?
THAT WOULD INVOLVE A CONSTRUCTIVE USE OF MAN-POWER. WHICH IS WHY I'M DOWN THE HALL SORTING THROUGH DEAD HOPES AND DREAMS.
F
HAPPY HUNTING!

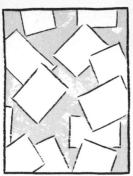

Flamer: YEAR ONE.
A reappraisal.

REJECTED
LEGAL DEPT.

Flamer: YEAR ONE.
A reappraisal.

Adding contemporary accounts
to the context of the early
TEMPUS FUGIT storyline.

All reference to
"Tempus Fugit"
erased from
continuity

J. Lehmann
copyright dept.

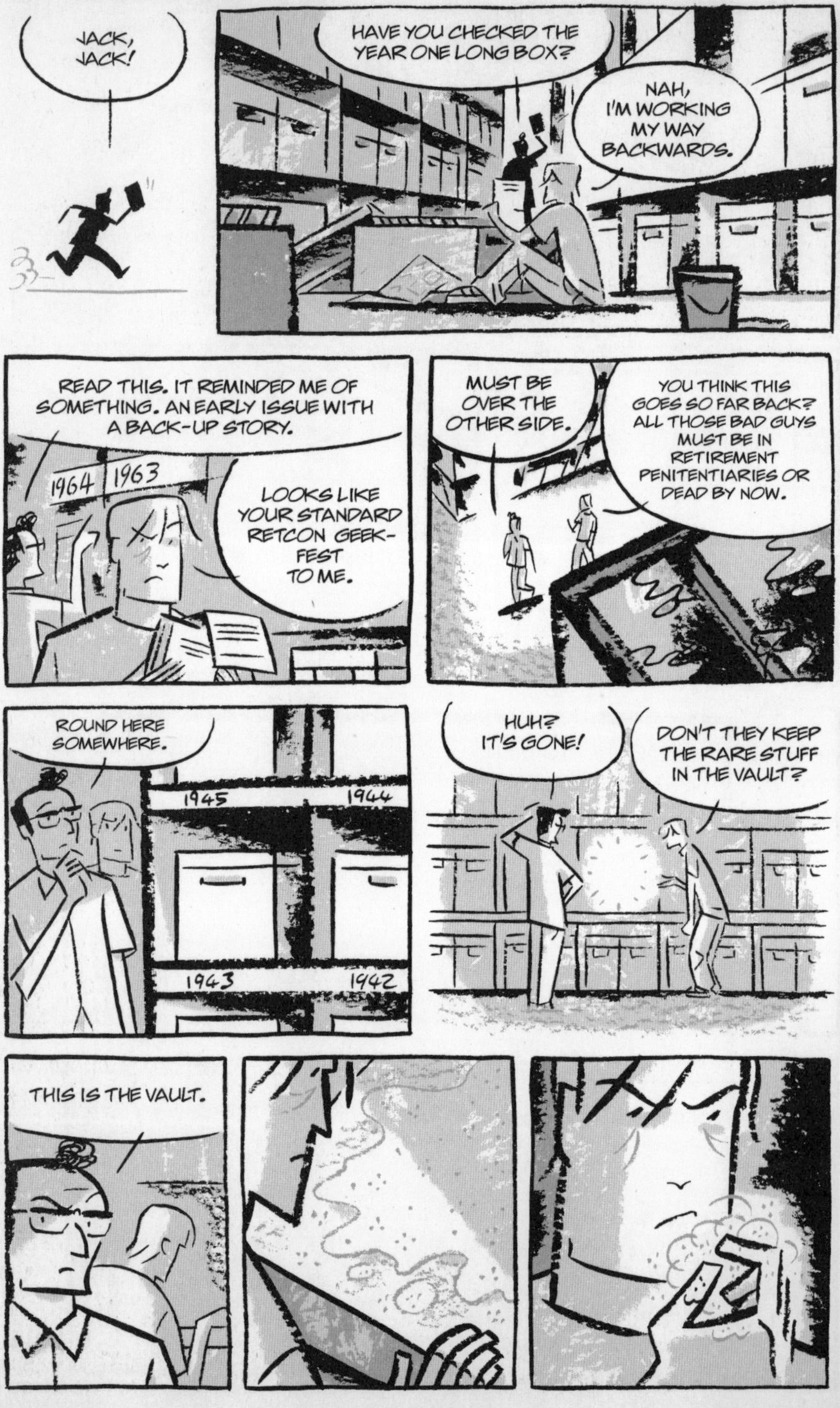
JACK, JACK!
HAVE YOU CHECKED THE YEAR ONE LONG BOX?
NAH, I'M WORKING MY WAY BACKWARDS.
READ THIS. IT REMINDED ME OF SOMETHING. AN EARLY ISSUE WITH A BACK-UP STORY.
1964
1963
LOOKS LIKE YOUR STANDARD RETCON GEEK-FEST TO ME.
MUST BE OVER THE OTHER SIDE.
YOU THINK THIS GOES SO FAR BACK? ALL THOSE BAD GUYS MUST BE IN RETIREMENT PENITENTIARIES OR DEAD BY NOW.
ROUND HERE SOMEWHERE.
1945
1944
1943
1942
HUH? IT'S GONE!
DON'T THEY KEEP THE RARE STUFF IN THE VAULT?
THIS IS THE VAULT.

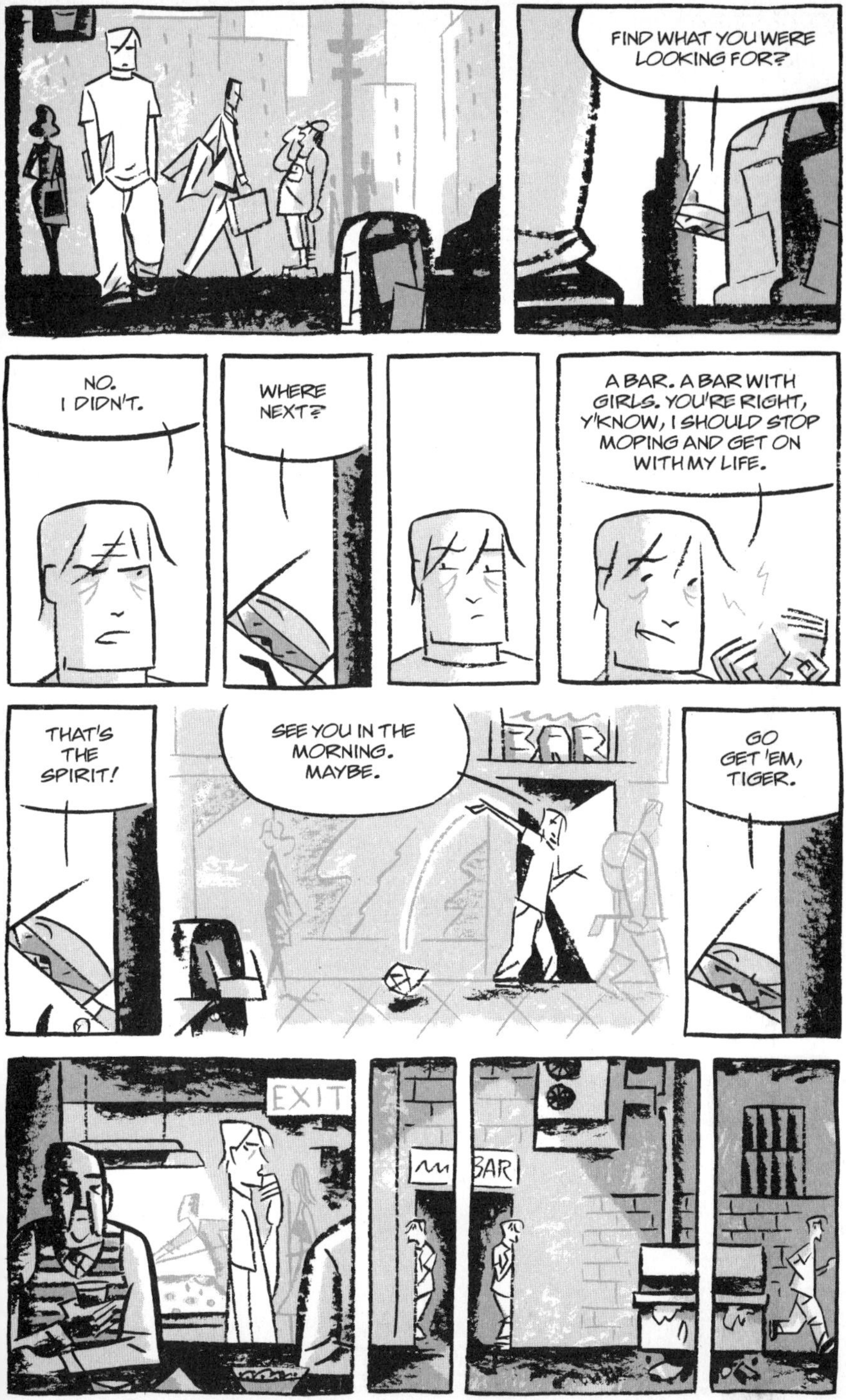
FIND WHAT YOU WERE LOOKING FOR?
NO. I DIDN'T.
WHERE NEXT?
A BAR. A BAR WITH GIRLS. YOU'RE RIGHT, Y'KNOW, I SHOULD STOP MOPING AND GET ON WITH MY LIFE.
THAT'S THE SPIRIT!
SEE YOU IN THE MORNING. MAYBE.
BAR
GO GET 'EM, TIGER.
EXIT
BAR

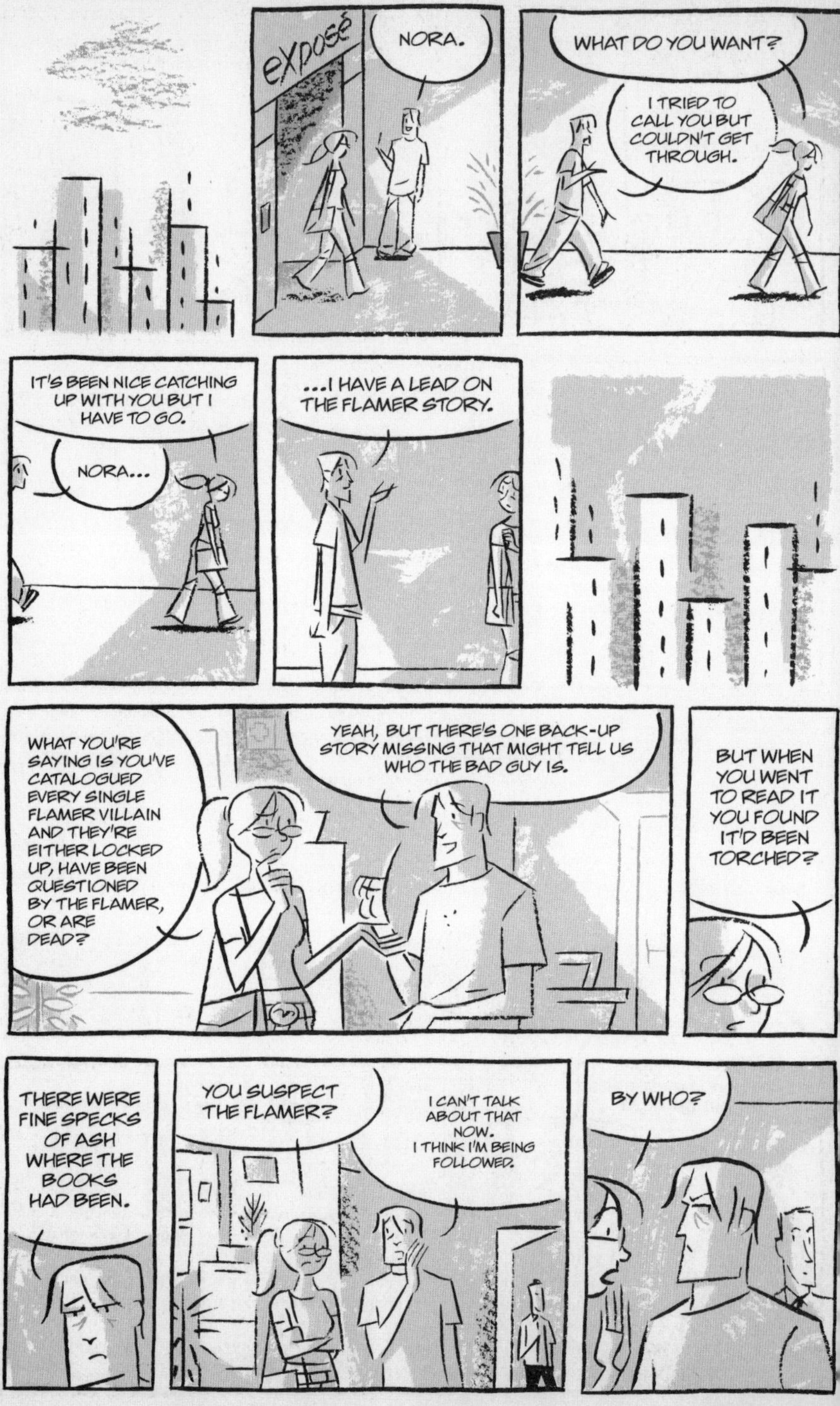
expose
NORA.
WHAT DO YOU WANT?
I TRIED TO CALL YOU BUT COULDN'T GET THROUGH.
IT'S BEEN NICE CATCHING UP WITH YOU BUT I HAVE TO GO.
NORA...
...I HAVE A LEAD ON THE FLAMER STORY.
WHAT YOU'RE SAYING IS YOU'VE CATALOGUED EVERY SINGLE FLAMER VILLAIN AND THEY'RE EITHER LOCKED UP, HAVE BEEN QUESTIONED BY THE FLAMER, OR ARE DEAD?
YEAH, BUT THERE'S ONE BACK-UP STORY MISSING THAT MIGHT TELL US WHO THE BAD GUY IS.
BUT WHEN YOU WENT TO READ IT YOU FOUND IT'D BEEN TORCHED?
THERE WERE FINE SPECKS OF ASH WHERE THE BOOKS HAD BEEN.
YOU SUSPECT THE FLAMER?
I CAN'T TALK ABOUT THAT NOW. I THINK I'M BEING FOLLOWED.
BY WHO?

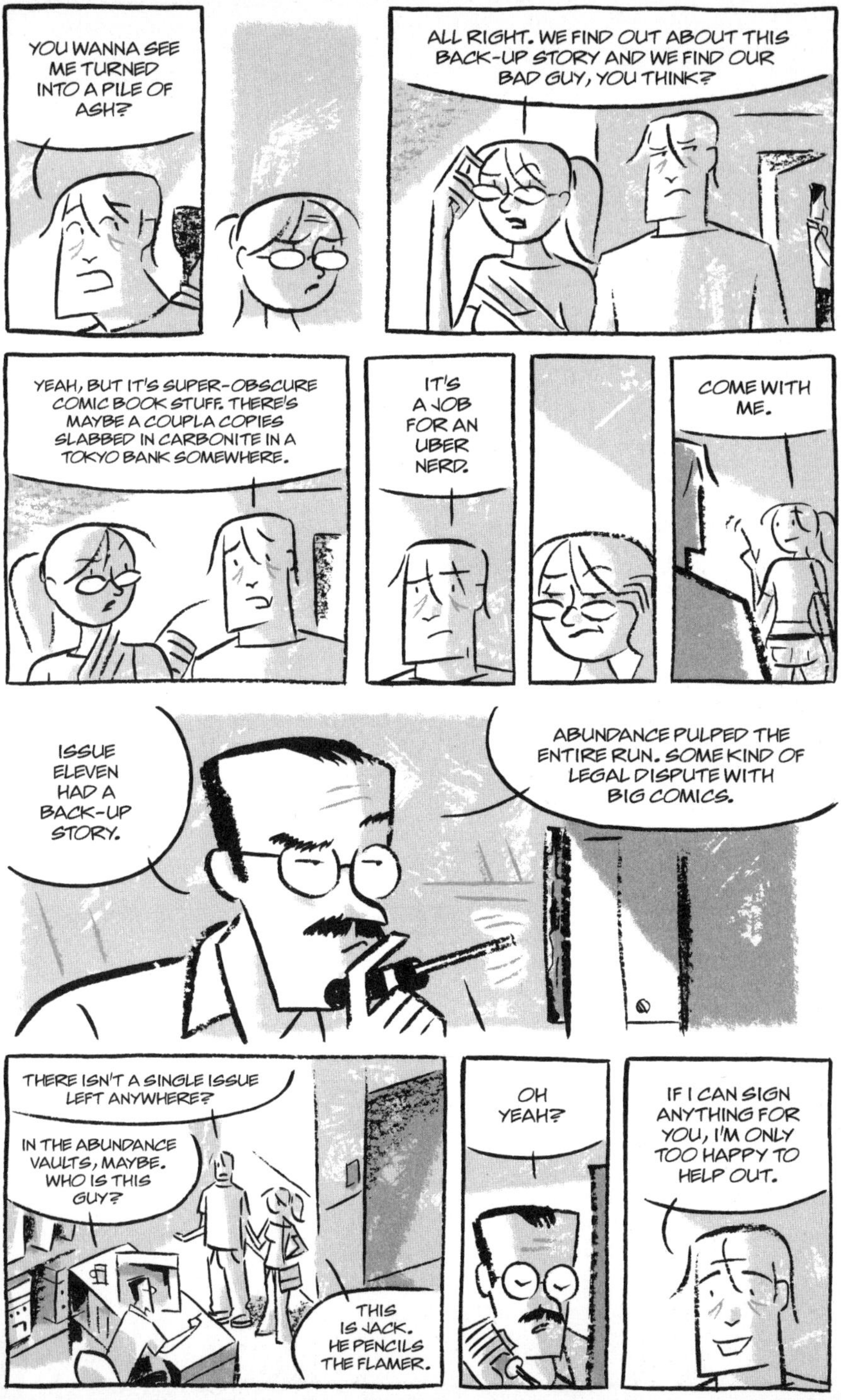
YOU WANNA SEE ME TURNED INTO A PILE OF ASH?
ALL RIGHT. WE FIND OUT ABOUT THIS BACK-UP STORY AND WE FIND OUR BAD GUY, YOU THINK?
YEAH, BUT IT'S SUPER-OBSCURE COMIC BOOK STUFF. THERE'S MAYBE A COUPLA COPIES SLABBED IN CARBONITE IN A TOKYO BANK SOMEWHERE.
IT'S A JOB FOR AN UBER NERD.
COME WITH ME.
ISSUE ELEVEN HAD A BACK-UP STORY.
ABUNDANCE PULPED THE ENTIRE RUN. SOME KIND OF LEGAL DISPUTE WITH BIG COMICS.
THERE ISN'T A SINGLE ISSUE LEFT ANYWHERE?
IN THE ABUNDANCE VAULTS, MAYBE. WHO IS THIS GUY?
THIS IS JACK. HE PENCILS THE FLAMER.
OH YEAH?
IF I CAN SIGN ANYTHING FOR YOU, I'M ONLY TOO HAPPY TO HELP OUT.

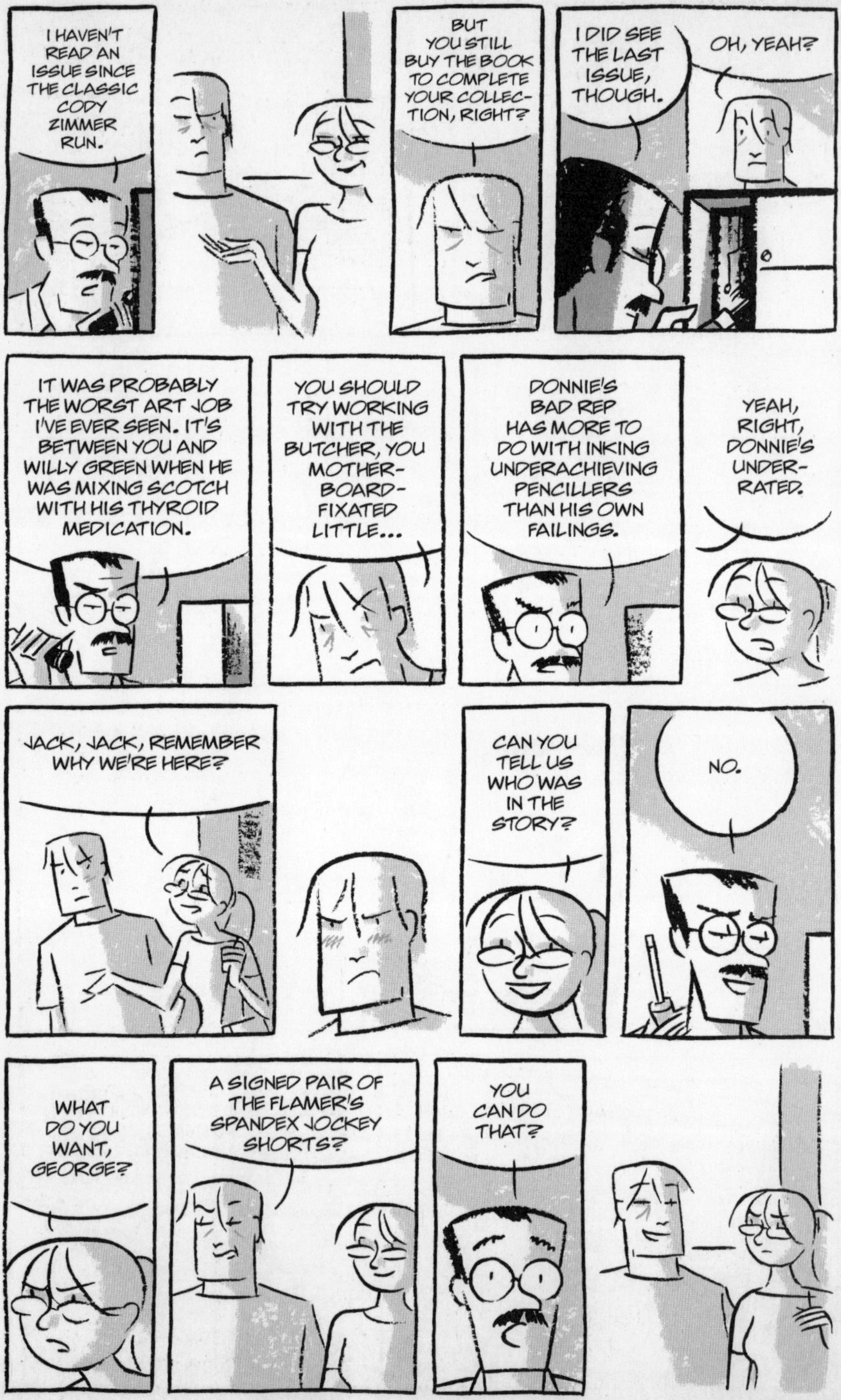
I HAVEN'T READ AN ISSUE SINCE THE CLASSIC CODY ZIMMER RUN.
BUT YOU STILL BUY THE BOOK TO COMPLETE YOUR COLLECTION, RIGHT?
I DID SEE THE LAST ISSUE, THOUGH.
OH, YEAH?
IT WAS PROBABLY THE WORST ART JOB I'VE EVER SEEN. IT'S BETWEEN YOU AND WILLY GREEN WHEN HE WAS MIXING SCOTCH WITH HIS THYROID MEDICATION.
YOU SHOULD TRY WORKING WITH THE BUTCHER, YOU MOTHER-BOARD-FIXATED LITTLE...
DONNIE'S BAD REP HAS MORE TO DO WITH INKING UNDERACHIEVING PENCILLERS THAN HIS OWN FAILINGS.
YEAH, RIGHT, DONNIE'S UNDER-RATED.
JACK, JACK, REMEMBER WHY WE'RE HERE?
CAN YOU TELL US WHO WAS IN THE STORY?
NO.
WHAT DO YOU WANT, GEORGE?
A SIGNED PAIR OF THE FLAMER'S SPANDEX JOCKEY SHORTS?
YOU CAN DO THAT?

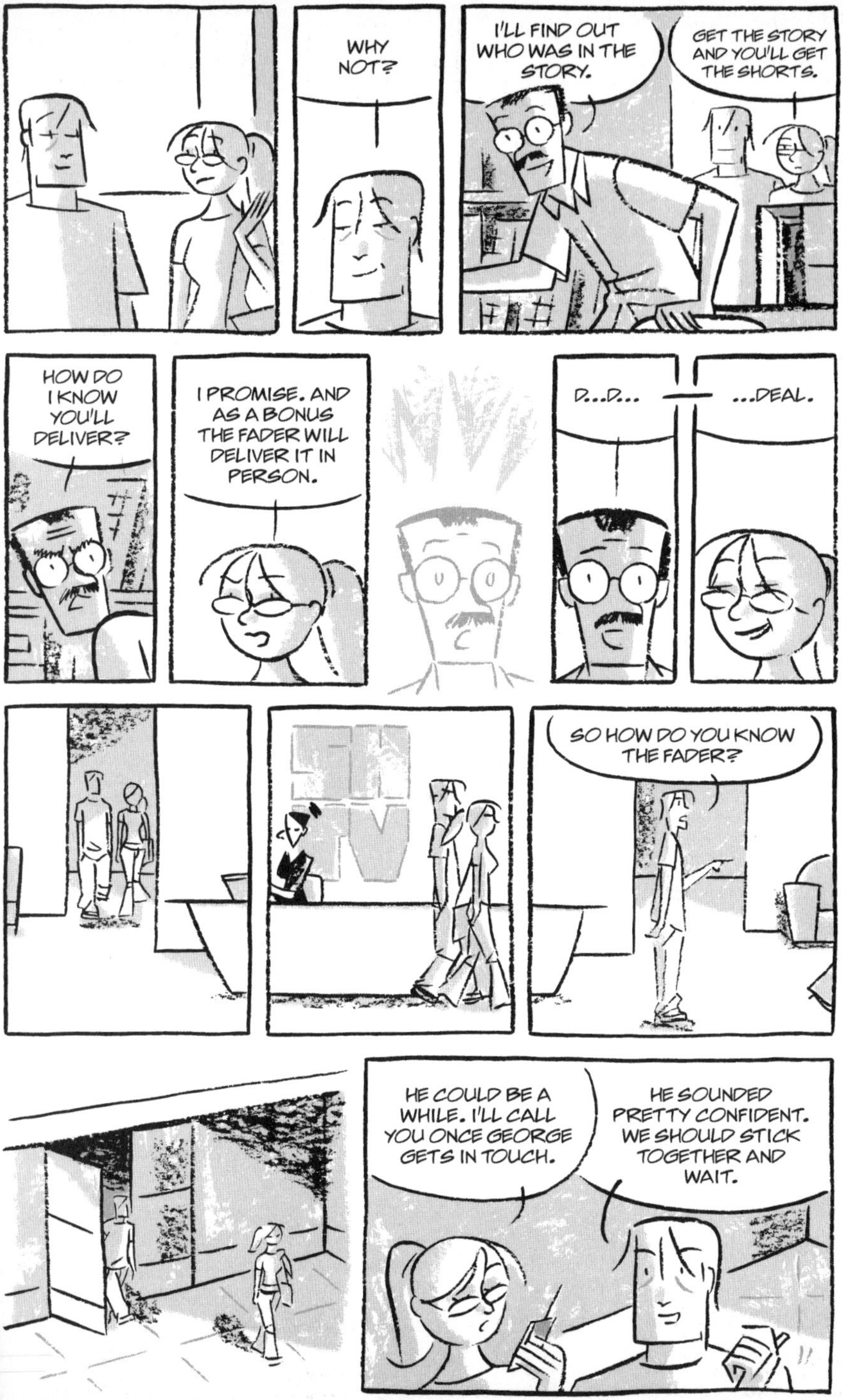
WHY NOT?
I'LL FIND OUT WHO WAS IN THE STORY.
GET THE STORY AND YOU'LL GET THE SHORTS.
HOW DO I KNOW YOU'LL DELIVER?
I PROMISE. AND AS A BONUS THE FADER WILL DELIVER IT IN PERSON.
D...D...
...DEAL.
SO HOW DO YOU KNOW THE FADER?
HE COULD BE A WHILE. I'LL CALL YOU ONCE GEORGE GETS IN TOUCH.
HE SOUNDED PRETTY CONFIDENT. WE SHOULD STICK TOGETHER AND WAIT.

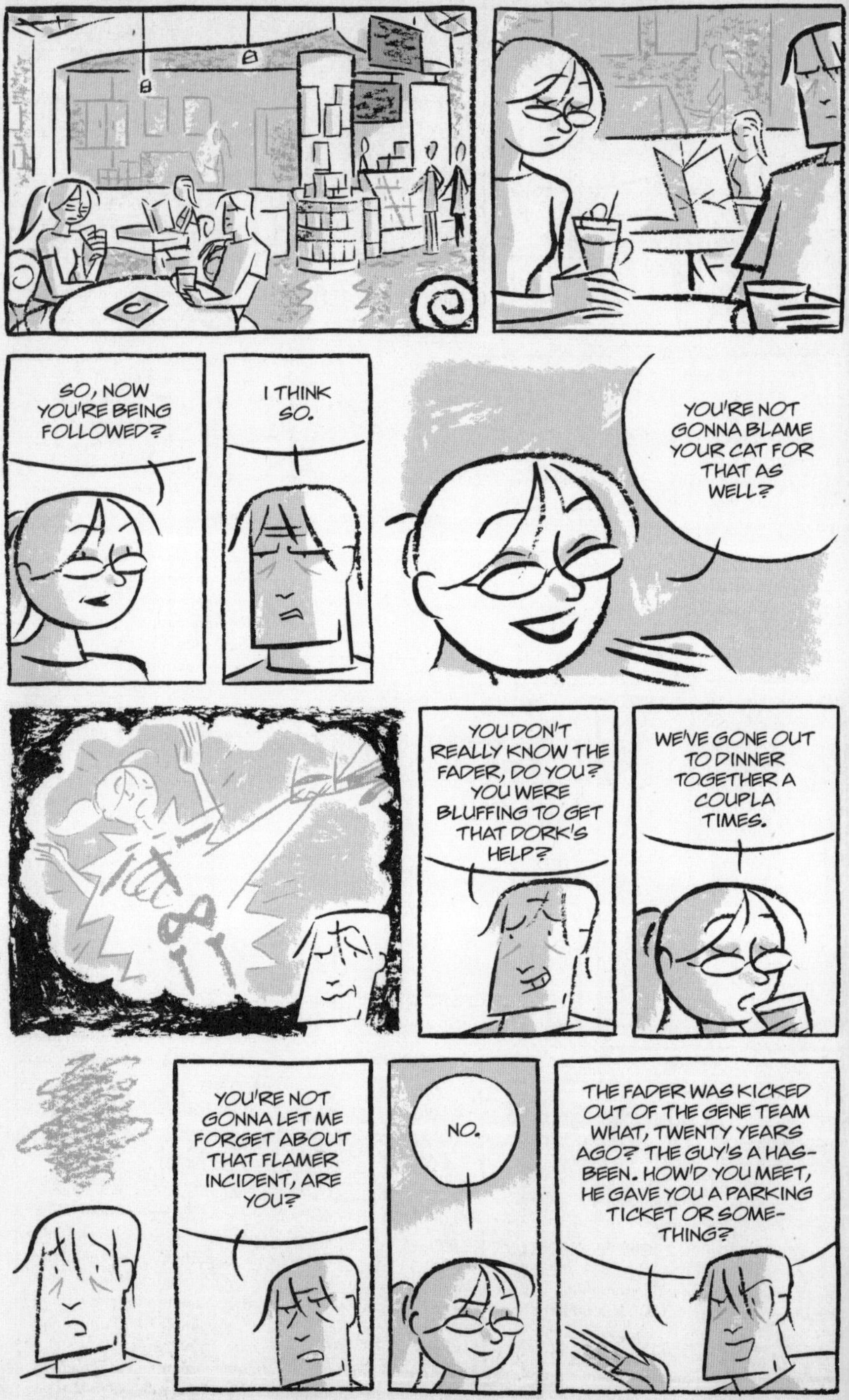

SO, NOW YOU'RE BEING FOLLOWED?
I THINK SO.
YOU'RE NOT GONNA BLAME YOUR CAT FOR THAT AS WELL?
YOU DON'T REALLY KNOW THE FADER, DO YOU? YOU WERE BLUFFING TO GET THAT DORK'S HELP?
WE'VE GONE OUT TO DINNER TOGETHER A COUPLA TIMES.
YOU'RE NOT GONNA LET ME FORGET ABOUT THAT FLAMER INCIDENT, ARE YOU?
NO.
THE FADER WAS KICKED OUT OF THE GENE TEAM WHAT, TWENTY YEARS AGO? THE GUY'S A HAS-BEEN. HOW'D YOU MEET, HE GAVE YOU A PARKING TICKET OR SOME-THING?

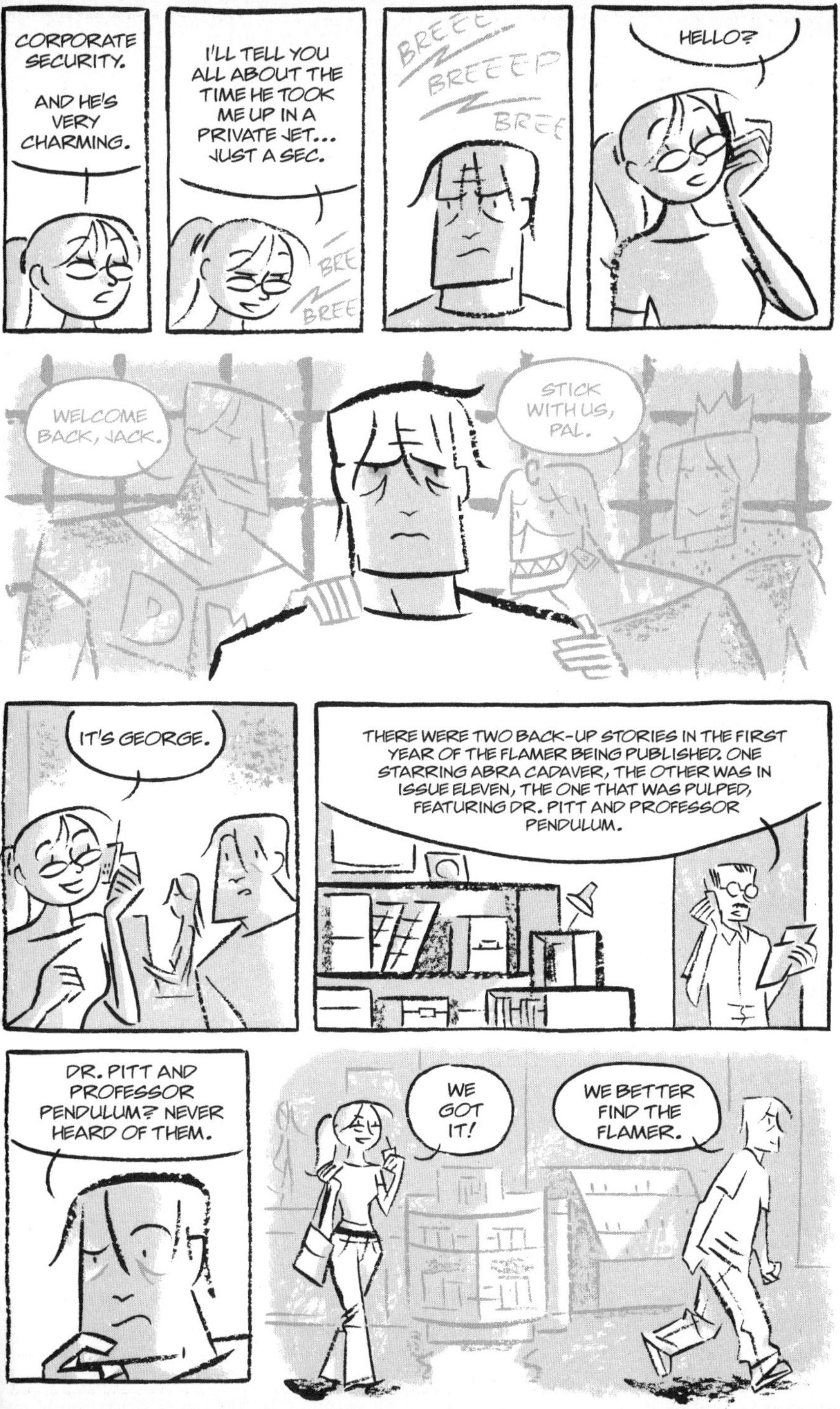
CORPORATE SECURITY.
AND HE'S VERY CHARMING.
I'LL TELL YOU ALL ABOUT THE TIME HE TOOK ME UP IN A PRIVATE JET... JUST A SEC.
BREE
BREE
BREEE
BREEEP
BREE
HELLO?
WELCOME BACK, JACK.
STICK WITH US, PAL.
IT'S GEORGE.
THERE WERE TWO BACK-UP STORIES IN THE FIRST YEAR OF THE FLAMER BEING PUBLISHED. ONE STARRING ABRA CADAVER, THE OTHER WAS IN ISSUE ELEVEN, THE ONE THAT WAS PULPED, FEATURING DR. PITT AND PROFESSOR PENDULUM.
DR. PITT AND PROFESSOR PENDULUM? NEVER HEARD OF THEM.
WE GOT IT!
WE BETTER FIND THE FLAMER.

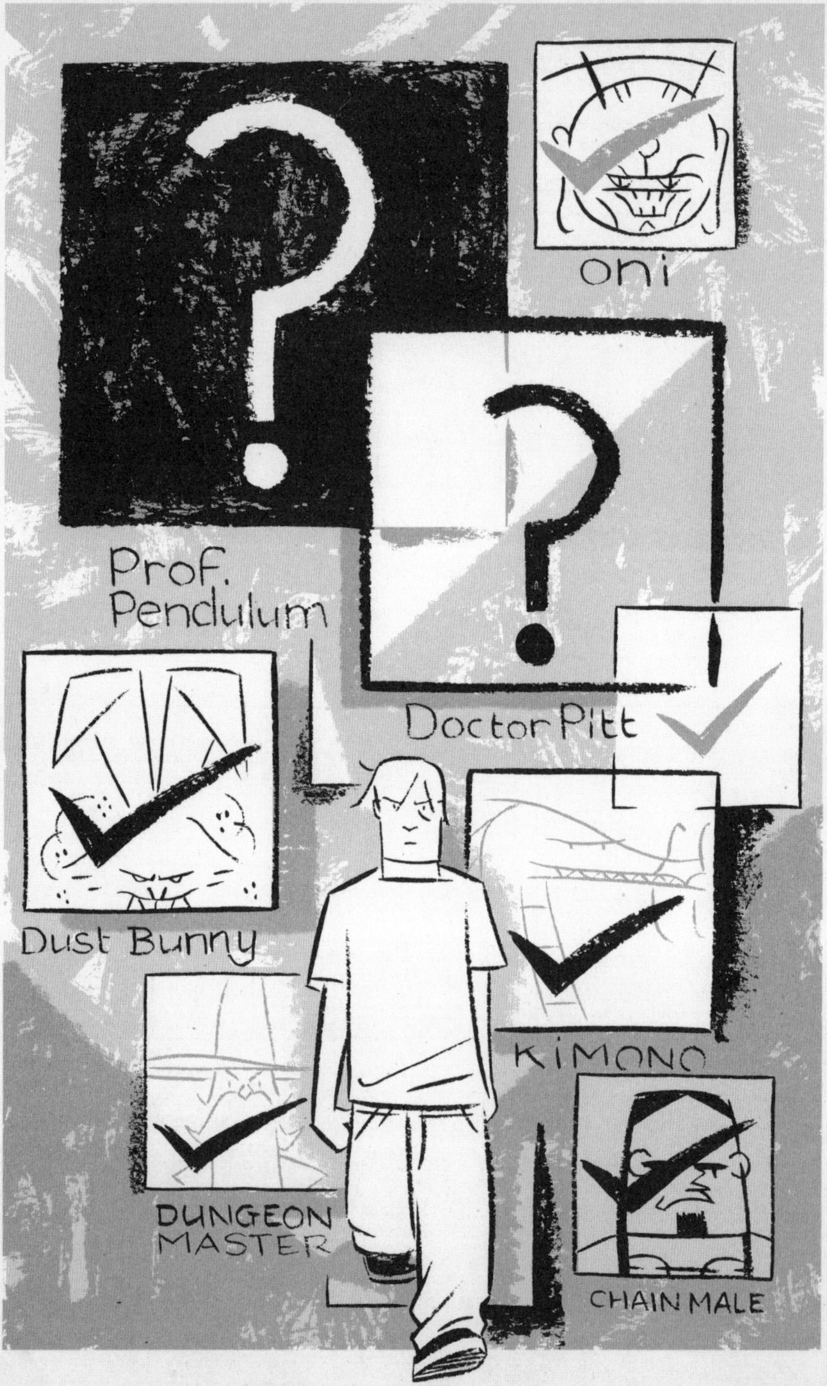
oni
Prof. Pendulum
Doctor Pitt
Dust Bunny
KIMONO
DUNGEON MASTER
CHAIN MALE

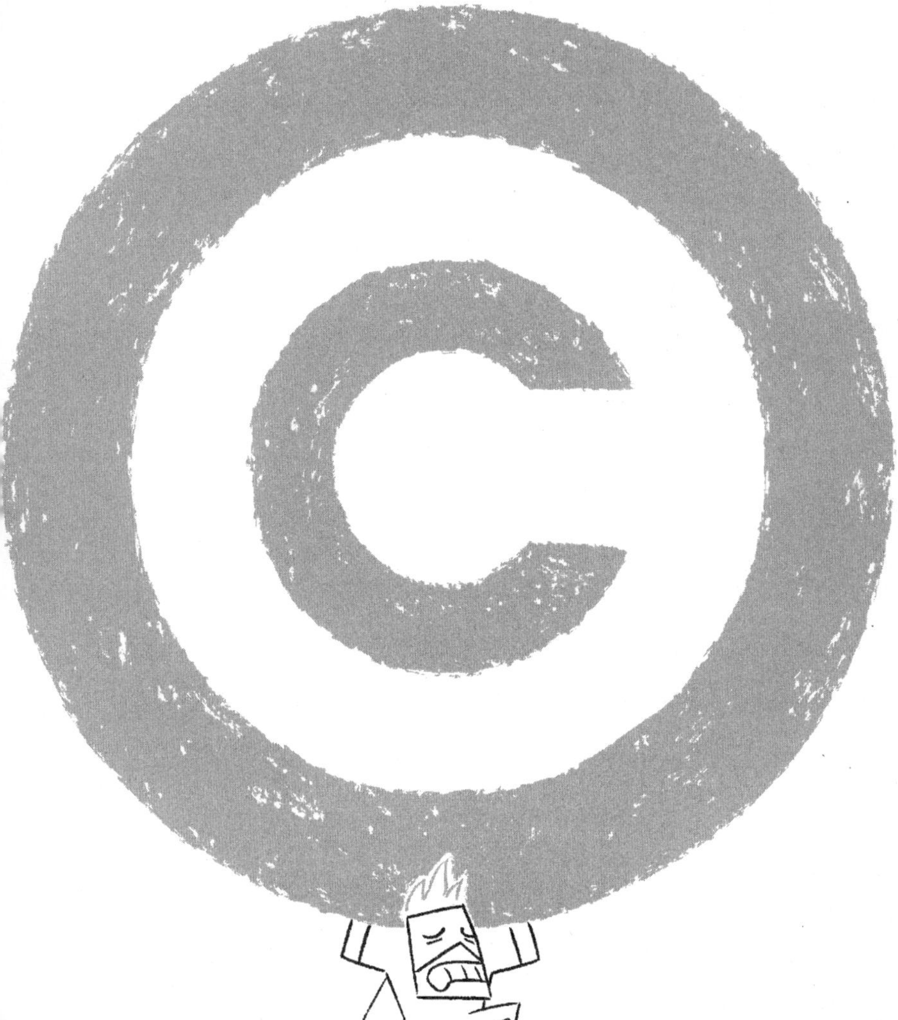

Love Fights™ #9

andi watson

ONI PRESS

$2.99 U.S., $4.60 CAN.

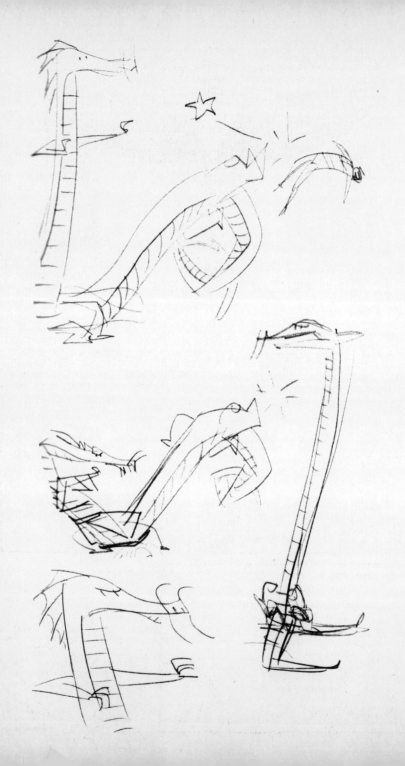

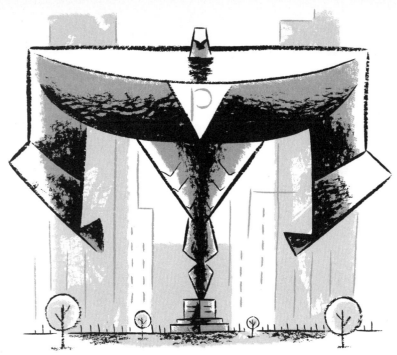

DR. CHILDERS? YES, IT'S NORA. I NEED YOU TO CONTACT THE FLAMER. TELL HIM TO MEET ME IN THE USUAL PLACE.

NO, I DON'T KNOW HOW I EXPECT YOU TO CONTACT HIM. USE THE FLAMER PHONE OR SMOKE SIGNALS, WHATEVER, JUST GET THE MESSAGE TO HIM.

I'M SURE HE'S VERY BUSY. I'LL BE WAITING.

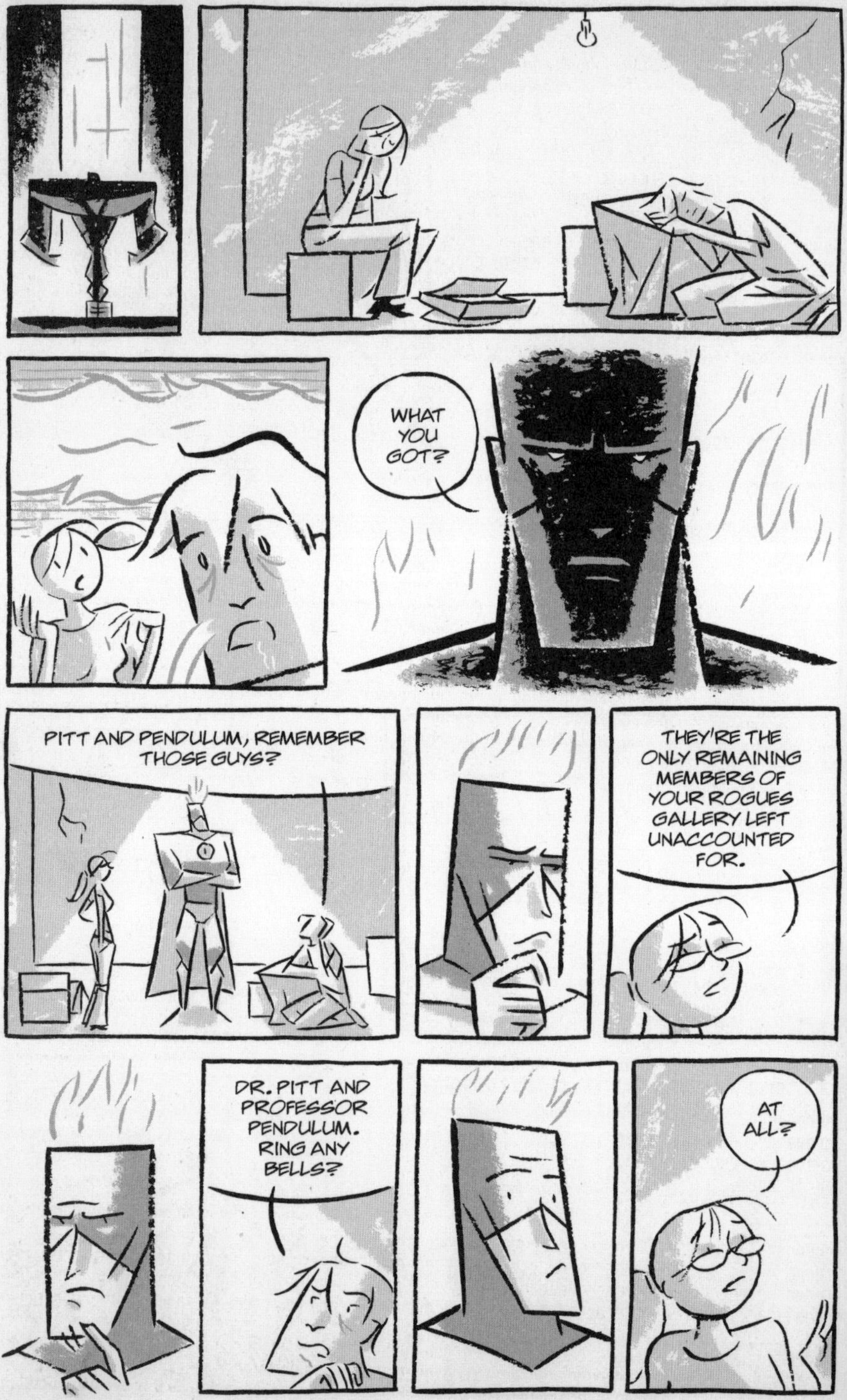
WHAT YOU GOT?
PITT AND PENDULUM, REMEMBER THOSE GUYS?
THEY'RE THE ONLY REMAINING MEMBERS OF YOUR ROGUES GALLERY LEFT UNACCOUNTED FOR.
DR. PITT AND PROFESSOR PENDULUM. RING ANY BELLS?
AT ALL?

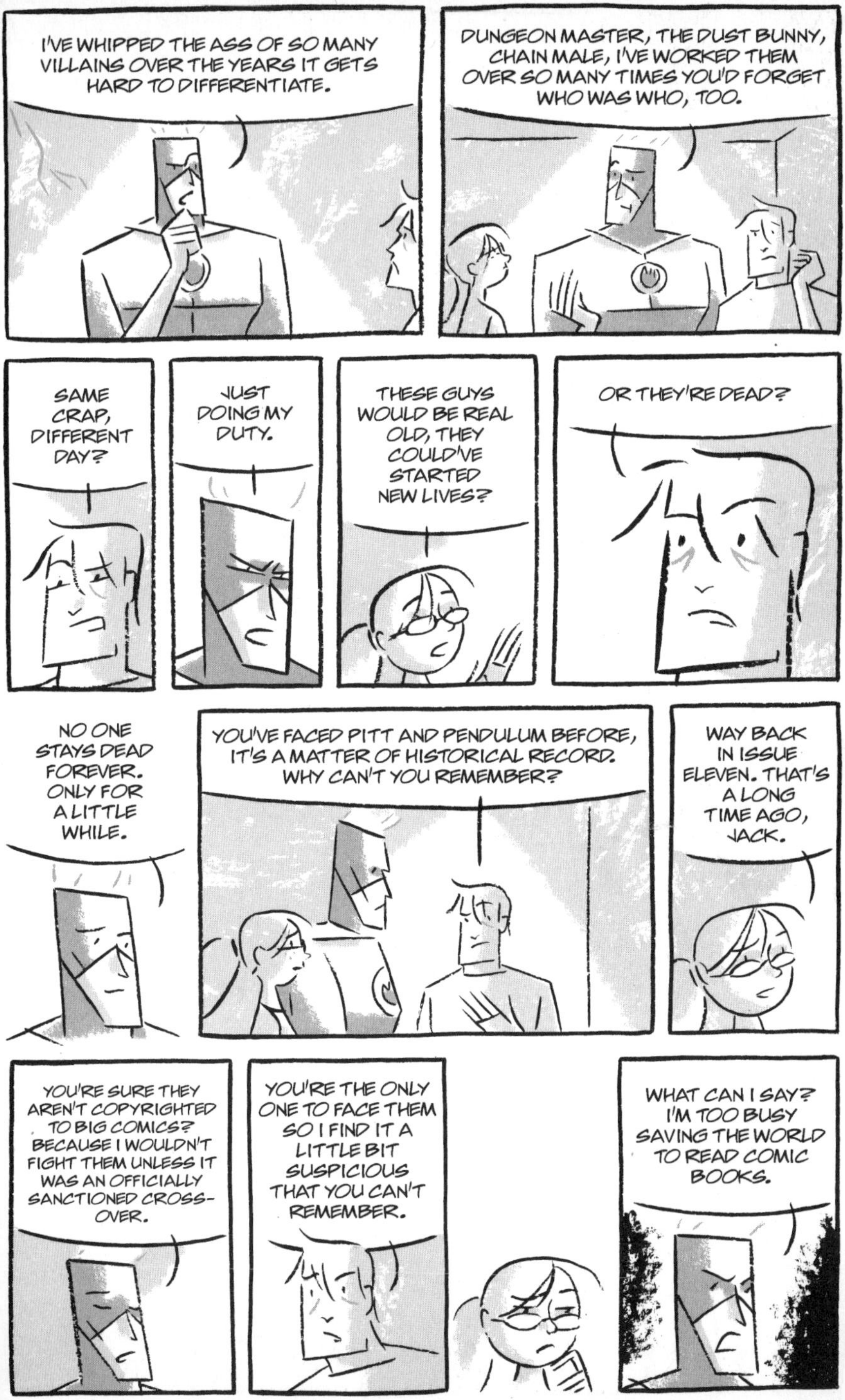
I'VE WHIPPED THE ASS OF SO MANY VILLAINS OVER THE YEARS IT GETS HARD TO DIFFERENTIATE.
DUNGEON MASTER, THE DUST BUNNY, CHAIN MALE, I'VE WORKED THEM OVER SO MANY TIMES YOU'D FORGET WHO WAS WHO, TOO.
SAME CRAP, DIFFERENT DAY?
JUST DOING MY DUTY.
THESE GUYS WOULD BE REAL OLD, THEY COULD'VE STARTED NEW LIVES?
OR THEY'RE DEAD?
NO ONE STAYS DEAD FOREVER. ONLY FOR A LITTLE WHILE.
YOU'VE FACED PITT AND PENDULUM BEFORE, IT'S A MATTER OF HISTORICAL RECORD. WHY CAN'T YOU REMEMBER?
WAY BACK IN ISSUE ELEVEN. THAT'S A LONG TIME AGO, JACK.
YOU'RE SURE THEY AREN'T COPYRIGHTED TO BIG COMICS? BECAUSE I WOULDN'T FIGHT THEM UNLESS IT WAS AN OFFICIALLY SANCTIONED CROSS-OVER.
YOU'RE THE ONLY ONE TO FACE THEM SO I FIND IT A LITTLE BIT SUSPICIOUS THAT YOU CAN'T REMEMBER.
WHAT CAN I SAY? I'M TOO BUSY SAVING THE WORLD TO READ COMIC BOOKS.

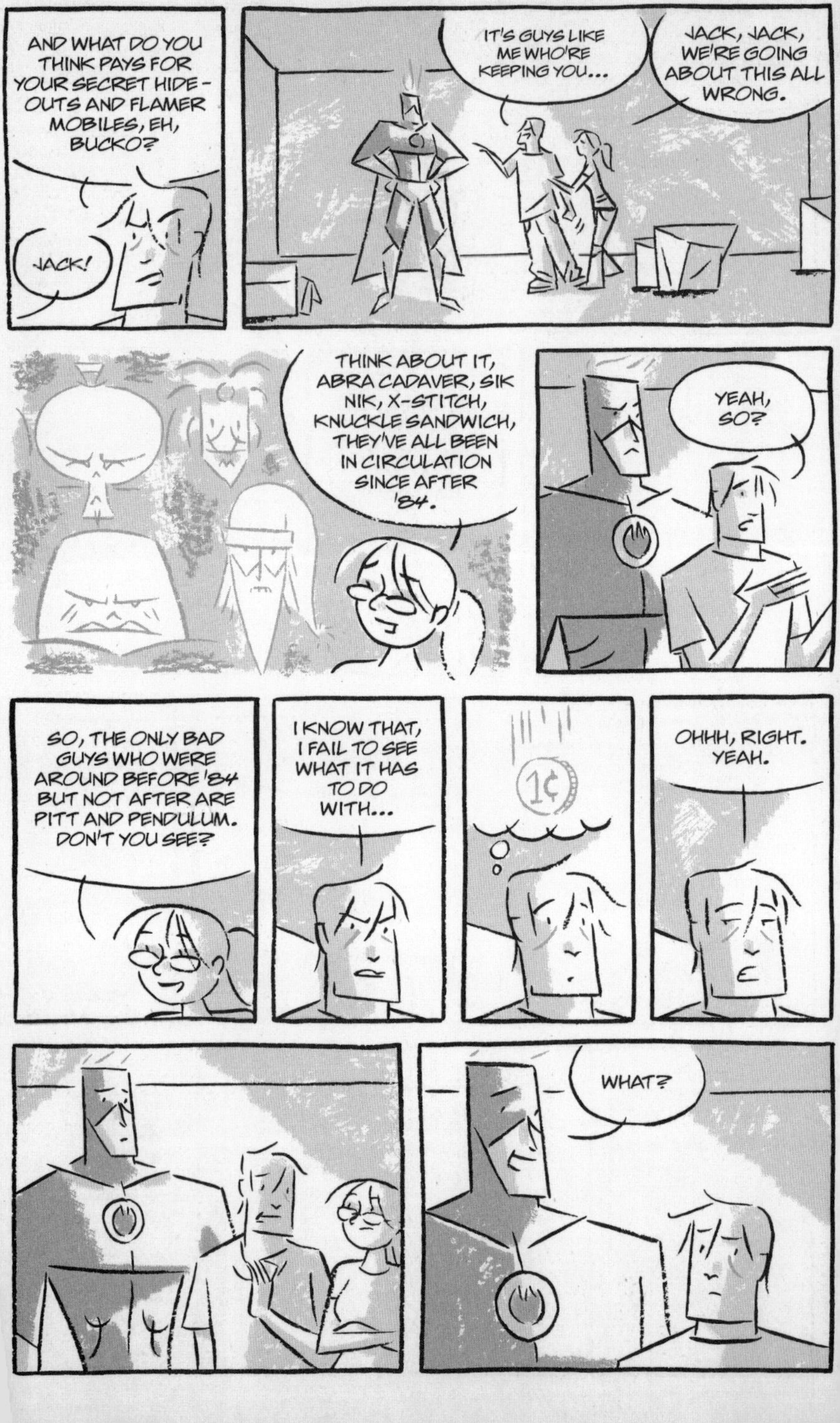
AND WHAT DO YOU THINK PAYS FOR YOUR SECRET HIDE-OUTS AND FLAMER MOBILES, EH, BUCKO?
JACK!
IT'S GUYS LIKE ME WHO'RE KEEPING YOU...
JACK, JACK, WE'RE GOING ABOUT THIS ALL WRONG.
THINK ABOUT IT, ABRA CADAVER, SIK NIK, X-STITCH, KNUCKLE SANDWICH, THEY'VE ALL BEEN IN CIRCULATION SINCE AFTER '84.
YEAH, SO?
SO, THE ONLY BAD GUYS WHO WERE AROUND BEFORE '84 BUT NOT AFTER ARE PITT AND PENDULUM. DON'T YOU SEE?
I KNOW THAT, I FAIL TO SEE WHAT IT HAS TO DO WITH...
1¢
OHHH, RIGHT. YEAH.
WHAT?

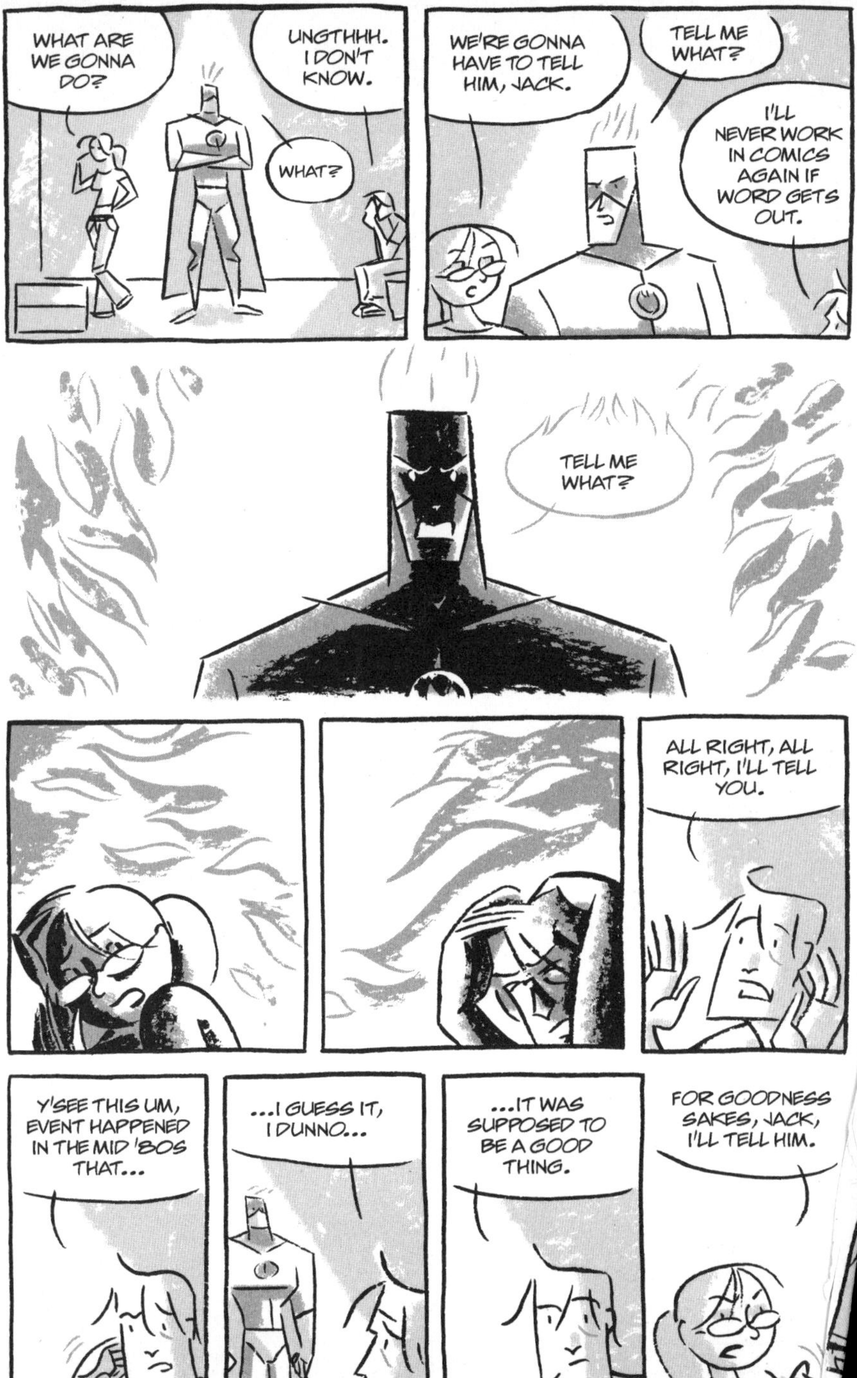
WHAT ARE WE GONNA DO?
UNGTHHH. I DON'T KNOW.
WHAT?
WE'RE GONNA HAVE TO TELL HIM, JACK.
TELL ME WHAT?
I'LL NEVER WORK IN COMICS AGAIN IF WORD GETS OUT.
TELL ME WHAT?
ALL RIGHT, ALL RIGHT, I'LL TELL YOU.
Y'SEE THIS UM, EVENT HAPPENED IN THE MID '80S THAT...
...I GUESS IT, I DUNNO...
...IT WAS SUPPOSED TO BE A GOOD THING.
FOR GOODNESS SAKES, JACK, I'LL TELL HIM.

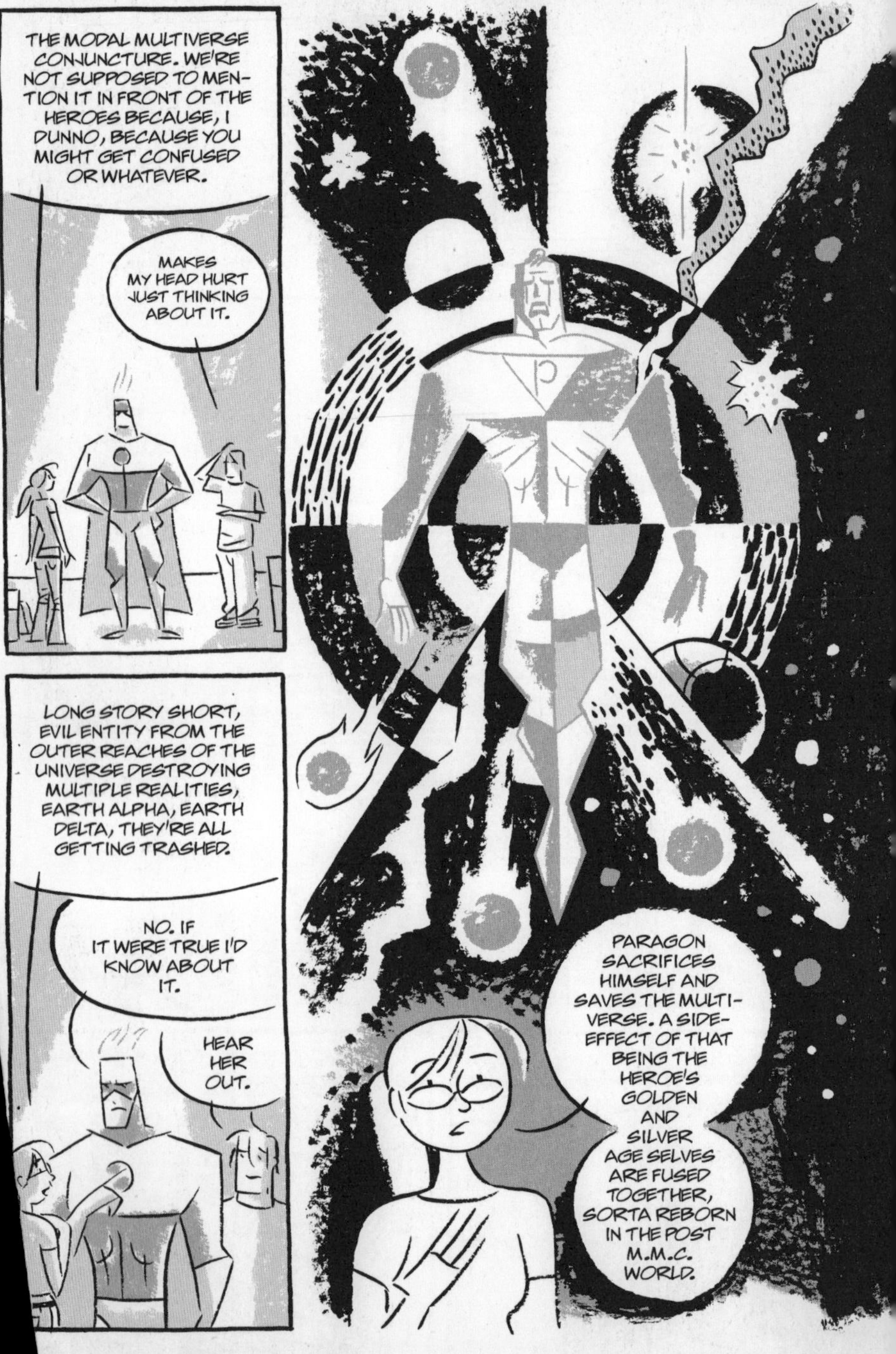
THE MODAL MULTIVERSE CONJUNCTURE. WE'RE NOT SUPPOSED TO MENTION IT IN FRONT OF THE HEROES BECAUSE, I DUNNO, BECAUSE YOU MIGHT GET CONFUSED OR WHATEVER.
MAKES MY HEAD HURT JUST THINKING ABOUT IT.
LONG STORY SHORT, EVIL ENTITY FROM THE OUTER REACHES OF THE UNIVERSE DESTROYING MULTIPLE REALITIES, EARTH ALPHA, EARTH DELTA, THEY'RE ALL GETTING TRASHED.
NO. IF IT WERE TRUE I'D KNOW ABOUT IT.
HEAR HER OUT.
PARAGON SACRIFICES HIMSELF AND SAVES THE MULTIVERSE. A SIDE-EFFECT OF THAT BEING THE HEROE'S GOLDEN AND SILVER AGE SELVES ARE FUSED TOGETHER, SORTA REBORN IN THE POST M.M.C. WORLD.

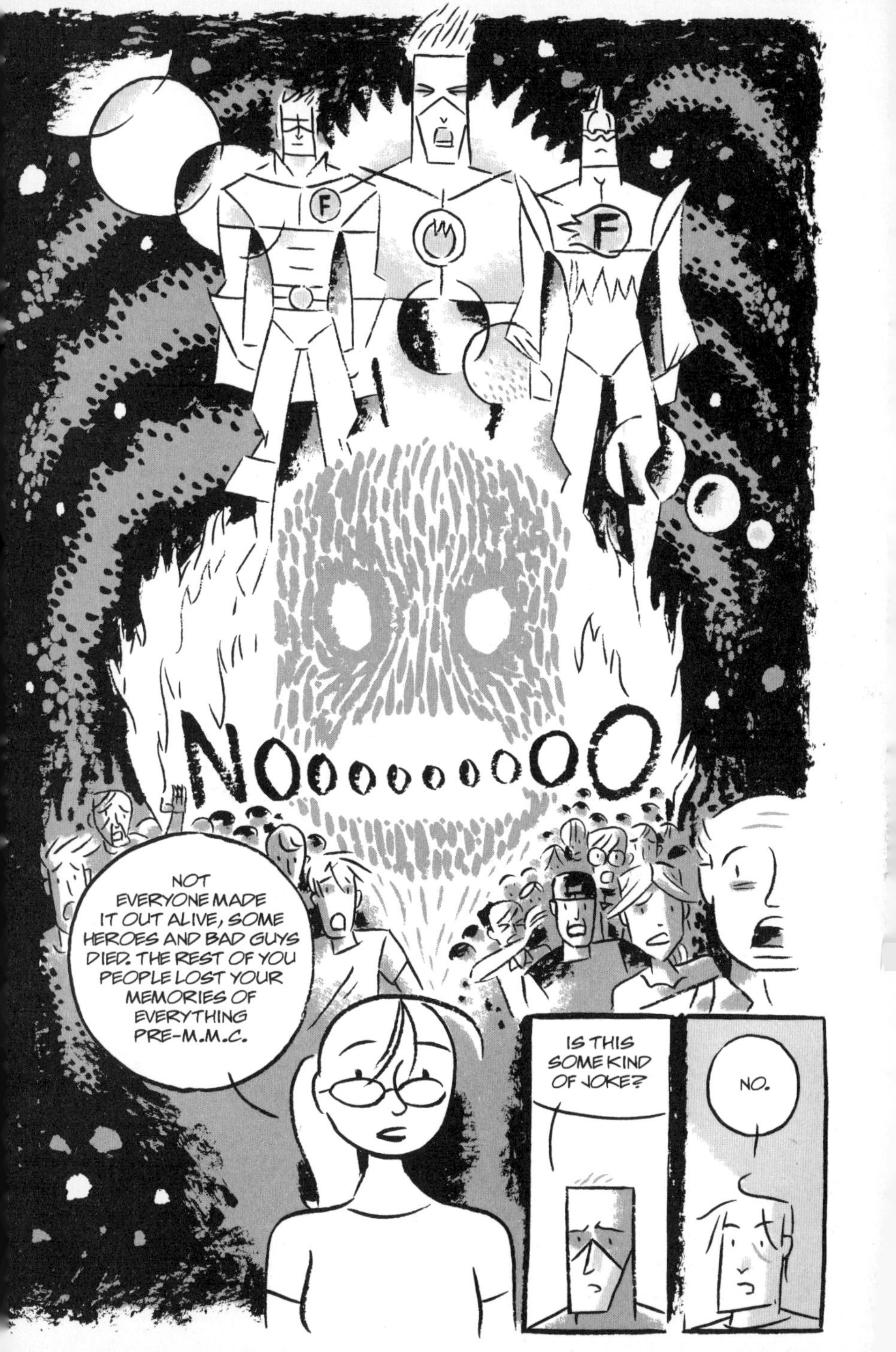
NOOOOOOOOO
NOT EVERYONE MADE IT OUT ALIVE, SOME HEROES AND BAD GUYS DIED. THE REST OF YOU PEOPLE LOST YOUR MEMORIES OF EVERYTHING PRE-M.M.C.
IS THIS SOME KIND OF JOKE?
NO.

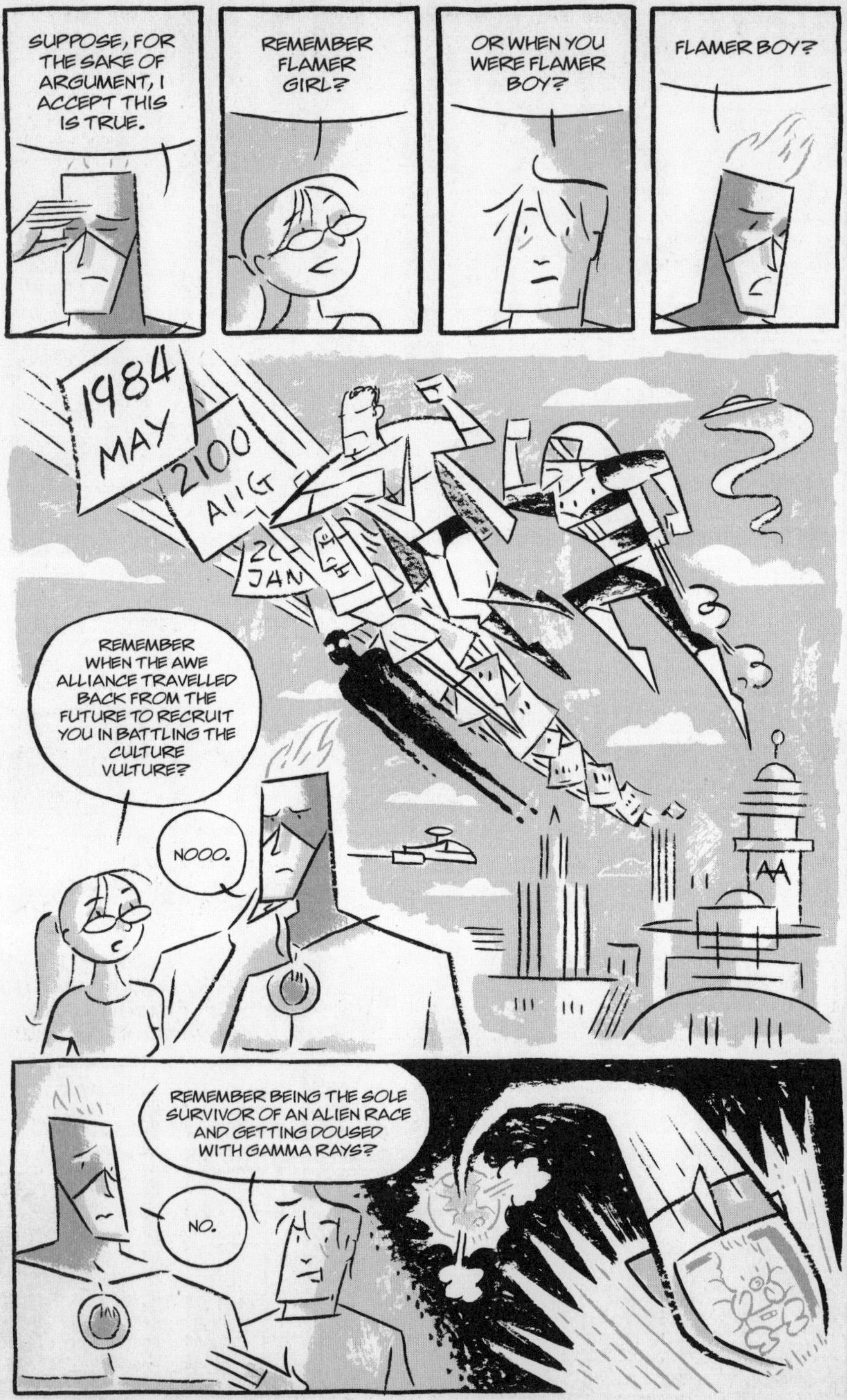
SUPPOSE, FOR THE SAKE OF ARGUMENT, I ACCEPT THIS IS TRUE.
REMEMBER FLAMER GIRL?
OR WHEN YOU WERE FLAMER BOY?
FLAMER BOY?
1984 MAY
2100 AUG
20 JAN
REMEMBER WHEN THE AWE ALLIANCE TRAVELLED BACK FROM THE FUTURE TO RECRUIT YOU IN BATTLING THE CULTURE VULTURE?
NOOO.
AA
REMEMBER BEING THE SOLE SURVIVOR OF AN ALIEN RACE AND GETTING DOUSED WITH GAMMA RAYS?
NO.

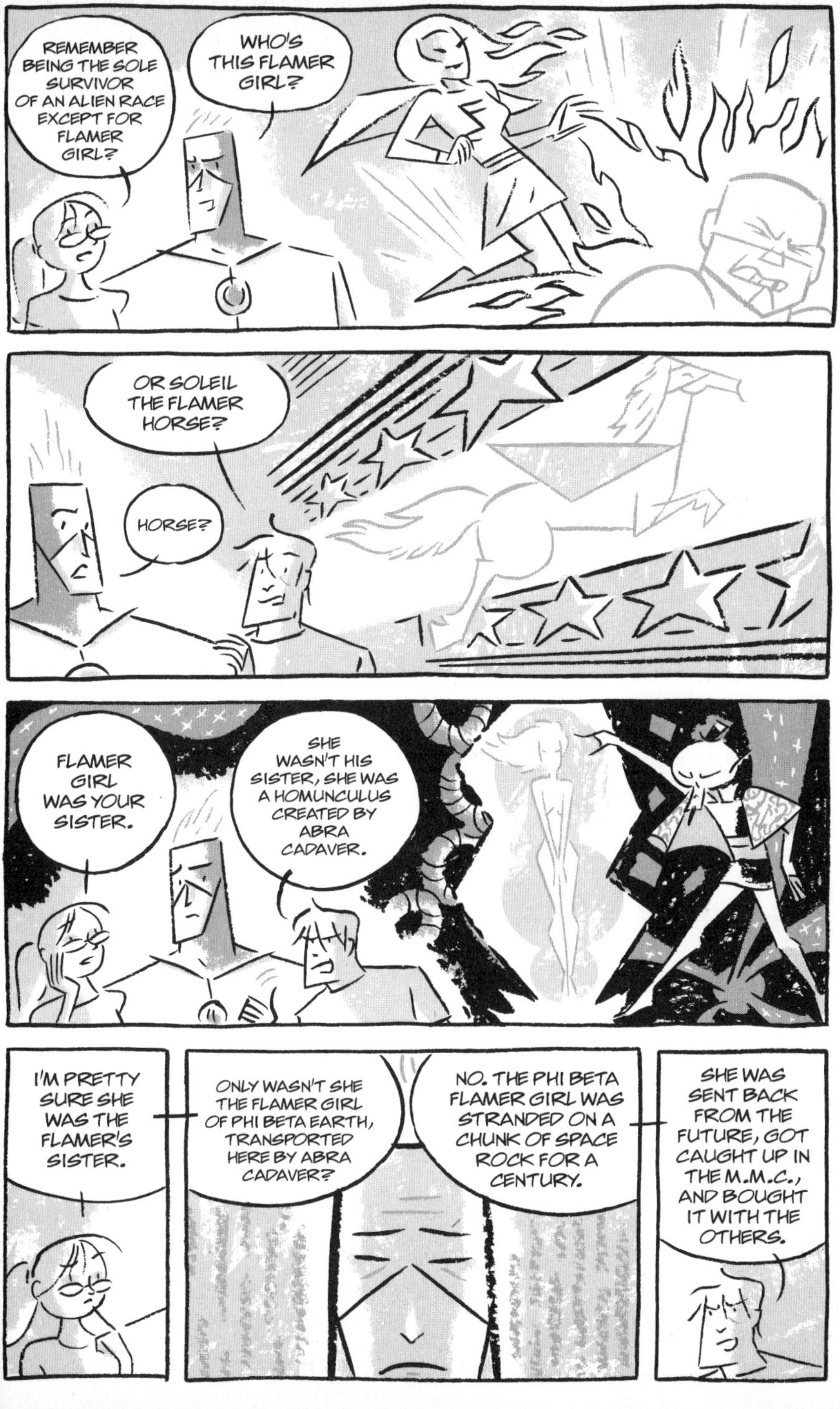
REMEMBER BEING THE SOLE SURVIVOR OF AN ALIEN RACE EXCEPT FOR FLAMER GIRL?
WHO'S THIS FLAMER GIRL?
OR SOLEIL THE FLAMER HORSE?
HORSE?
FLAMER GIRL WAS YOUR SISTER.
SHE WASN'T HIS SISTER, SHE WAS A HOMUNCULUS CREATED BY ABRA CADAVER.
I'M PRETTY SURE SHE WAS THE FLAMER'S SISTER.
ONLY WASN'T SHE THE FLAMER GIRL OF PHI BETA EARTH, TRANSPORTED HERE BY ABRA CADAVER?
NO. THE PHI BETA FLAMER GIRL WAS STRANDED ON A CHUNK OF SPACE ROCK FOR A CENTURY.
SHE WAS SENT BACK FROM THE FUTURE, GOT CAUGHT UP IN THE M.M.C., AND BOUGHT IT WITH THE OTHERS.

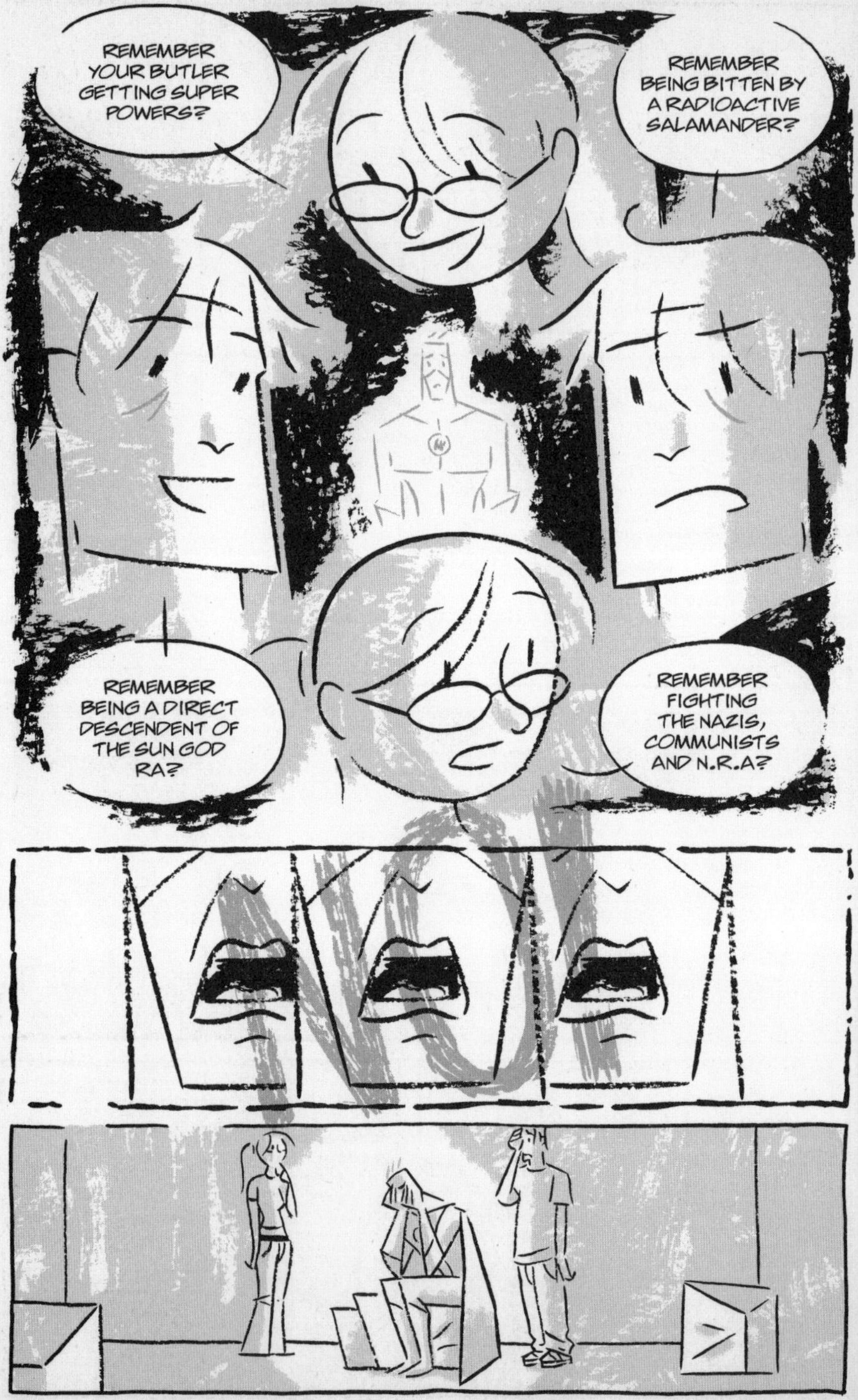
REMEMBER YOUR BUTLER GETTING SUPER POWERS?
REMEMBER BEING BITTEN BY A RADIOACTIVE SALAMANDER?
REMEMBER BEING A DIRECT DESCENDENT OF THE SUN GOD RA?
REMEMBER FIGHTING THE NAZIS, COMMUNISTS AND N.R.A?

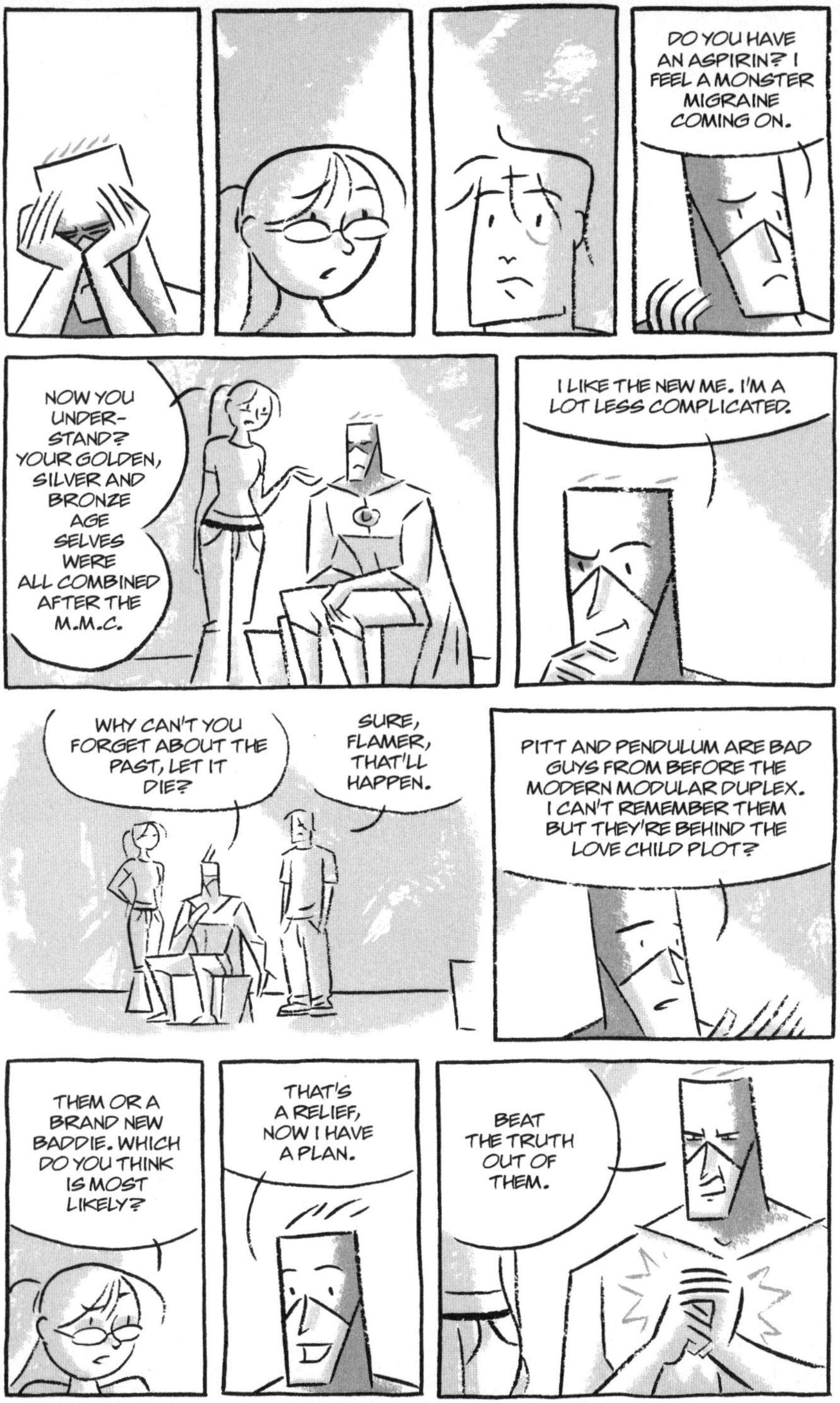
DO YOU HAVE AN ASPIRIN? I FEEL A MONSTER MIGRAINE COMING ON.
NOW YOU UNDER-STAND? YOUR GOLDEN, SILVER AND BRONZE AGE SELVES WERE ALL COMBINED AFTER THE M.M.C.
I LIKE THE NEW ME. I'M A LOT LESS COMPLICATED.
WHY CAN'T YOU FORGET ABOUT THE PAST, LET IT DIE?
SURE, FLAMER, THAT'LL HAPPEN.
PITT AND PENDULUM ARE BAD GUYS FROM BEFORE THE MODERN MODULAR DUPLEX. I CAN'T REMEMBER THEM BUT THEY'RE BEHIND THE LOVE CHILD PLOT?
THEM OR A BRAND NEW BADDIE. WHICH DO YOU THINK IS MOST LIKELY?
THAT'S A RELIEF, NOW I HAVE A PLAN.
BEAT THE TRUTH OUT OF THEM.

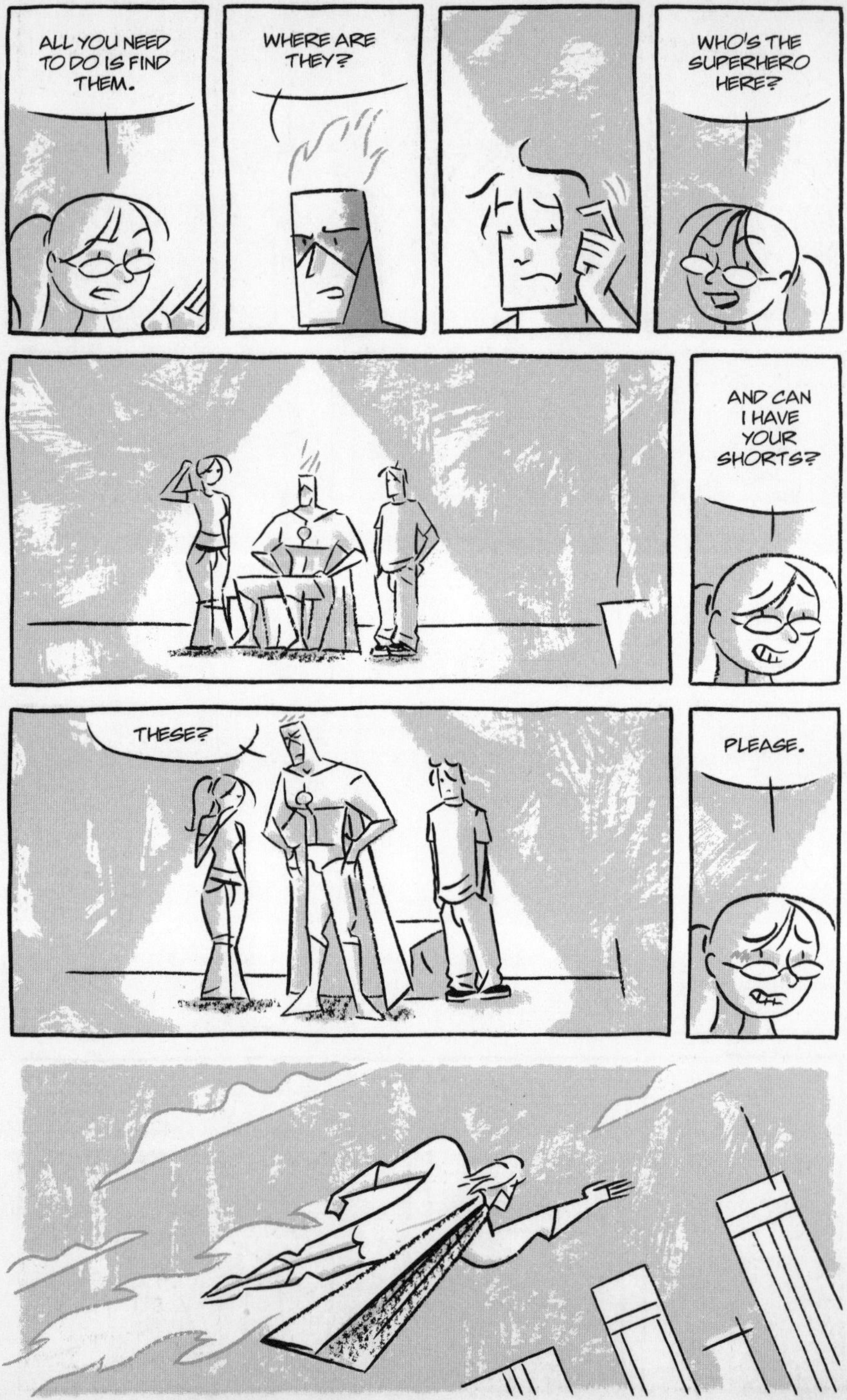
ALL YOU NEED TO DO IS FIND THEM.
WHERE ARE THEY?
WHO'S THE SUPERHERO HERE?
AND CAN I HAVE YOUR SHORTS?
THESE?
PLEASE.

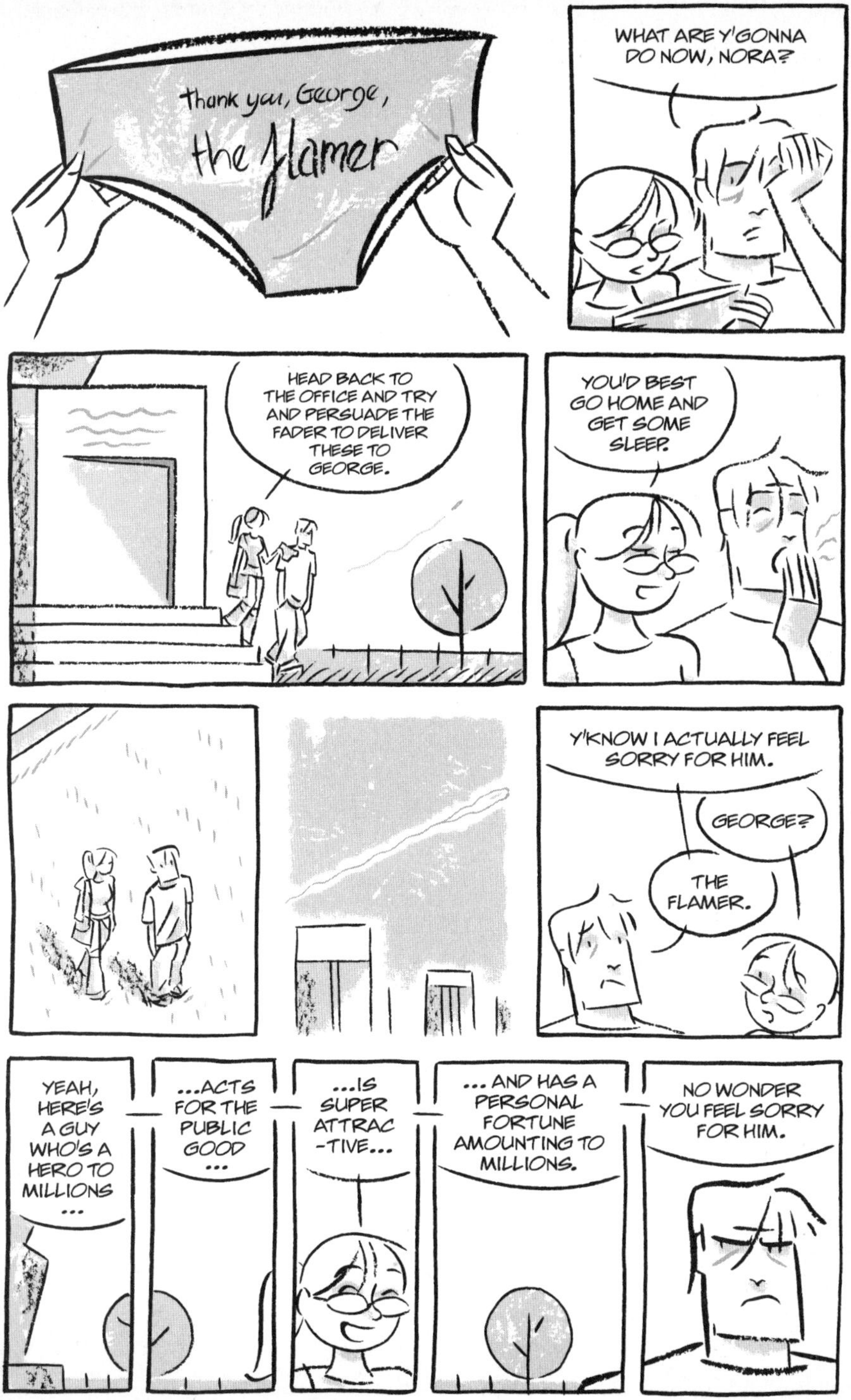
thank you, George,
the flamer
WHAT ARE Y'GONNA DO NOW, NORA?
HEAD BACK TO THE OFFICE AND TRY AND PERSUADE THE FADER TO DELIVER THESE TO GEORGE.
YOU'D BEST GO HOME AND GET SOME SLEEP.
Y'KNOW I ACTUALLY FEEL SORRY FOR HIM.
GEORGE?
THE FLAMER.
YEAH, HERE'S A GUY WHO'S A HERO TO MILLIONS ...
...ACTS FOR THE PUBLIC GOOD ...
...IS SUPER ATTRAC -TIVE...
... AND HAS A PERSONAL FORTUNE AMOUNTING TO MILLIONS.
NO WONDER YOU FEEL SORRY FOR HIM.

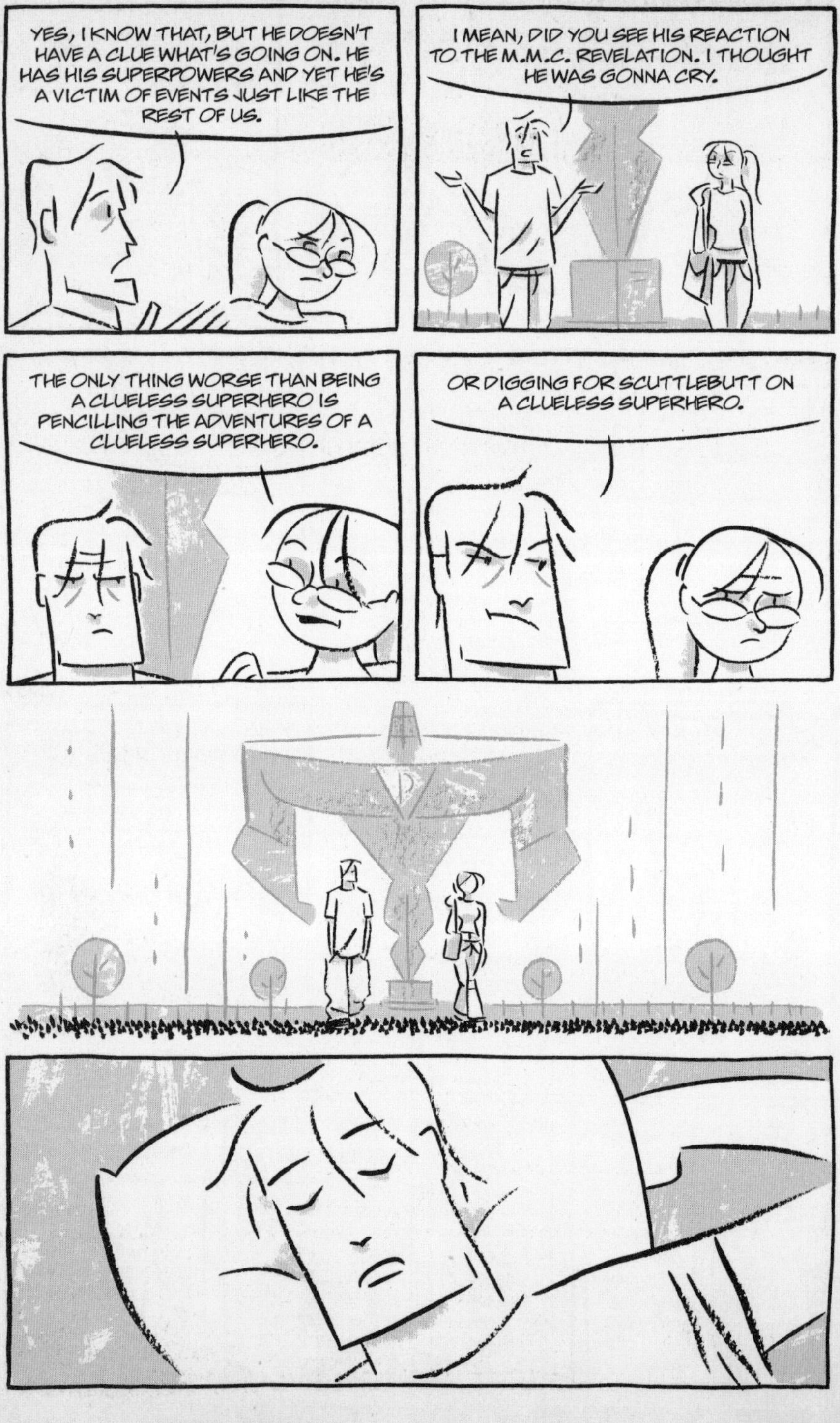
YES, I KNOW THAT, BUT HE DOESN'T HAVE A CLUE WHAT'S GOING ON. HE HAS HIS SUPERPOWERS AND YET HE'S A VICTIM OF EVENTS JUST LIKE THE REST OF US.
I MEAN, DID YOU SEE HIS REACTION TO THE M.M.C. REVELATION. I THOUGHT HE WAS GONNA CRY.
THE ONLY THING WORSE THAN BEING A CLUELESS SUPERHERO IS PENCILLING THE ADVENTURES OF A CLUELESS SUPERHERO.
OR DIGGING FOR SCUTTLEBUTT ON A CLUELESS SUPERHERO.

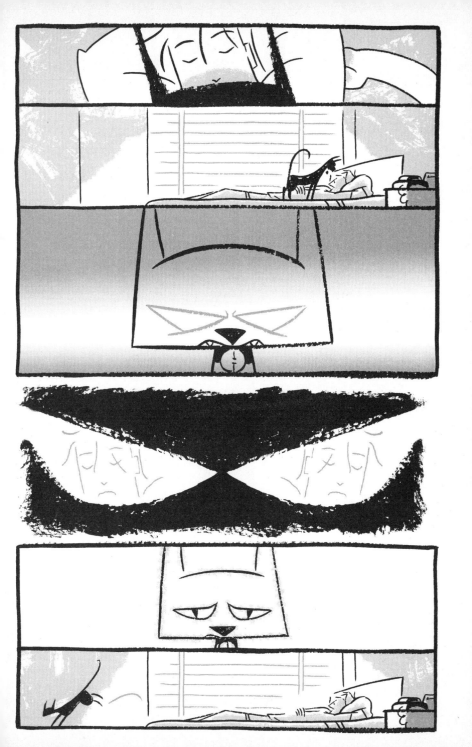

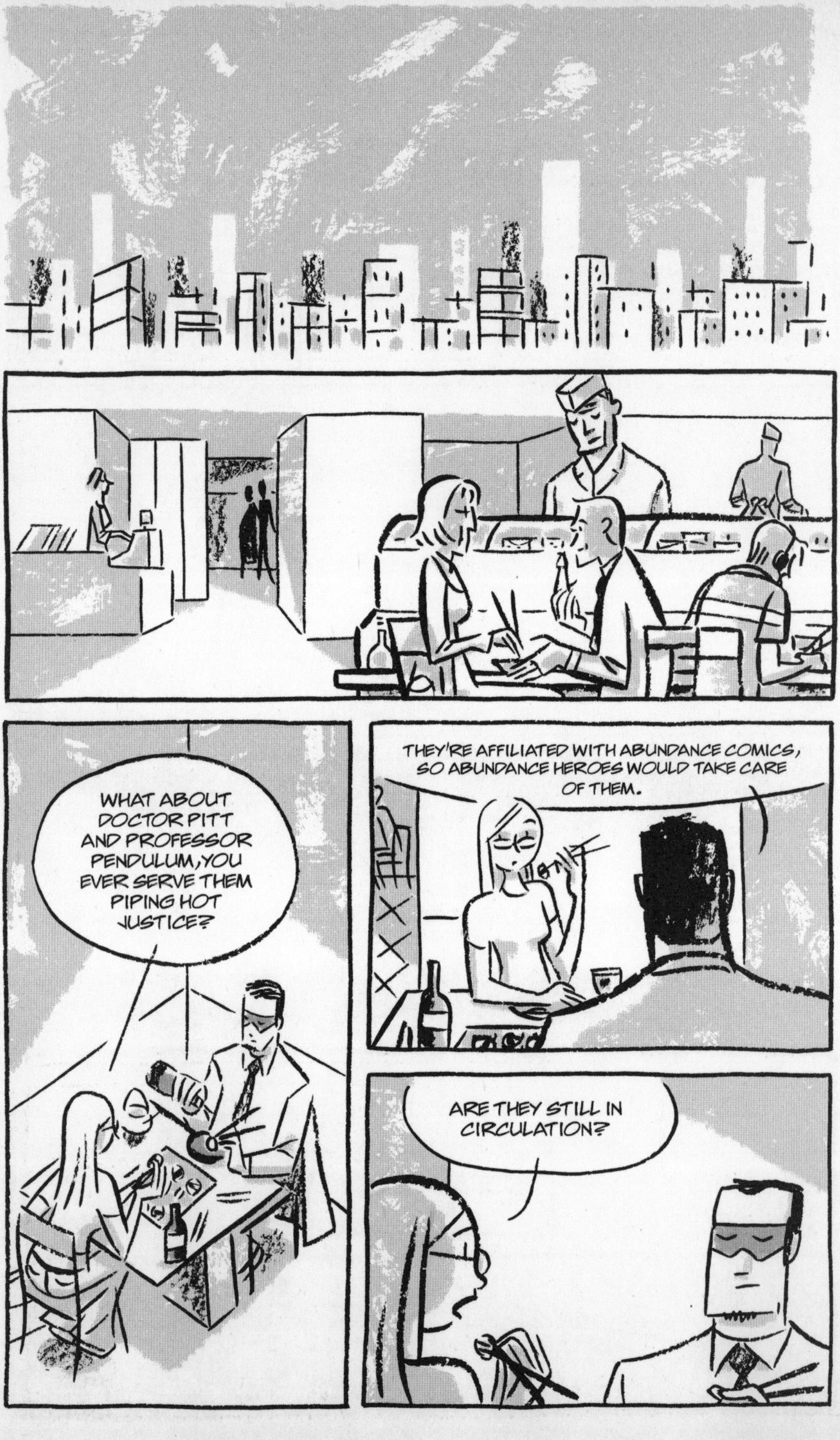
WHAT ABOUT DOCTOR PITT AND PROFESSOR PENDULUM, YOU EVER SERVE THEM PIPING HOT JUSTICE?
THEY'RE AFFILIATED WITH ABUNDANCE COMICS, SO ABUNDANCE HEROES WOULD TAKE CARE OF THEM.
ARE THEY STILL IN CIRCULATION?

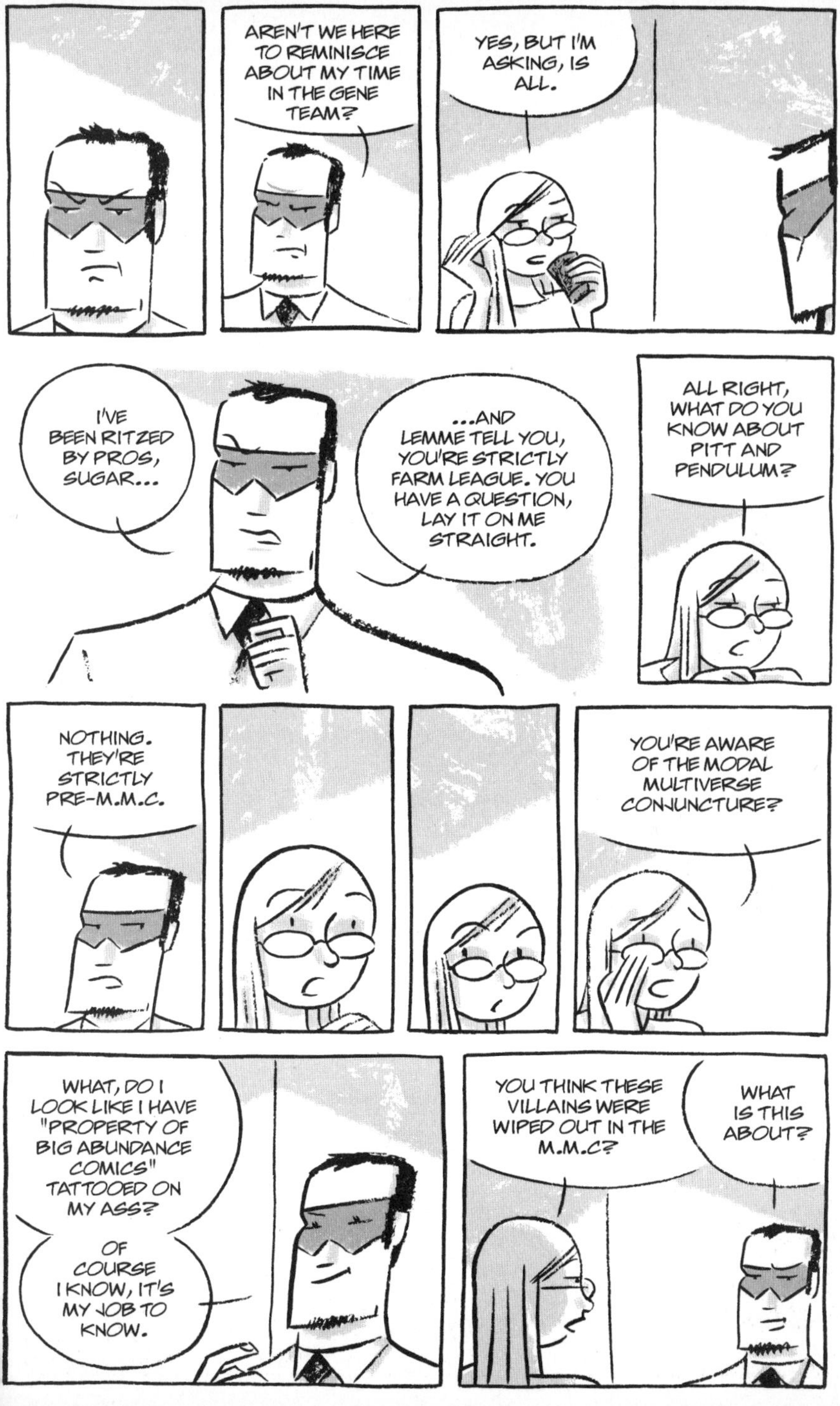
AREN'T WE HERE TO REMINISCE ABOUT MY TIME IN THE GENE TEAM?
YES, BUT I'M ASKING, IS ALL.
I'VE BEEN RITZED BY PROS, SUGAR...
...AND LEMME TELL YOU, YOU'RE STRICTLY FARM LEAGUE. YOU HAVE A QUESTION, LAY IT ON ME STRAIGHT.
ALL RIGHT, WHAT DO YOU KNOW ABOUT PITT AND PENDULUM?
NOTHING. THEY'RE STRICTLY PRE-M.M.C.
YOU'RE AWARE OF THE MODAL MULTIVERSE CONJUNCTURE?
WHAT, DO I LOOK LIKE I HAVE "PROPERTY OF BIG ABUNDANCE COMICS" TATTOOED ON MY ASS?
OF COURSE I KNOW, IT'S MY JOB TO KNOW.
YOU THINK THESE VILLAINS WERE WIPED OUT IN THE M.M.C?
WHAT IS THIS ABOUT?

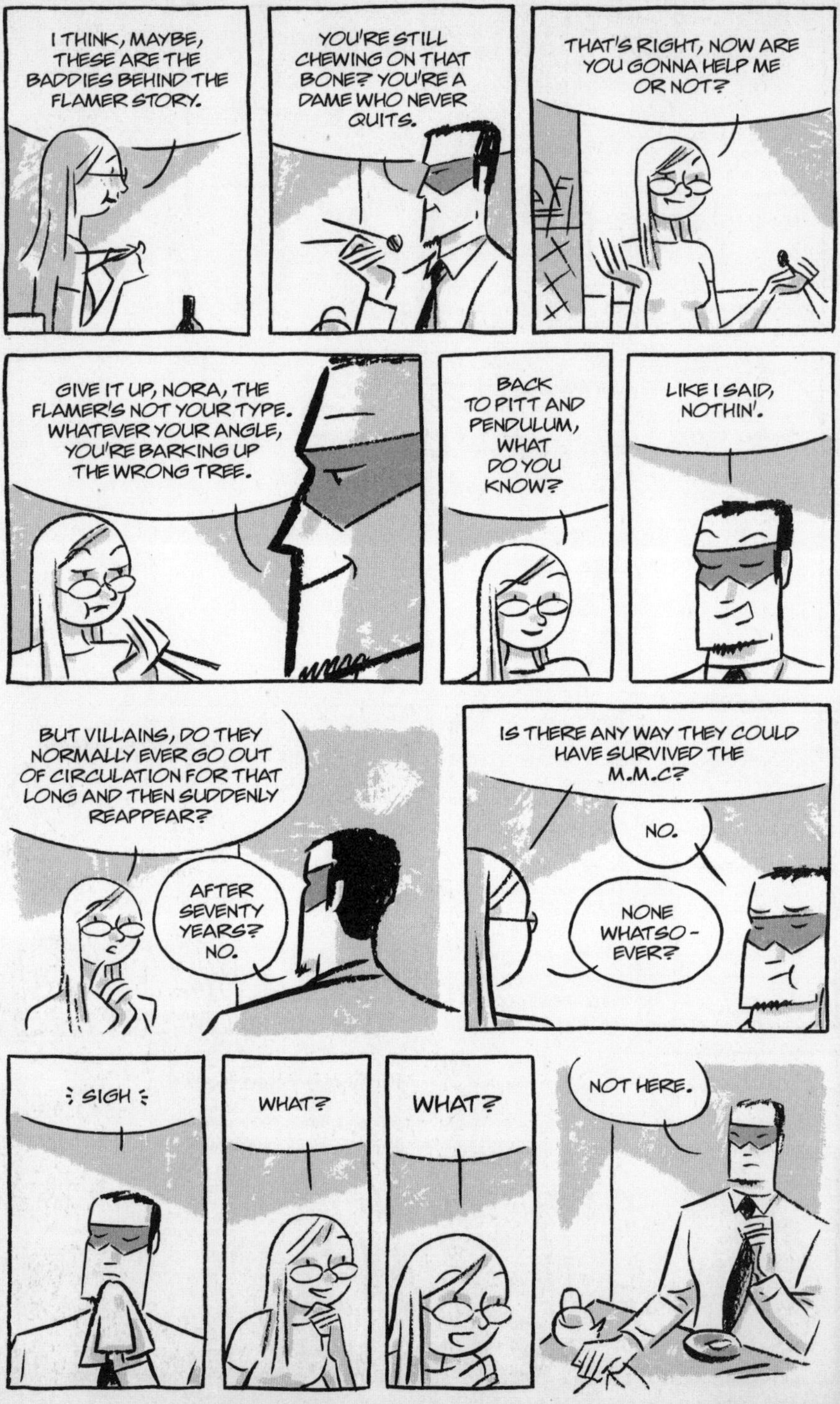
I THINK, MAYBE, THESE ARE THE BADDIES BEHIND THE FLAMER STORY.
YOU'RE STILL CHEWING ON THAT BONE? YOU'RE A DAME WHO NEVER QUITS.
THAT'S RIGHT, NOW ARE YOU GONNA HELP ME OR NOT?
GIVE IT UP, NORA, THE FLAMER'S NOT YOUR TYPE. WHATEVER YOUR ANGLE, YOU'RE BARKING UP THE WRONG TREE.
BACK TO PITT AND PENDULUM, WHAT DO YOU KNOW?
LIKE I SAID, NOTHIN'.
BUT VILLAINS, DO THEY NORMALLY EVER GO OUT OF CIRCULATION FOR THAT LONG AND THEN SUDDENLY REAPPEAR?
AFTER SEVENTY YEARS? NO.
IS THERE ANY WAY THEY COULD HAVE SURVIVED THE M.M.C?
NO.
NONE WHATSO-EVER?
SIGH
WHAT?
WHAT?
NOT HERE.

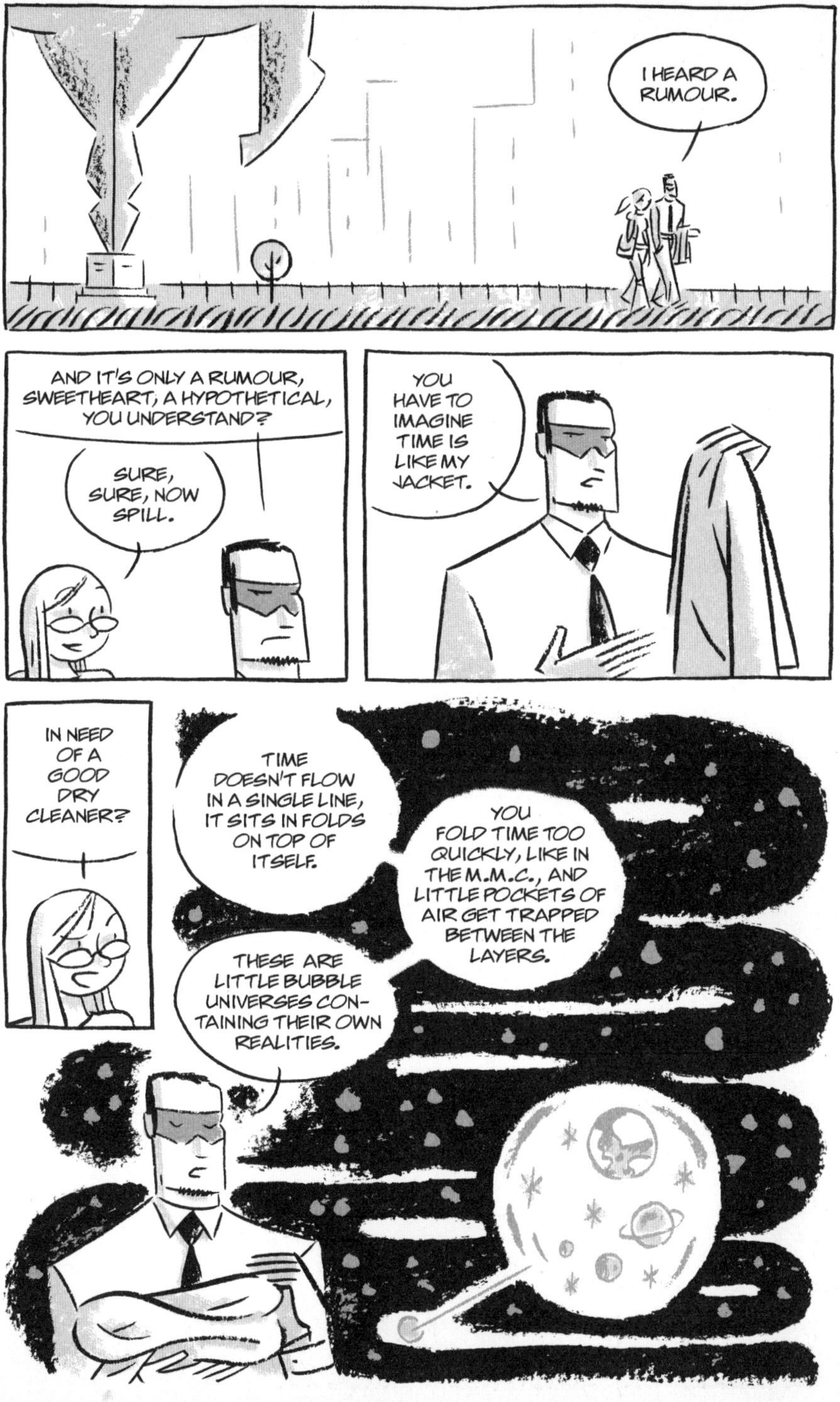
I HEARD A RUMOUR.
AND IT'S ONLY A RUMOUR, SWEETHEART, A HYPOTHETICAL, YOU UNDERSTAND?
SURE, SURE, NOW SPILL.
YOU HAVE TO IMAGINE TIME IS LIKE MY JACKET.
IN NEED OF A GOOD DRY CLEANER?
TIME DOESN'T FLOW IN A SINGLE LINE, IT SITS IN FOLDS ON TOP OF ITSELF.
YOU FOLD TIME TOO QUICKLY, LIKE IN THE M.M.C., AND LITTLE POCKETS OF AIR GET TRAPPED BETWEEN THE LAYERS.
THESE ARE LITTLE BUBBLE UNIVERSES CONTAINING THEIR OWN REALITIES.

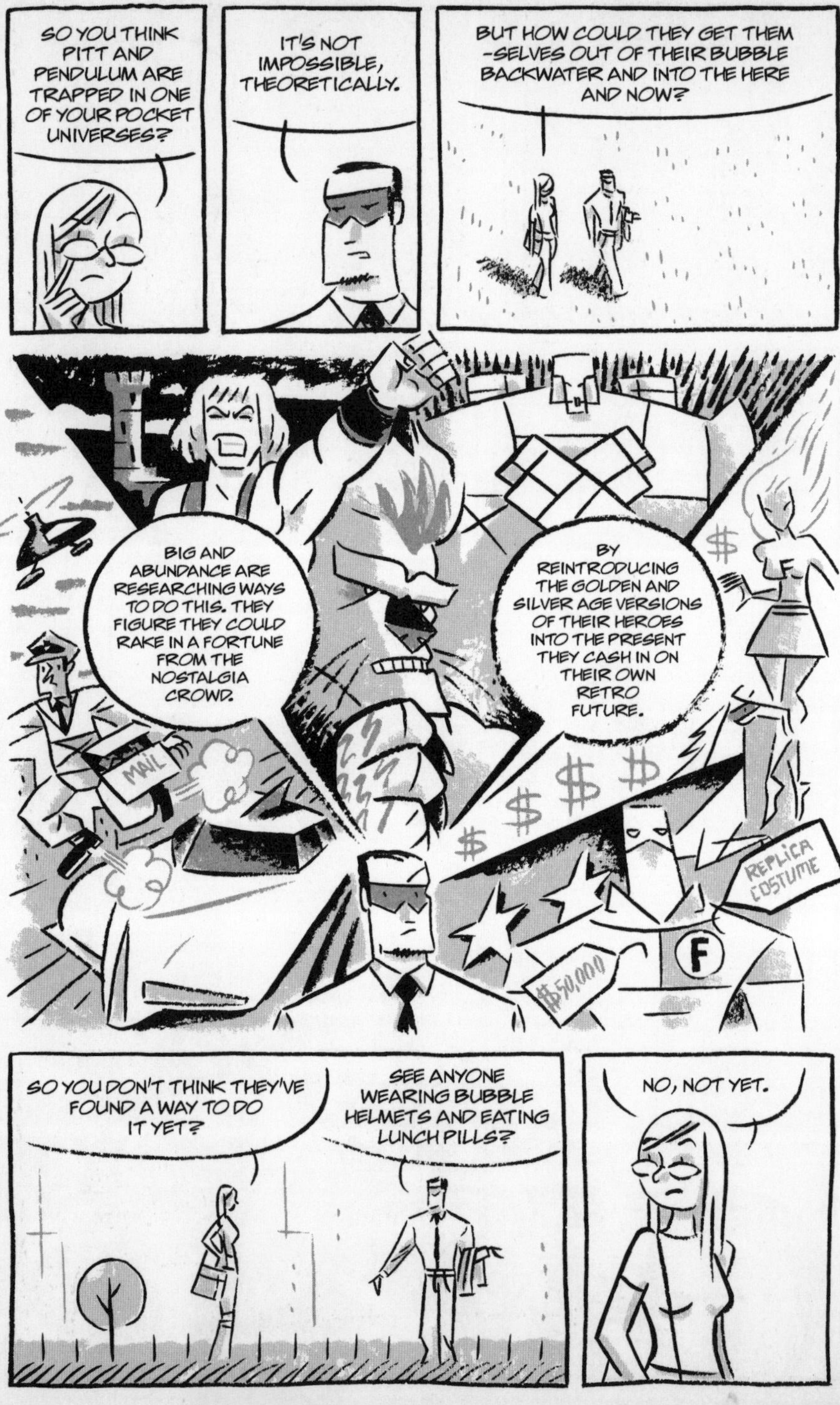
SO YOU THINK PITT AND PENDULUM ARE TRAPPED IN ONE OF YOUR POCKET UNIVERSES?
IT'S NOT IMPOSSIBLE, THEORETICALLY.
BUT HOW COULD THEY GET THEM -SELVES OUT OF THEIR BUBBLE BACKWATER AND INTO THE HERE AND NOW?
BIG AND ABUNDANCE ARE RESEARCHING WAYS TO DO THIS. THEY FIGURE THEY COULD RAKE IN A FORTUNE FROM THE NOSTALGIA CROWD.
BY REINTRODUCING THE GOLDEN AND SILVER AGE VERSIONS OF THEIR HEROES INTO THE PRESENT THEY CASH IN ON THEIR OWN RETRO FUTURE.
MAIL
REPLICA COSTUME
$50,000
SO YOU DON'T THINK THEY'VE FOUND A WAY TO DO IT YET?
SEE ANYONE WEARING BUBBLE HELMETS AND EATING LUNCH PILLS?
NO, NOT YET.

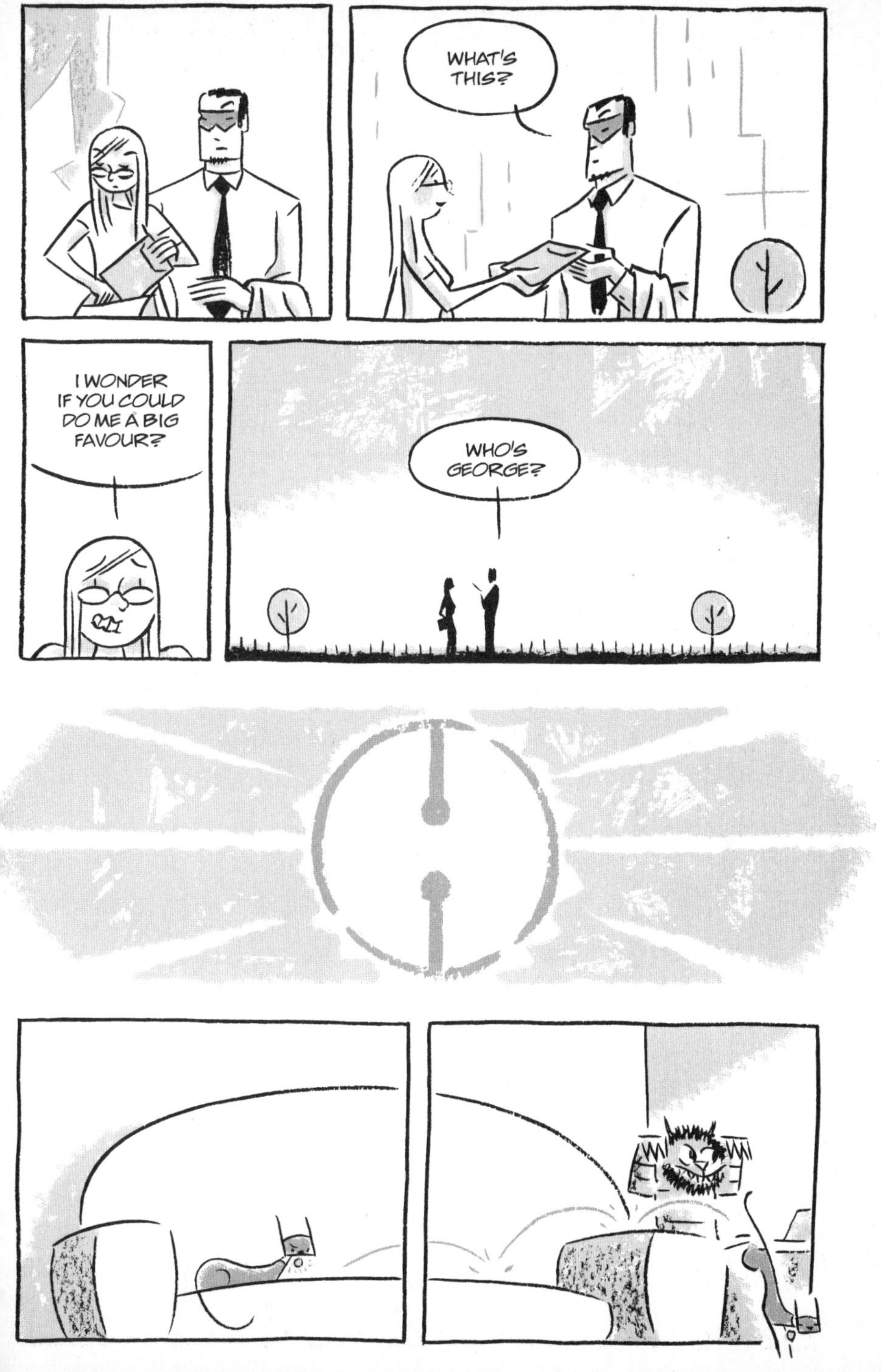
WHAT'S THIS?
I WONDER IF YOU COULD DO ME A BIG FAVOUR?
WHO'S GEORGE?

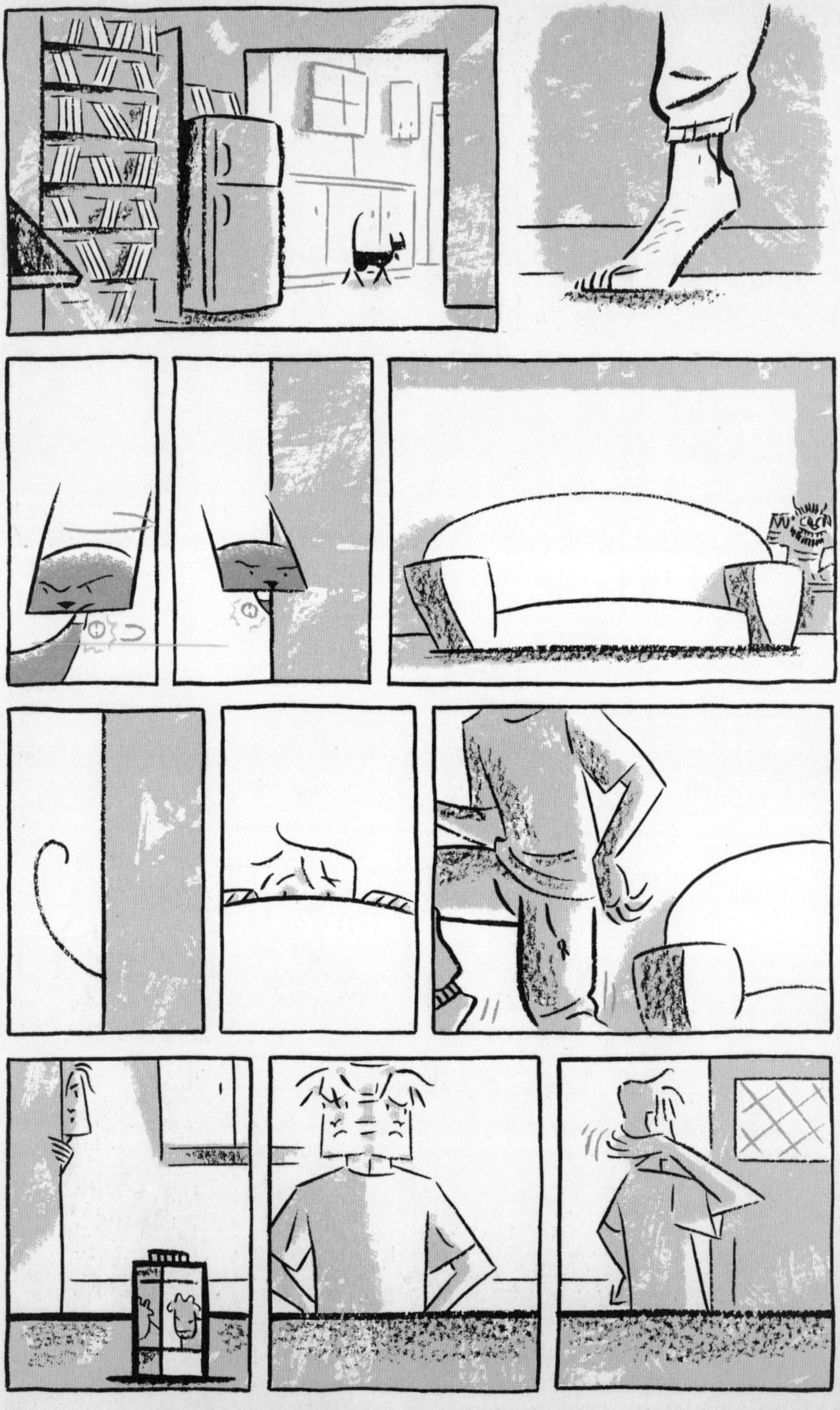

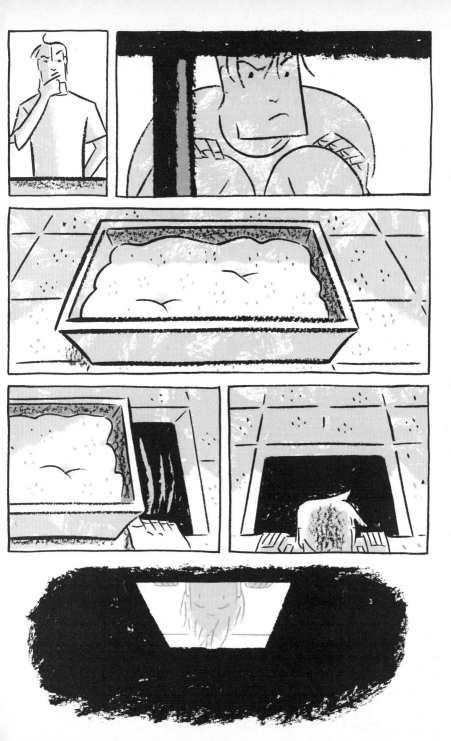

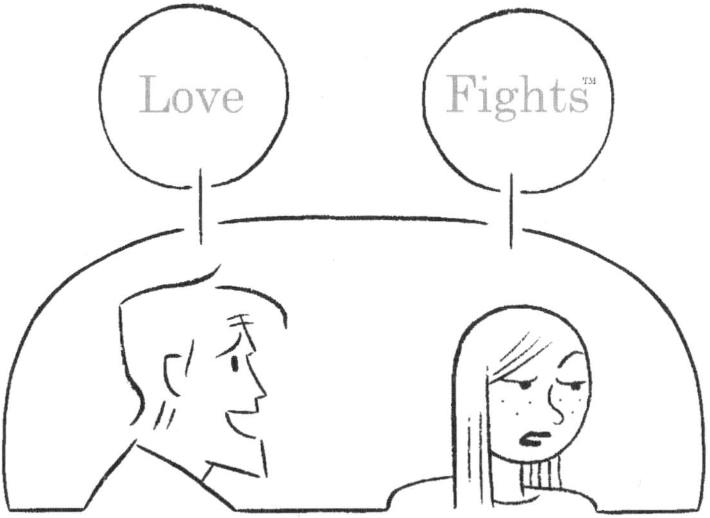
Love
Fights™

andi watson #10 ONI PRESS $2.99 U.S., $4.60 CAN.

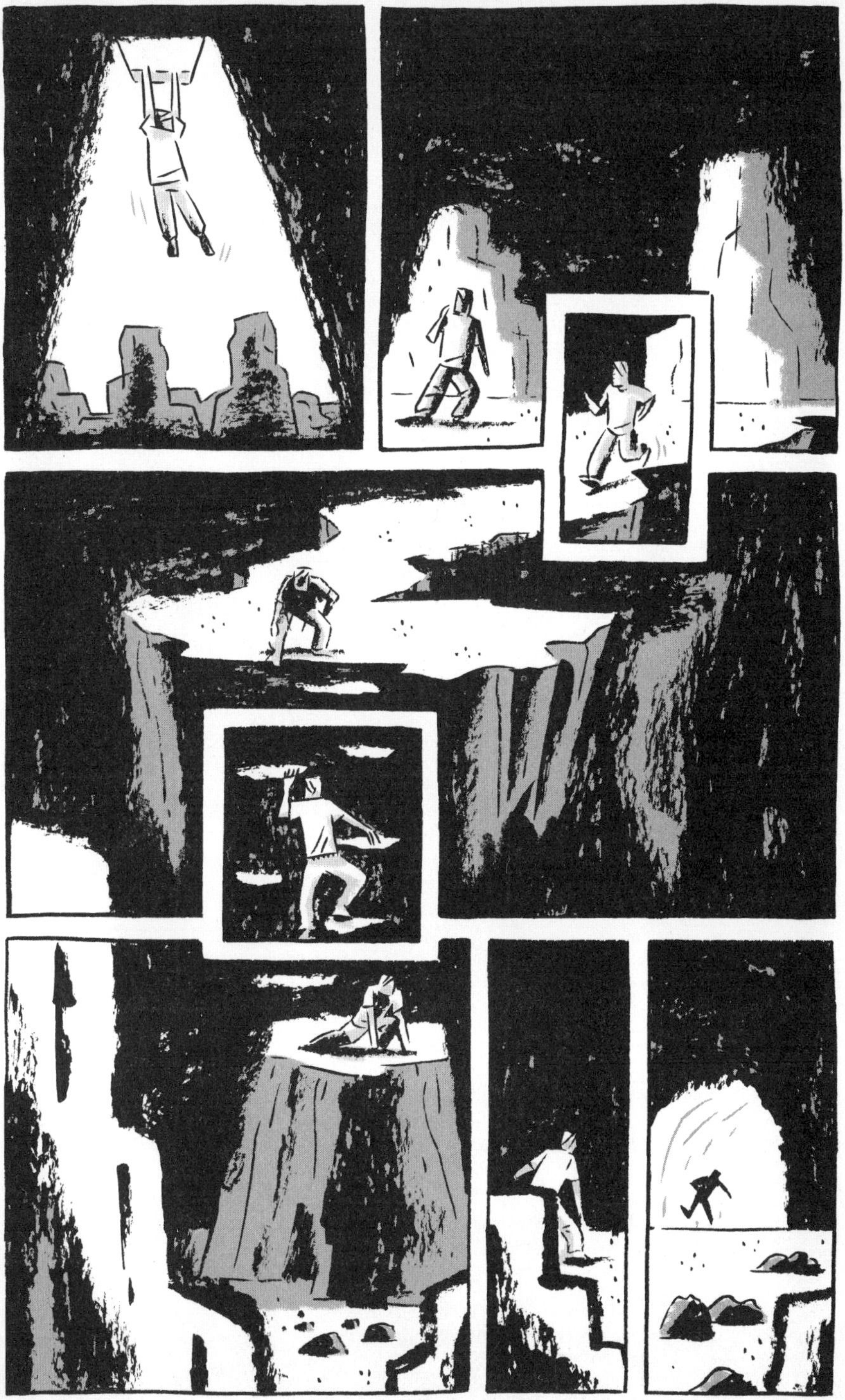

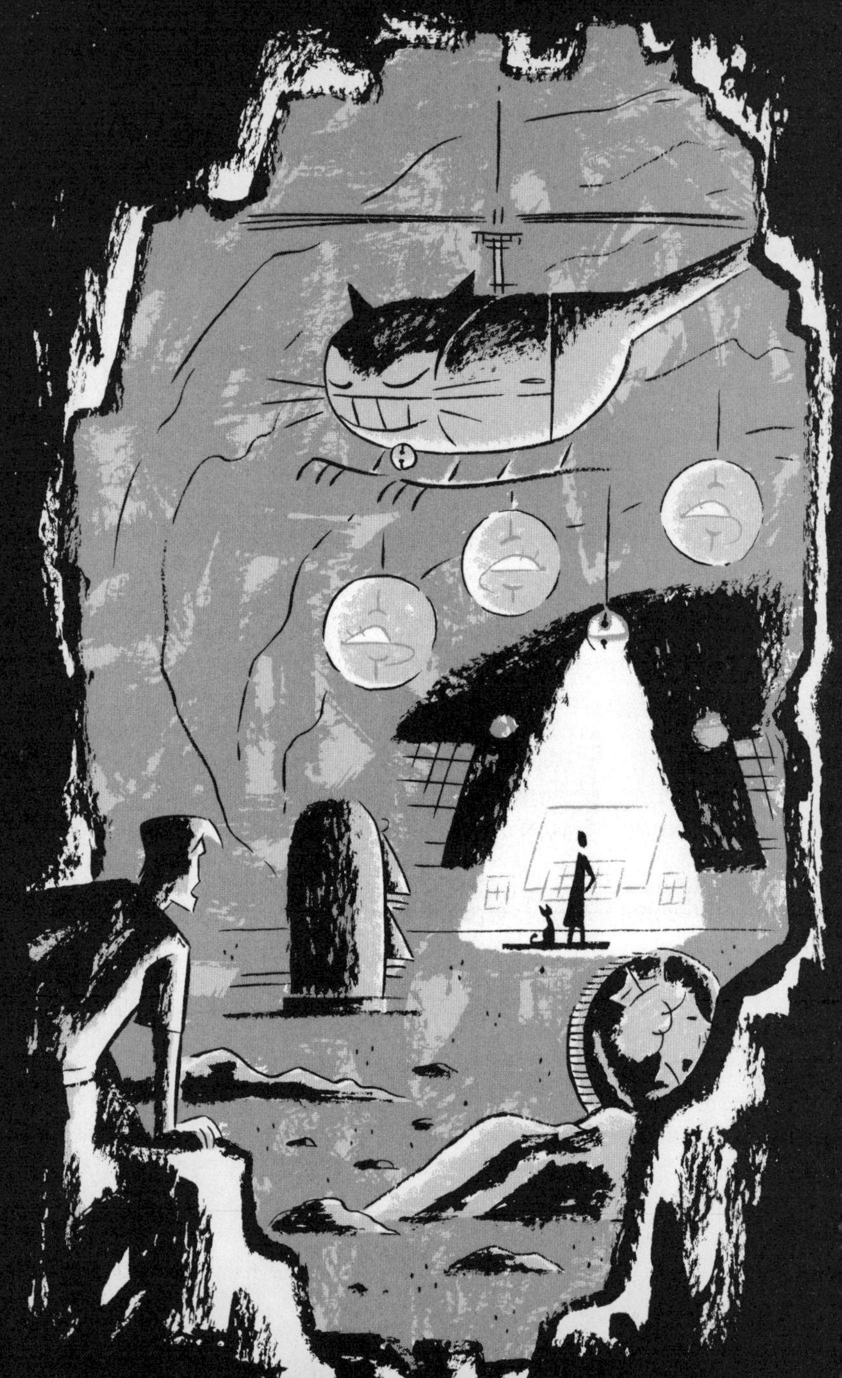

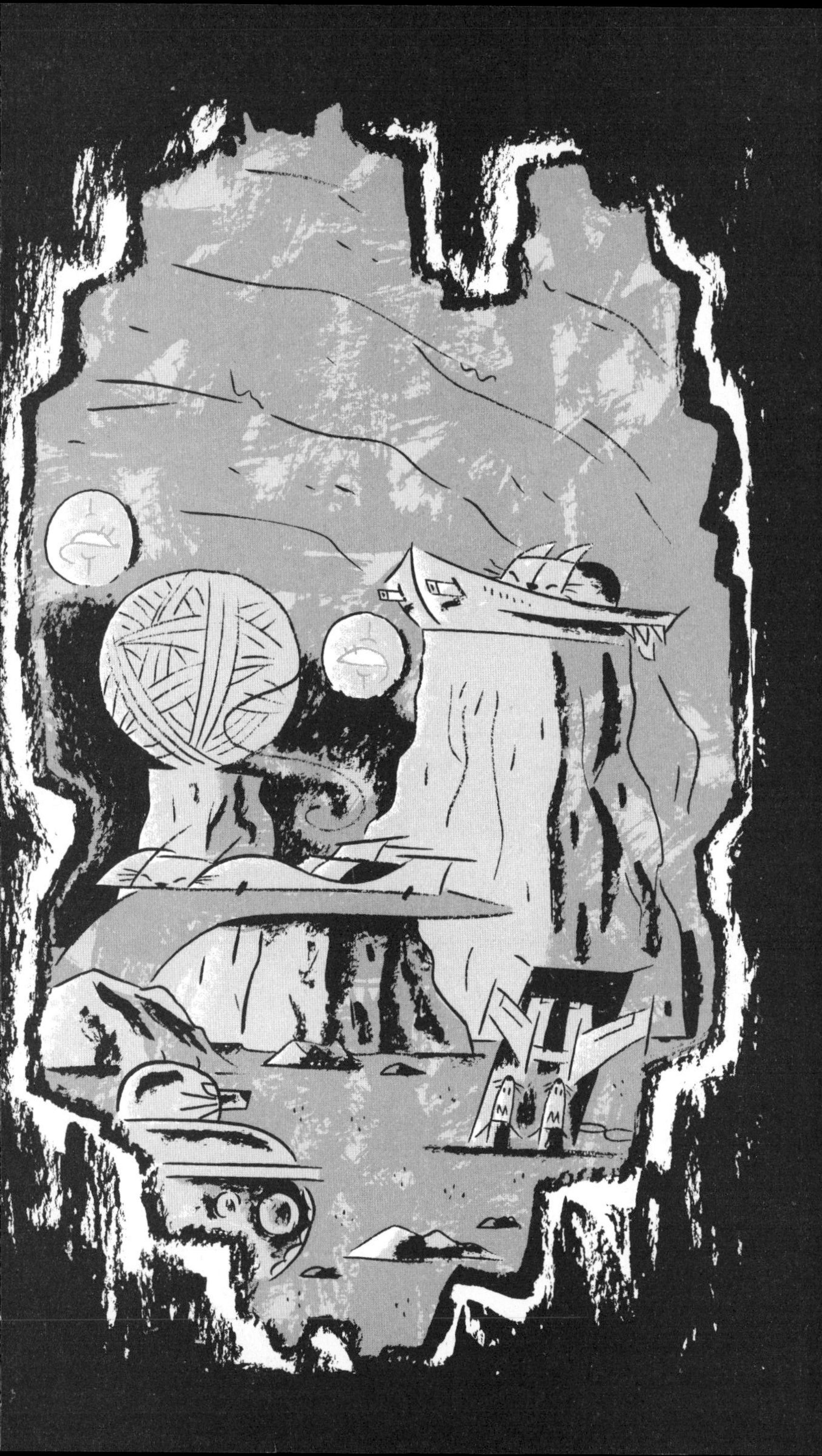

...ABOUT HER TEST, IS IT AT THE LAB YET?

NO.

MROWWW

DO IT NOW.

AND PUT ASIDE ANY THOUGHTS OF KILLING JACK. UNDERSTAND? YOU KNOW THE REPERCUSSIONS WOULD BE DISASTEROUS. NOW GO.

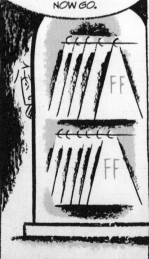
FF

FF

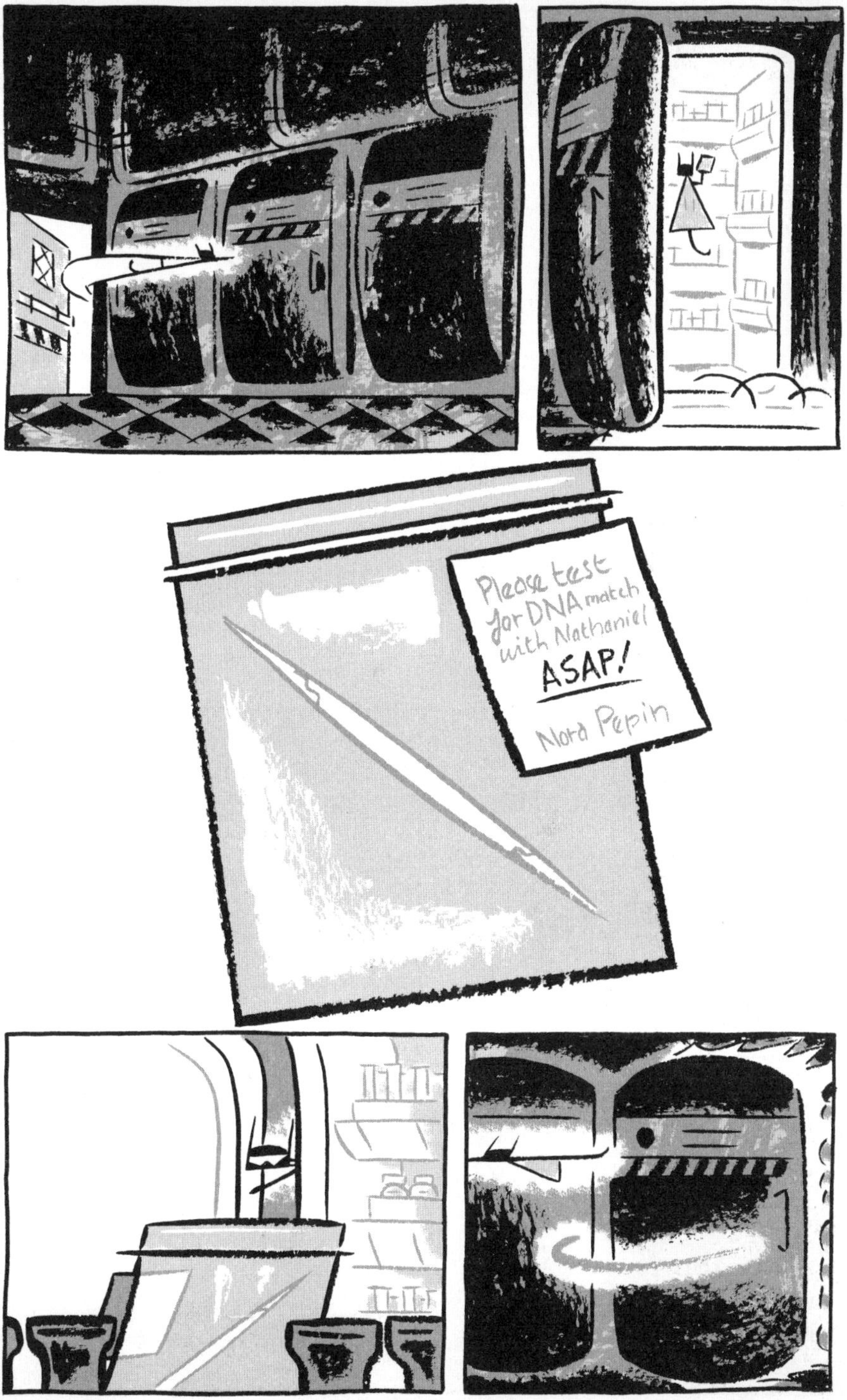
Please test for DNA match with Nathaniel
ASAP!
Nora Pepin

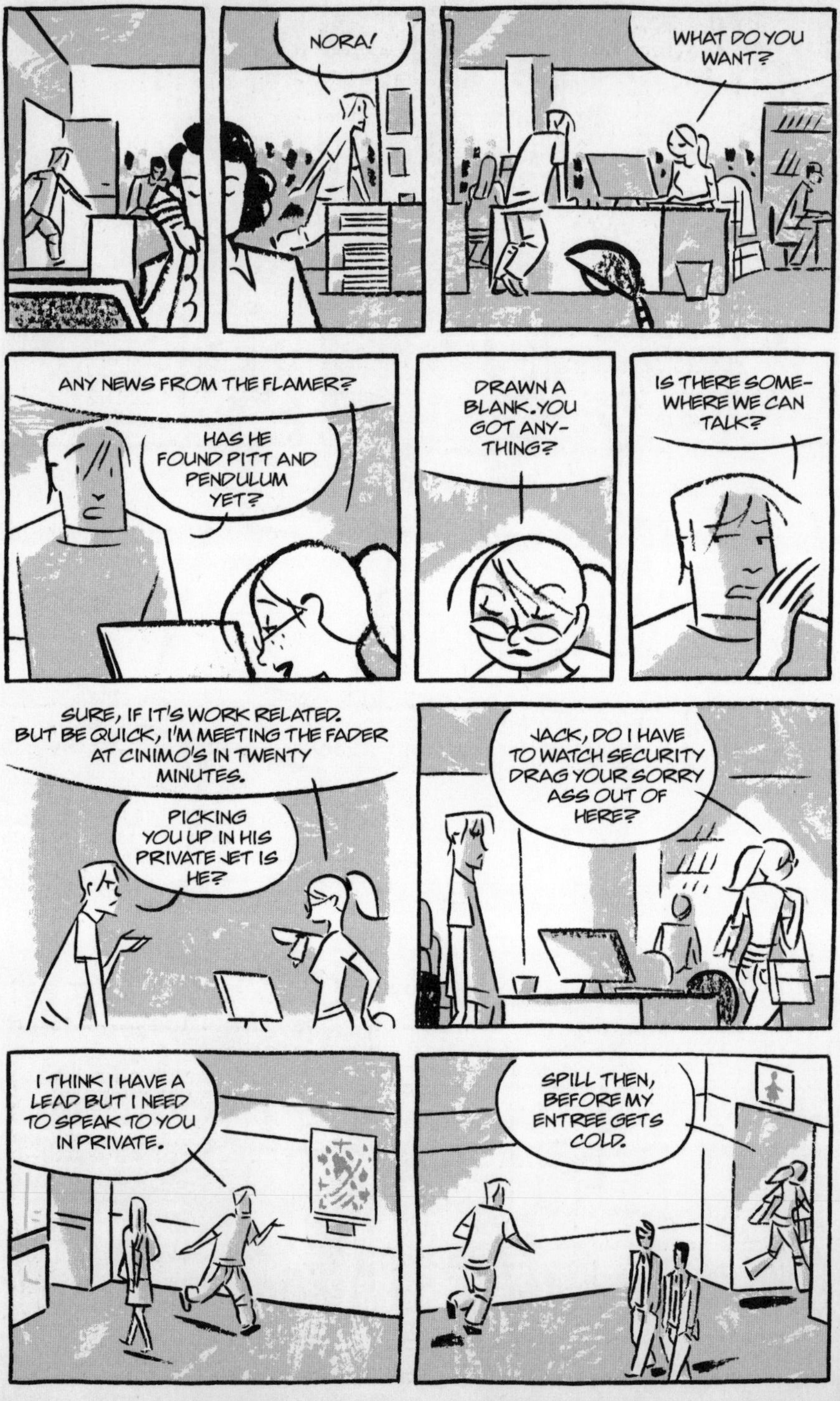
NORA!
WHAT DO YOU WANT?
ANY NEWS FROM THE FLAMER?
HAS HE FOUND PITT AND PENDULUM YET?
DRAWN A BLANK. YOU GOT ANY-THING?
IS THERE SOME-WHERE WE CAN TALK?
SURE, IF IT'S WORK RELATED. BUT BE QUICK, I'M MEETING THE FADER AT CINIMO'S IN TWENTY MINUTES.
PICKING YOU UP IN HIS PRIVATE JET IS HE?
JACK, DO I HAVE TO WATCH SECURITY DRAG YOUR SORRY ASS OUT OF HERE?
I THINK I HAVE A LEAD BUT I NEED TO SPEAK TO YOU IN PRIVATE.
SPILL THEN, BEFORE MY ENTREE GETS COLD.

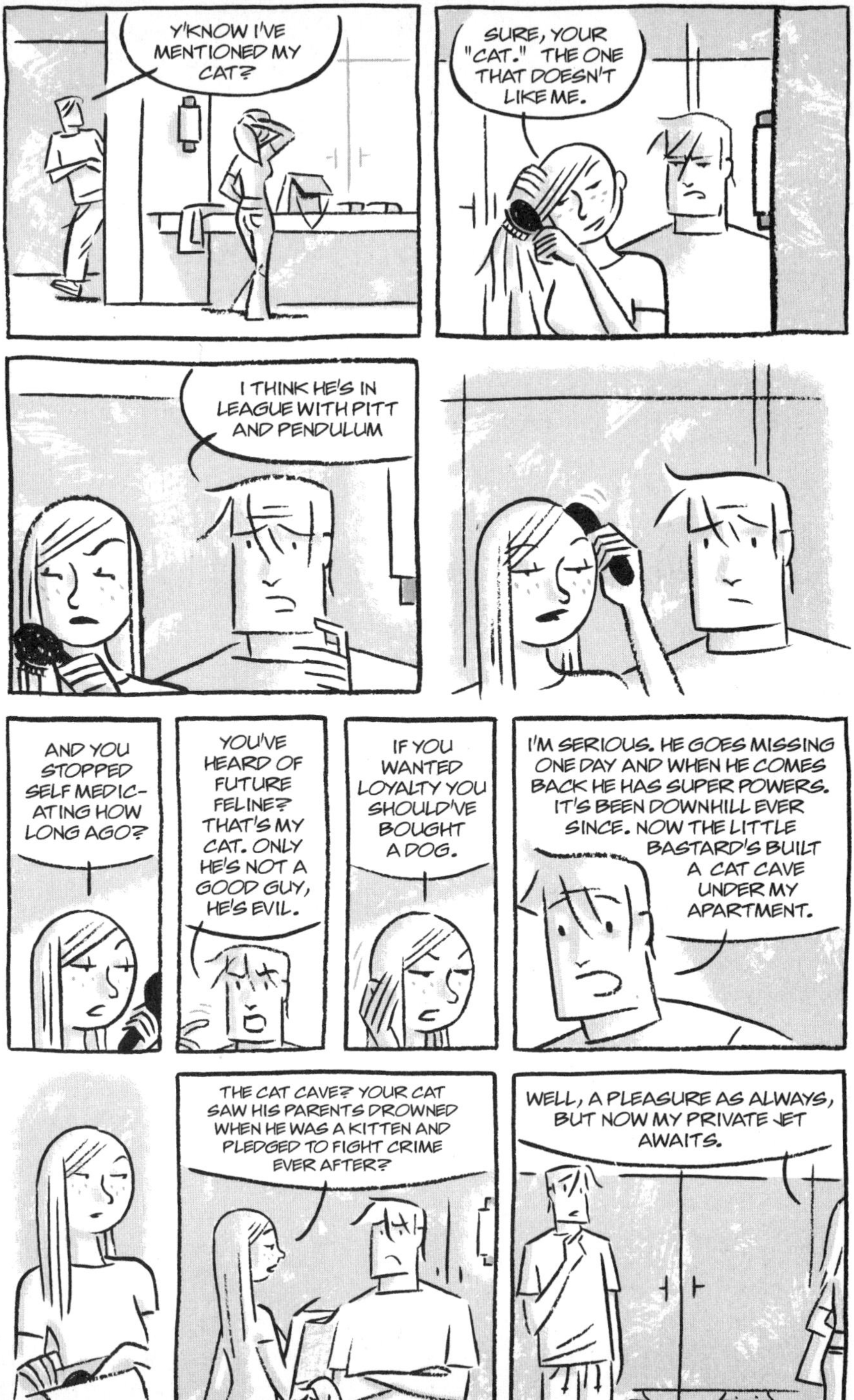
Y'KNOW I'VE MENTIONED MY CAT?
SURE, YOUR "CAT." THE ONE THAT DOESN'T LIKE ME.
I THINK HE'S IN LEAGUE WITH PITT AND PENDULUM
AND YOU STOPPED SELF MEDIC-ATING HOW LONG AGO?
YOU'VE HEARD OF FUTURE FELINE? THAT'S MY CAT. ONLY HE'S NOT A GOOD GUY, HE'S EVIL.
IF YOU WANTED LOYALTY YOU SHOULD'VE BOUGHT A DOG.
I'M SERIOUS. HE GOES MISSING ONE DAY AND WHEN HE COMES BACK HE HAS SUPER POWERS. IT'S BEEN DOWNHILL EVER SINCE. NOW THE LITTLE BASTARD'S BUILT A CAT CAVE UNDER MY APARTMENT.
THE CAT CAVE? YOUR CAT SAW HIS PARENTS DROWNED WHEN HE WAS A KITTEN AND PLEDGED TO FIGHT CRIME EVER AFTER?
WELL, A PLEASURE AS ALWAYS, BUT NOW MY PRIVATE JET AWAITS.

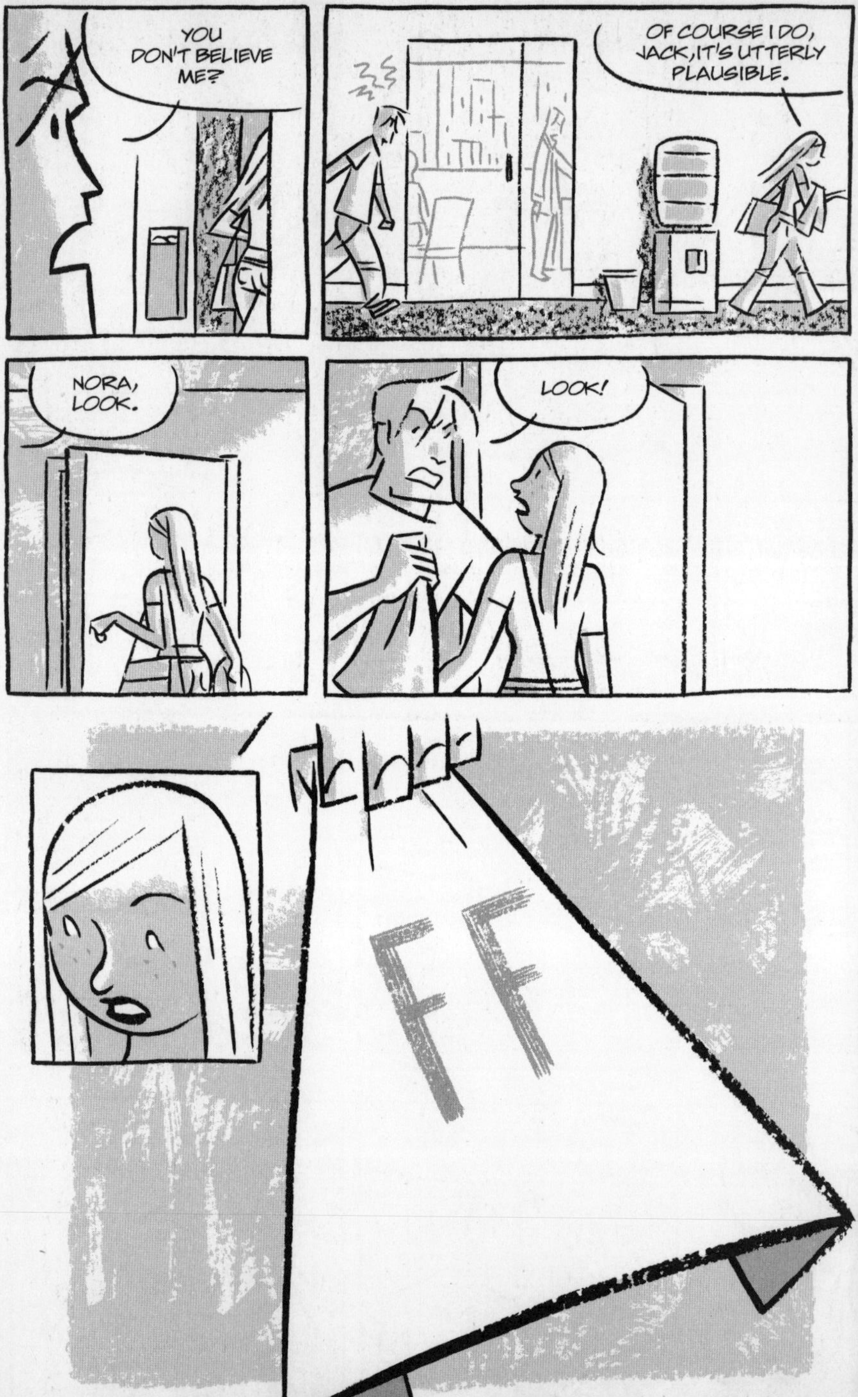
YOU DON'T BELIEVE ME?
OF COURSE I DO, JACK, IT'S UTTERLY PLAUSIBLE.
NORA, LOOK.
LOOK!
FF

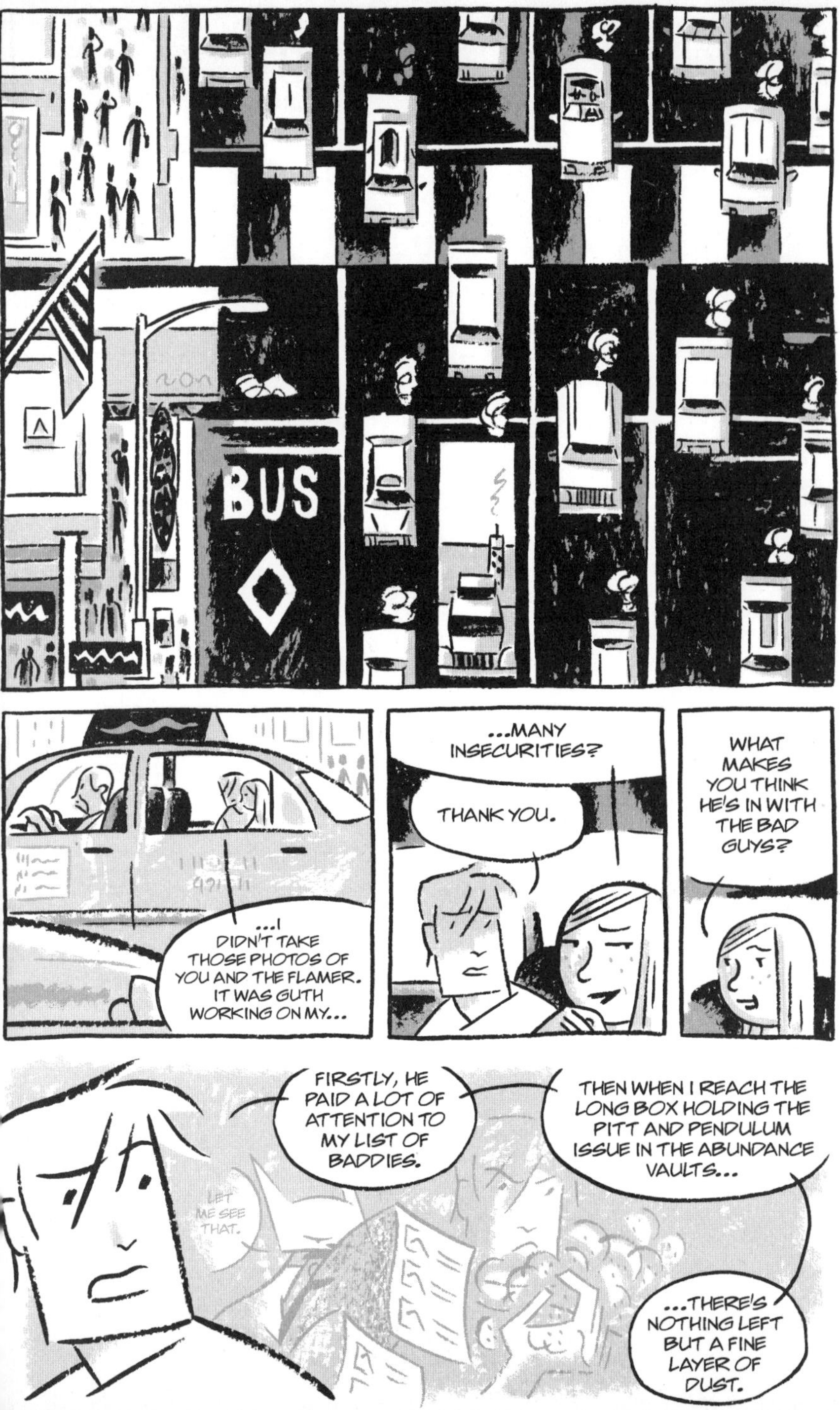
BUS
...I DIDN'T TAKE THOSE PHOTOS OF YOU AND THE FLAMER. IT WAS GUTH WORKING ON MY...
...MANY INSECURITIES?
THANK YOU.
WHAT MAKES YOU THINK HE'S IN WITH THE BAD GUYS?
FIRSTLY, HE PAID A LOT OF ATTENTION TO MY LIST OF BADDIES.
LET ME SEE THAT.
THEN WHEN I REACH THE LONG BOX HOLDING THE PITT AND PENDULUM ISSUE IN THE ABUNDANCE VAULTS...
...THERE'S NOTHING LEFT BUT A FINE LAYER OF DUST.

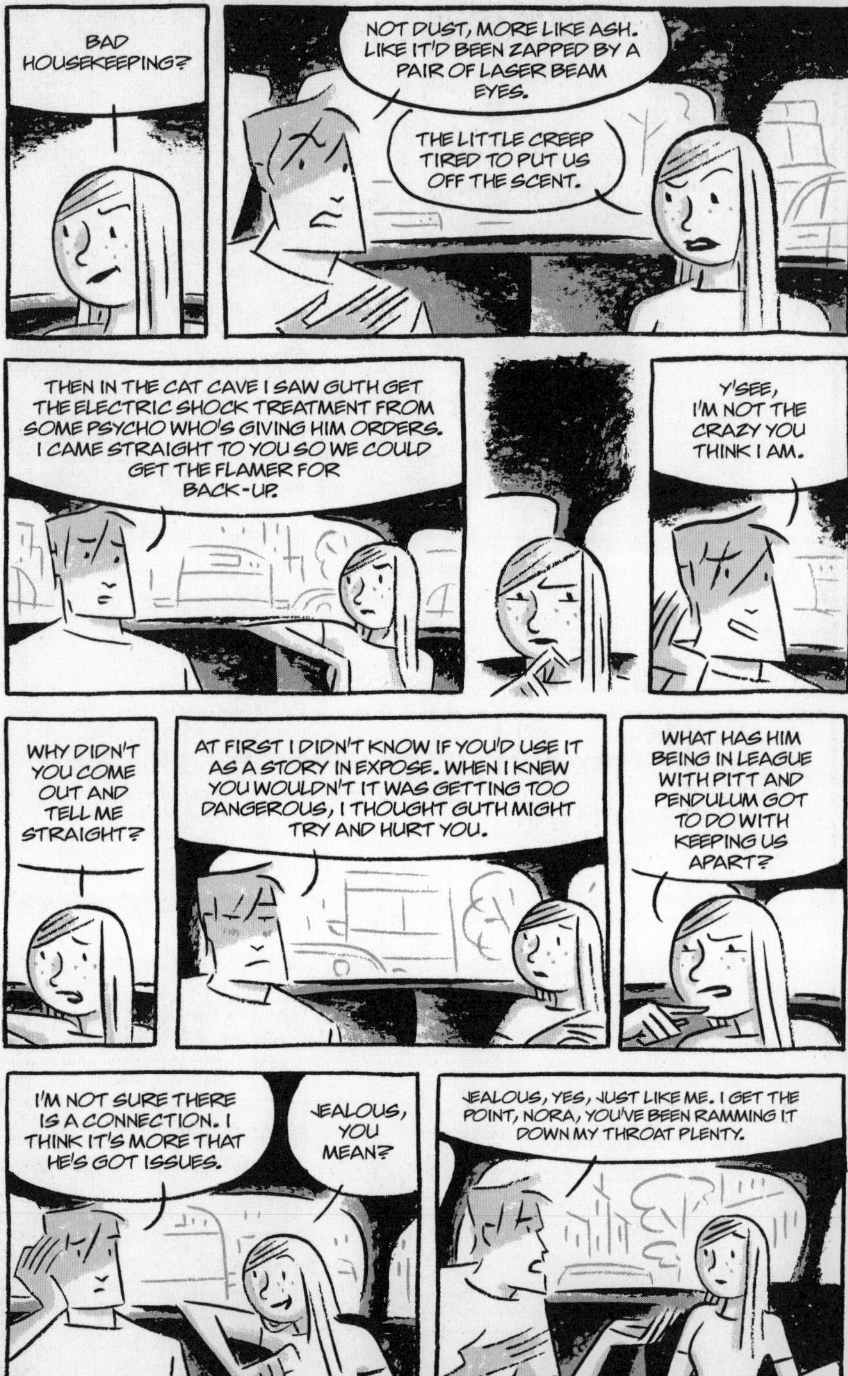
BAD HOUSEKEEPING?
NOT DUST, MORE LIKE ASH. LIKE IT'D BEEN ZAPPED BY A PAIR OF LASER BEAM EYES.
THE LITTLE CREEP TIRED TO PUT US OFF THE SCENT.
THEN IN THE CAT CAVE I SAW GUTH GET THE ELECTRIC SHOCK TREATMENT FROM SOME PSYCHO WHO'S GIVING HIM ORDERS. I CAME STRAIGHT TO YOU SO WE COULD GET THE FLAMER FOR BACK-UP.
Y'SEE, I'M NOT THE CRAZY YOU THINK I AM.
WHY DIDN'T YOU COME OUT AND TELL ME STRAIGHT?
AT FIRST I DIDN'T KNOW IF YOU'D USE IT AS A STORY IN EXPOSE. WHEN I KNEW YOU WOULDN'T IT WAS GETTING TOO DANGEROUS, I THOUGHT GUTH MIGHT TRY AND HURT YOU.
WHAT HAS HIM BEING IN LEAGUE WITH PITT AND PENDULUM GOT TO DO WITH KEEPING US APART?
I'M NOT SURE THERE IS A CONNECTION. I THINK IT'S MORE THAT HE'S GOT ISSUES.
JEALOUS, YOU MEAN?
JEALOUS, YES, JUST LIKE ME. I GET THE POINT, NORA, YOU'VE BEEN RAMMING IT DOWN MY THROAT PLENTY.

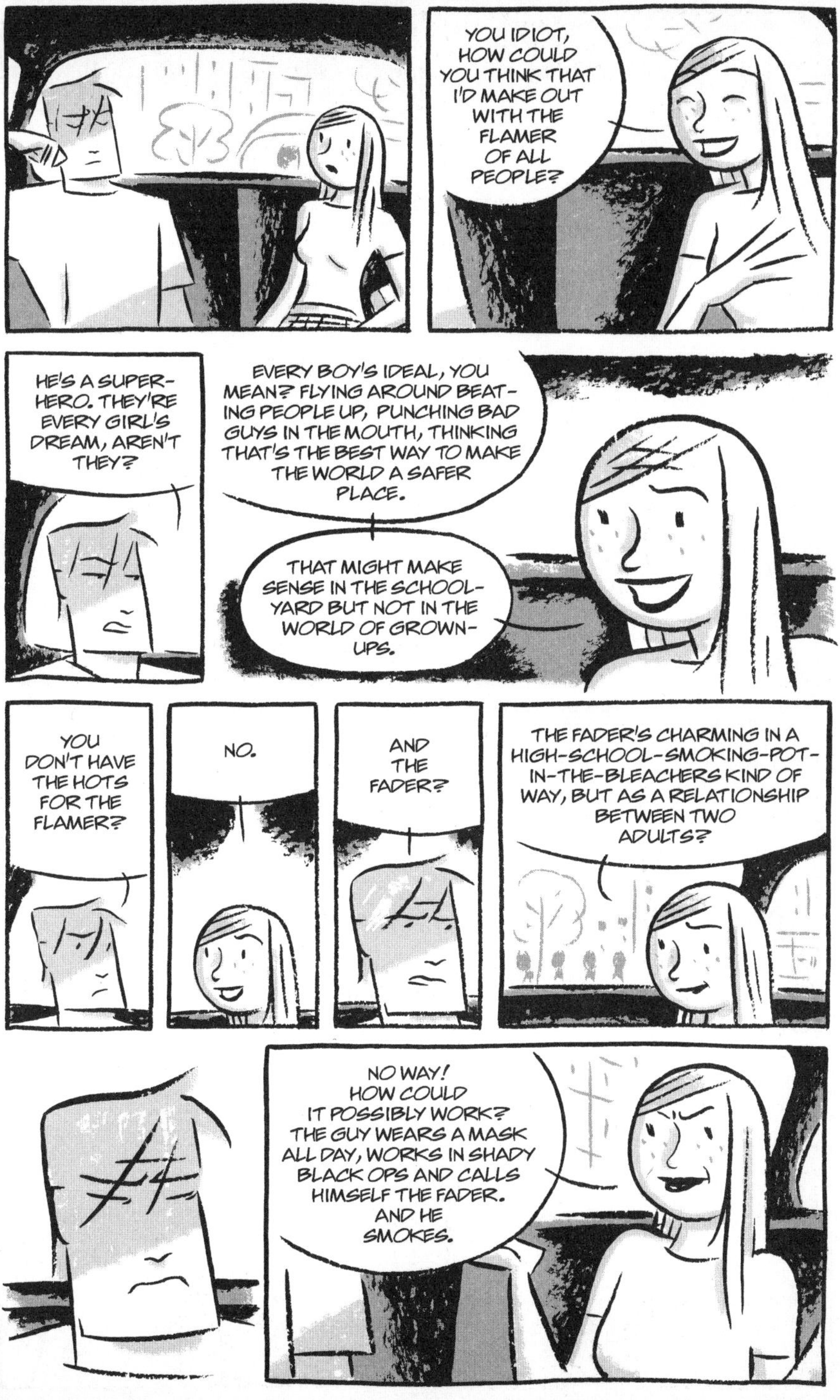
YOU IDIOT, HOW COULD YOU THINK THAT I'D MAKE OUT WITH THE FLAMER OF ALL PEOPLE?
HE'S A SUPER-HERO. THEY'RE EVERY GIRL'S DREAM, AREN'T THEY?
EVERY BOY'S IDEAL, YOU MEAN? FLYING AROUND BEAT-ING PEOPLE UP, PUNCHING BAD GUYS IN THE MOUTH, THINKING THAT'S THE BEST WAY TO MAKE THE WORLD A SAFER PLACE.
THAT MIGHT MAKE SENSE IN THE SCHOOL-YARD BUT NOT IN THE WORLD OF GROWN-UPS.
YOU DON'T HAVE THE HOTS FOR THE FLAMER?
NO.
AND THE FADER?
THE FADER'S CHARMING IN A HIGH-SCHOOL-SMOKING-POT-IN-THE-BLEACHERS KIND OF WAY, BUT AS A RELATIONSHIP BETWEEN TWO ADULTS?
NO WAY! HOW COULD IT POSSIBLY WORK? THE GUY WEARS A MASK ALL DAY, WORKS IN SHADY BLACK OPS AND CALLS HIMSELF THE FADER. AND HE SMOKES.

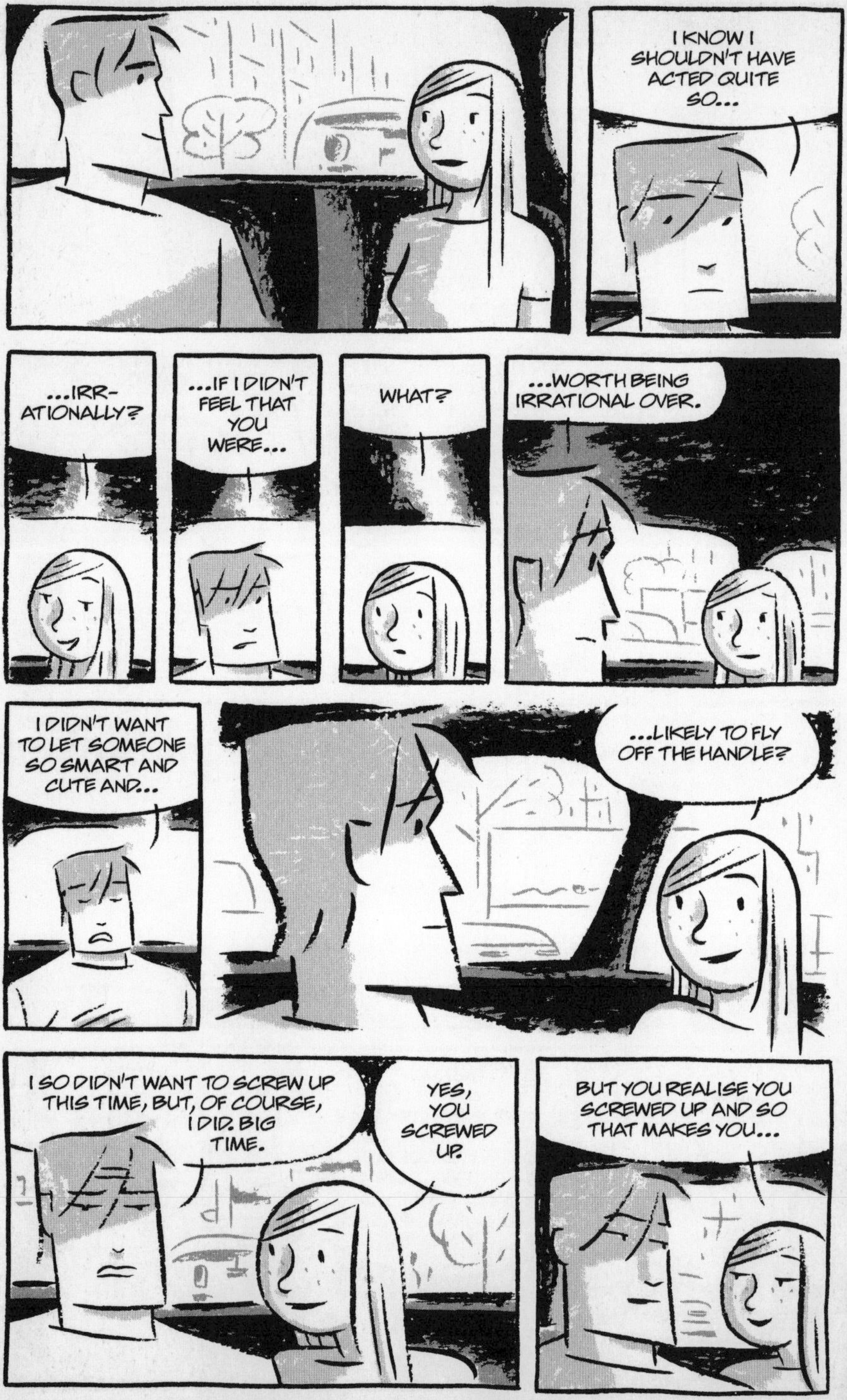
I KNOW I SHOULDN'T HAVE ACTED QUITE SO...
...IRR-ATIONALLY?
...IF I DIDN'T FEEL THAT YOU WERE...
WHAT?
...WORTH BEING IRRATIONAL OVER.
I DIDN'T WANT TO LET SOMEONE SO SMART AND CUTE AND...
...LIKELY TO FLY OFF THE HANDLE?
I SO DIDN'T WANT TO SCREW UP THIS TIME, BUT, OF COURSE, I DID. BIG TIME.
YES, YOU SCREWED UP.
BUT YOU REALISE YOU SCREWED UP AND SO THAT MAKES YOU...

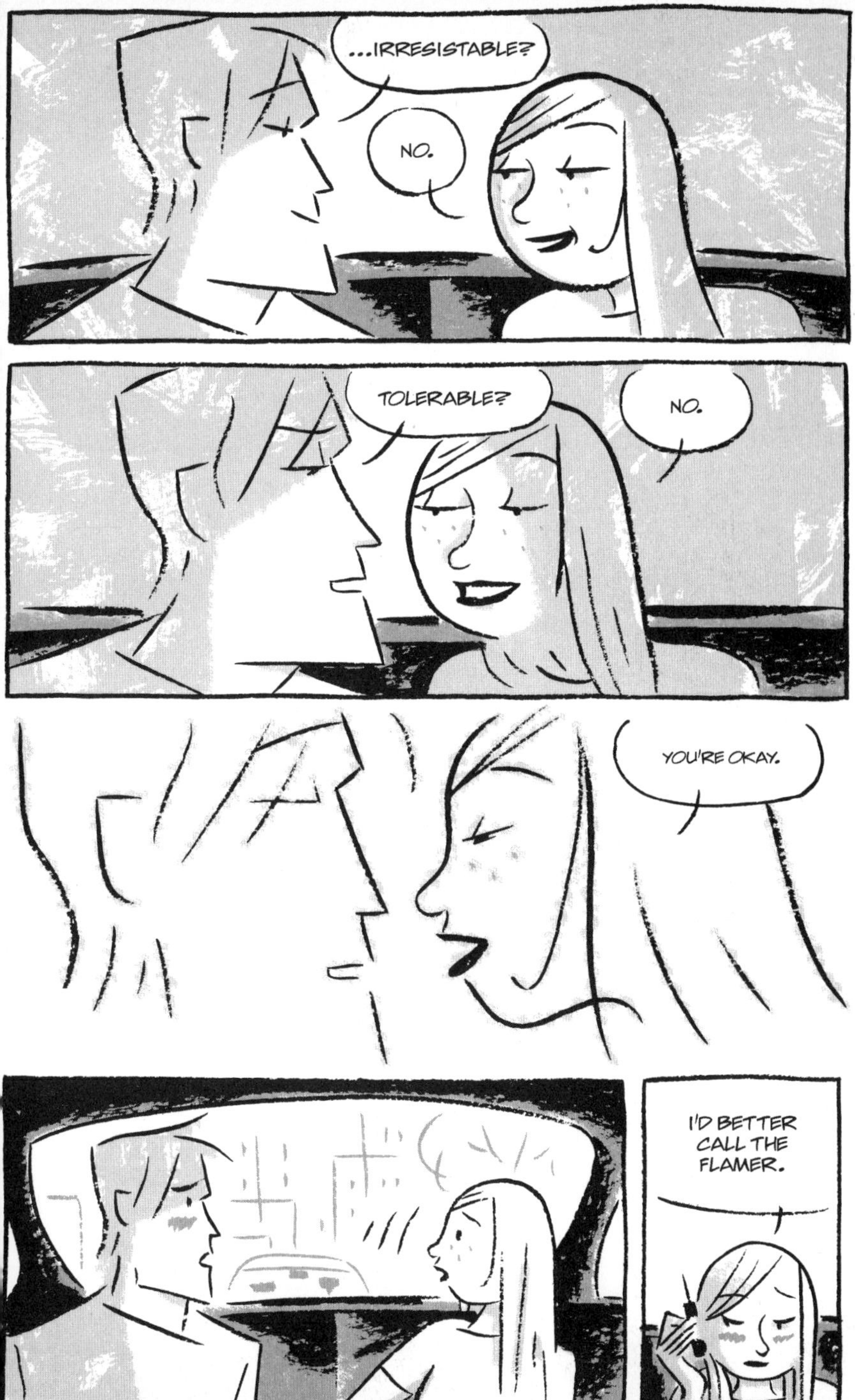
...IRRESISTABLE?
NO.
TOLERABLE?
NO.
YOU'RE OKAY.
I'D BETTER CALL THE FLAMER.

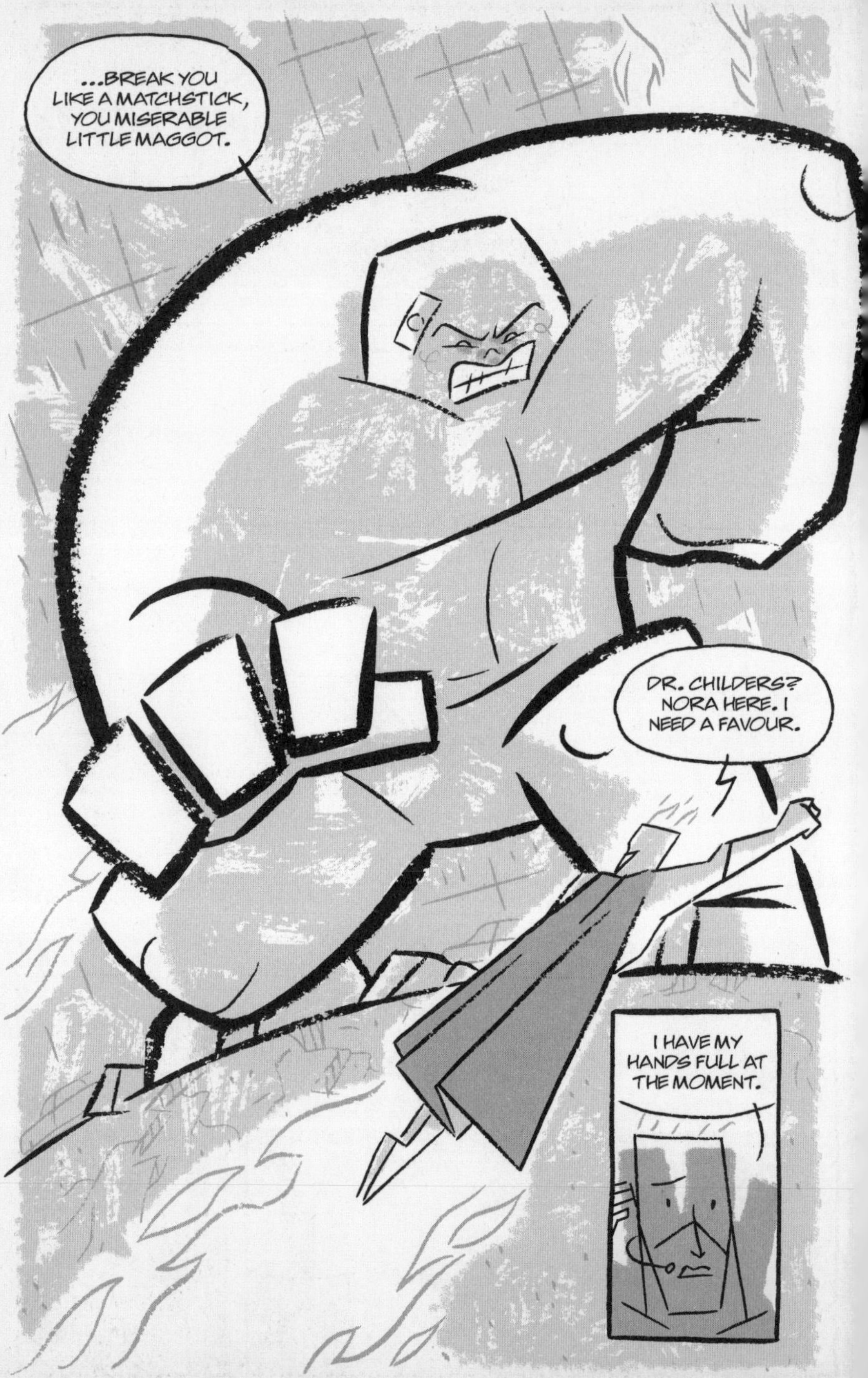
...BREAK YOU LIKE A MATCHSTICK, YOU MISERABLE LITTLE MAGGOT.
DR. CHILDERS? NORA HERE. I NEED A FAVOUR.
I HAVE MY HANDS FULL AT THE MOMENT.

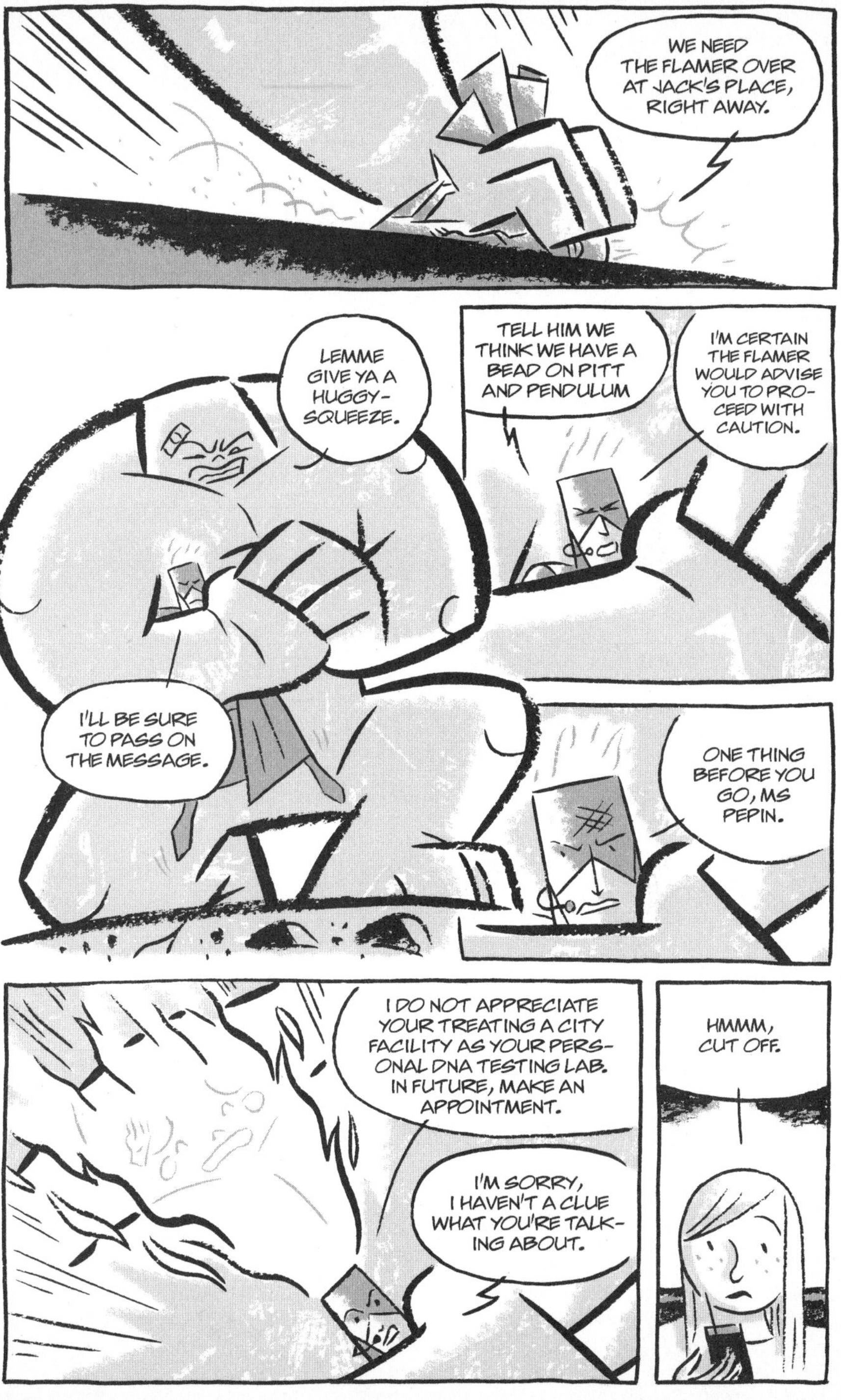
WE NEED THE FLAMER OVER AT JACK'S PLACE, RIGHT AWAY.
LEMME GIVE YA A HUGGY-SQUEEZE.
TELL HIM WE THINK WE HAVE A BEAD ON PITT AND PENDULUM
I'M CERTAIN THE FLAMER WOULD ADVISE YOU TO PRO-CEED WITH CAUTION.
I'LL BE SURE TO PASS ON THE MESSAGE.
ONE THING BEFORE YOU GO, MS PEPIN.
I DO NOT APPRECIATE YOUR TREATING A CITY FACILITY AS YOUR PERS-ONAL DNA TESTING LAB. IN FUTURE, MAKE AN APPOINTMENT.
I'M SORRY, I HAVEN'T A CLUE WHAT YOU'RE TALK-ING ABOUT.
HMMM, CUT OFF.

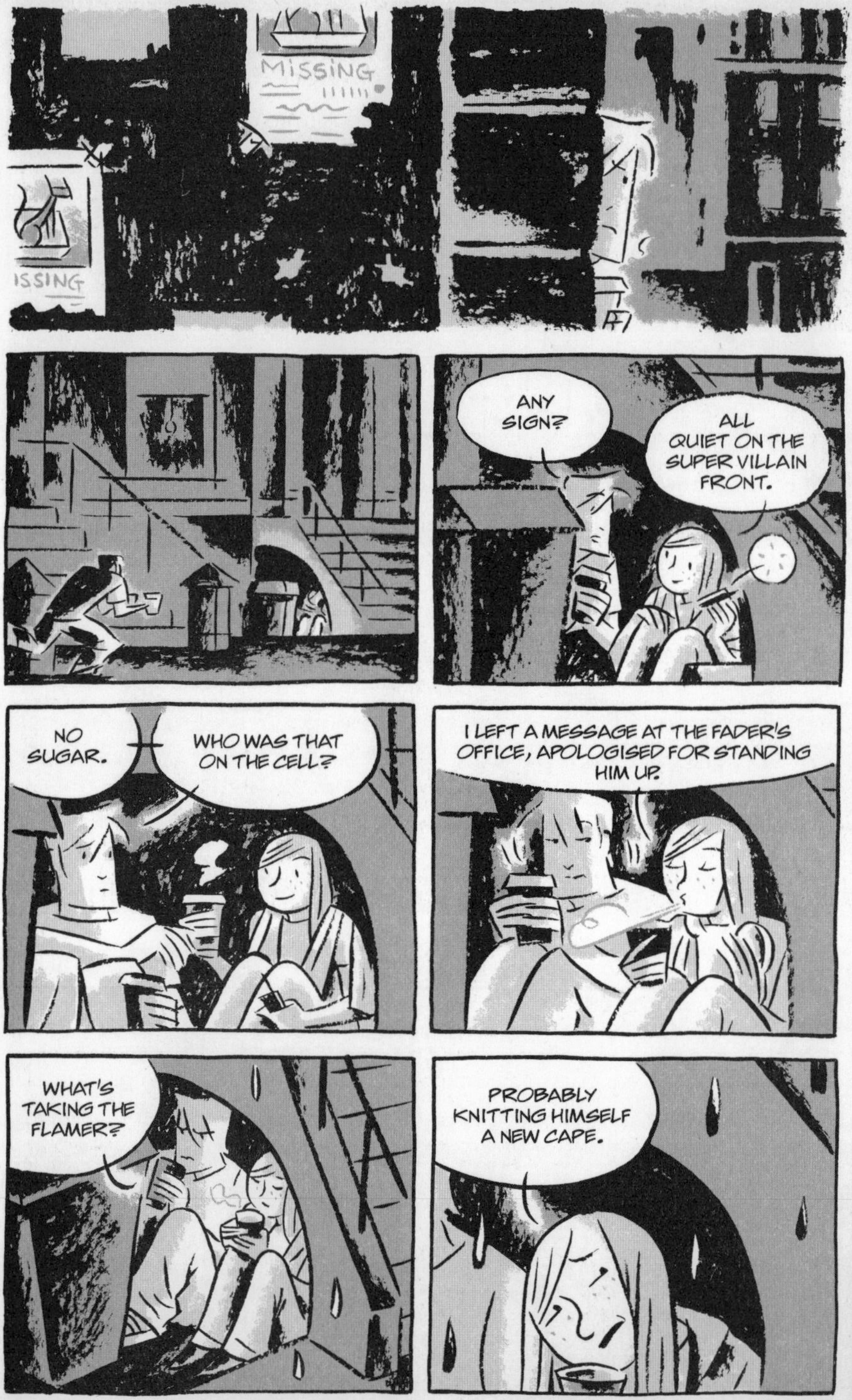
MISSING
ISSING
ANY SIGN?
ALL QUIET ON THE SUPER VILLAIN FRONT.
NO SUGAR.
WHO WAS THAT ON THE CELL?
I LEFT A MESSAGE AT THE FADER'S OFFICE, APOLOGISED FOR STANDING HIM UP.
WHAT'S TAKING THE FLAMER?
PROBABLY KNITTING HIMSELF A NEW CAPE.

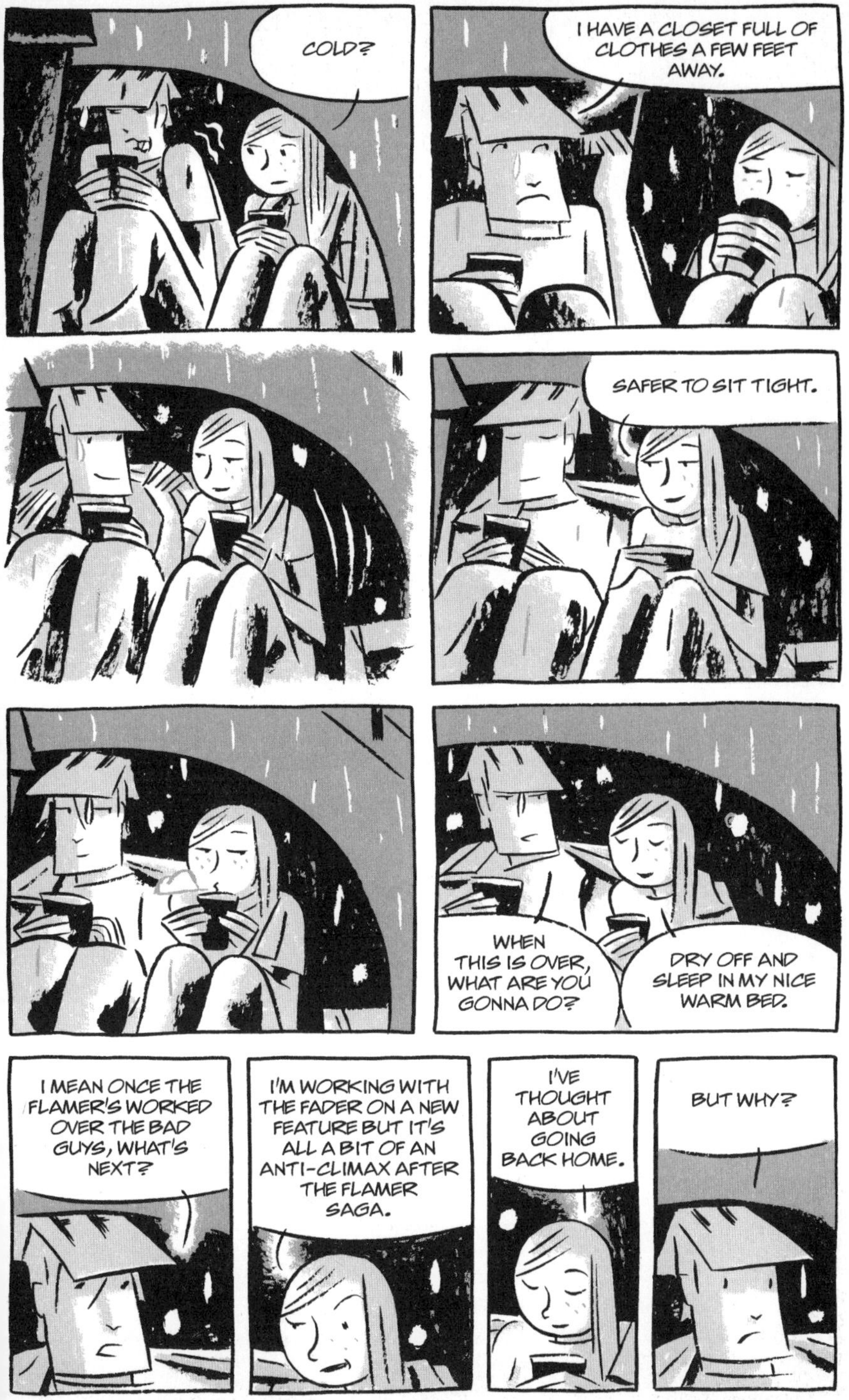
COLD?
I HAVE A CLOSET FULL OF CLOTHES A FEW FEET AWAY.
SAFER TO SIT TIGHT.
WHEN THIS IS OVER, WHAT ARE YOU GONNA DO?
DRY OFF AND SLEEP IN MY NICE WARM BED.
I MEAN ONCE THE FLAMER'S WORKED OVER THE BAD GUYS, WHAT'S NEXT?
I'M WORKING WITH THE FADER ON A NEW FEATURE BUT IT'S ALL A BIT OF AN ANTI-CLIMAX AFTER THE FLAMER SAGA.
I'VE THOUGHT ABOUT GOING BACK HOME.
BUT WHY?

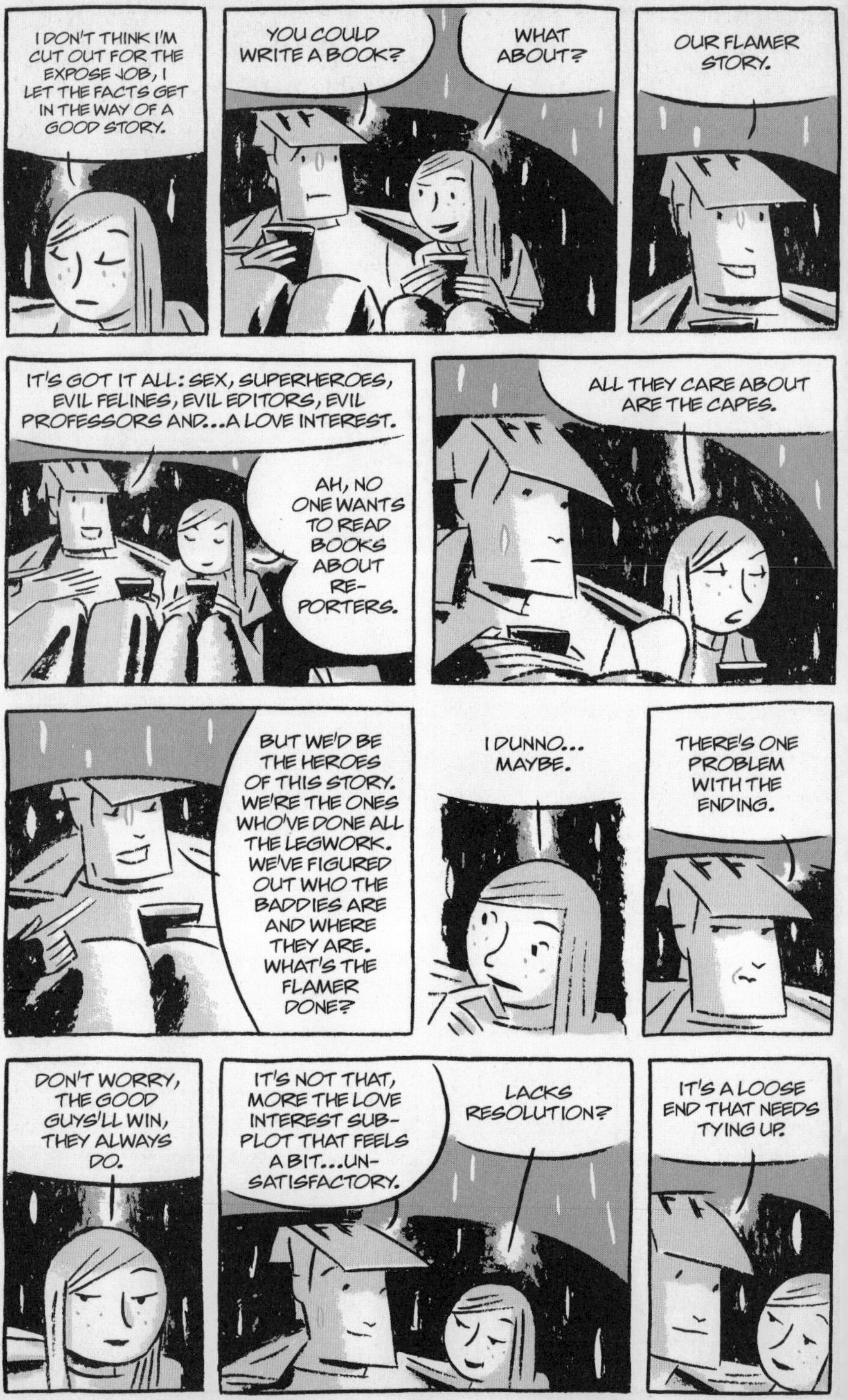
I DON'T THINK I'M CUT OUT FOR THE EXPOSE JOB, I LET THE FACTS GET IN THE WAY OF A GOOD STORY.
YOU COULD WRITE A BOOK?
WHAT ABOUT?
OUR FLAMER STORY.
IT'S GOT IT ALL: SEX, SUPERHEROES, EVIL FELINES, EVIL EDITORS, EVIL PROFESSORS AND...A LOVE INTEREST.
AH, NO ONE WANTS TO READ BOOKS ABOUT RE-PORTERS.
ALL THEY CARE ABOUT ARE THE CAPES.
BUT WE'D BE THE HEROES OF THIS STORY. WE'RE THE ONES WHO'VE DONE ALL THE LEGWORK. WE'VE FIGURED OUT WHO THE BADDIES ARE AND WHERE THEY ARE. WHAT'S THE FLAMER DONE?
I DUNNO... MAYBE.
THERE'S ONE PROBLEM WITH THE ENDING.
DON'T WORRY, THE GOOD GUYS'LL WIN, THEY ALWAYS DO.
IT'S NOT THAT, MORE THE LOVE INTEREST SUB-PLOT THAT FEELS A BIT...UN-SATISFACTORY.
LACKS RESOLUTION?
IT'S A LOOSE END THAT NEEDS TYING UP.

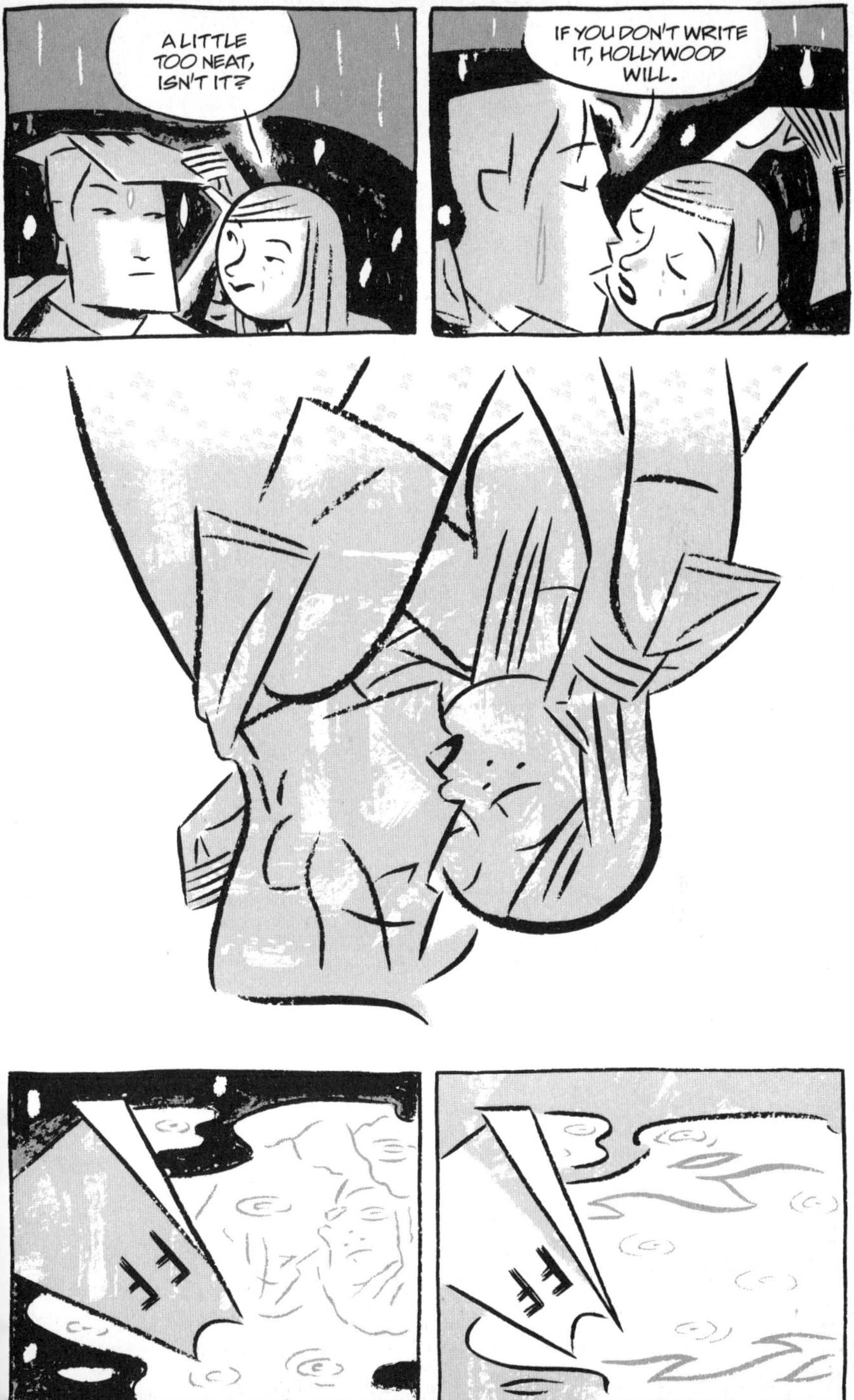
A LITTLE TOO NEAT, ISN'T IT?
IF YOU DON'T WRITE IT, HOLLYWOOD WILL.

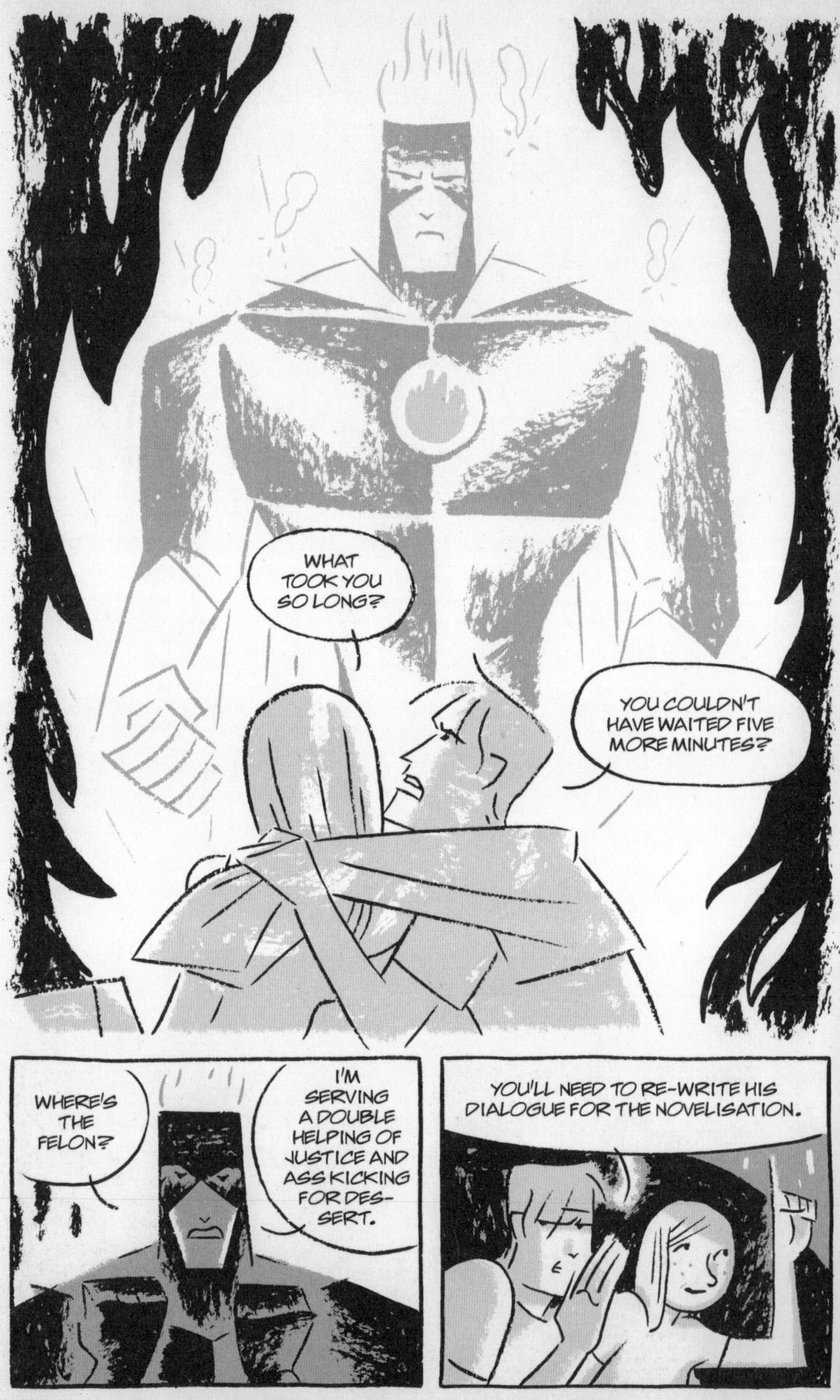
WHAT TOOK YOU SO LONG?
YOU COULDN'T HAVE WAITED FIVE MORE MINUTES?
WHERE'S THE FELON?
I'M SERVING A DOUBLE HELPING OF JUSTICE AND ASS KICKING FOR DES-SERT.
YOU'LL NEED TO RE-WRITE HIS DIALOGUE FOR THE NOVELISATION.

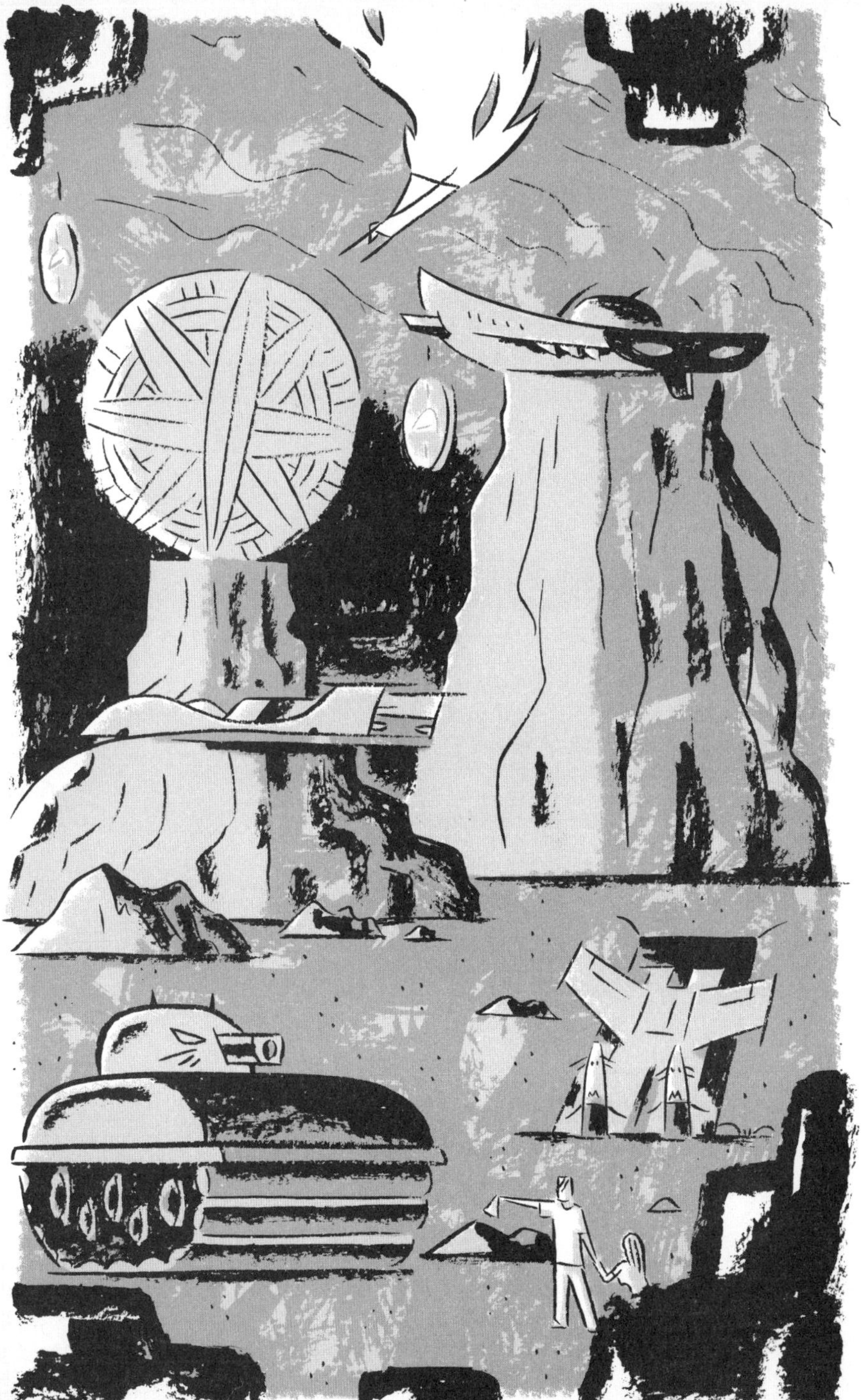

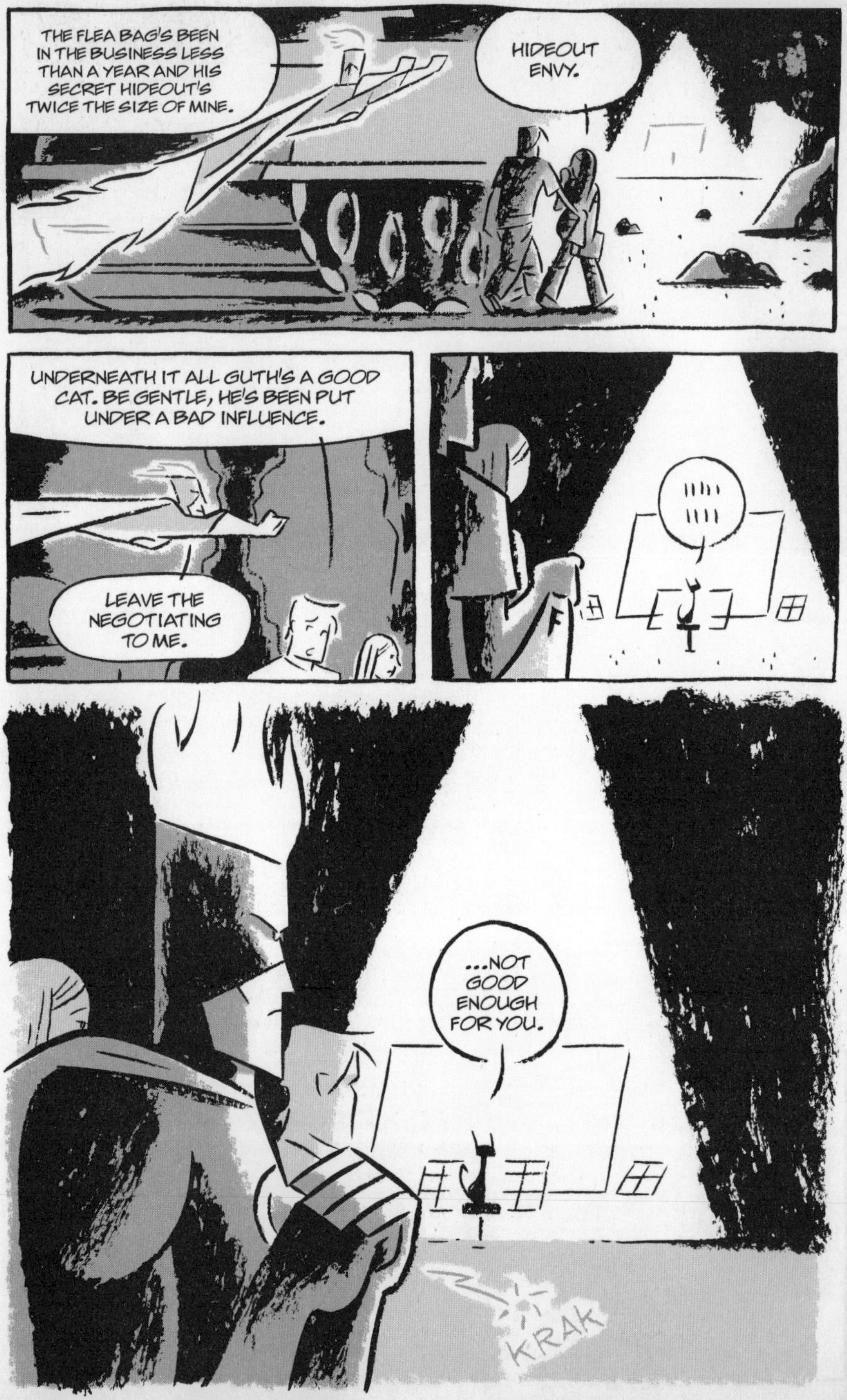
THE FLEA BAG'S BEEN IN THE BUSINESS LESS THAN A YEAR AND HIS SECRET HIDEOUT'S TWICE THE SIZE OF MINE.
HIDEOUT ENVY.
UNDERNEATH IT ALL GUTH'S A GOOD CAT. BE GENTLE, HE'S BEEN PUT UNDER A BAD INFLUENCE.
LEAVE THE NEGOTIATING TO ME.
...NOT GOOD ENOUGH FOR YOU.
KRAK

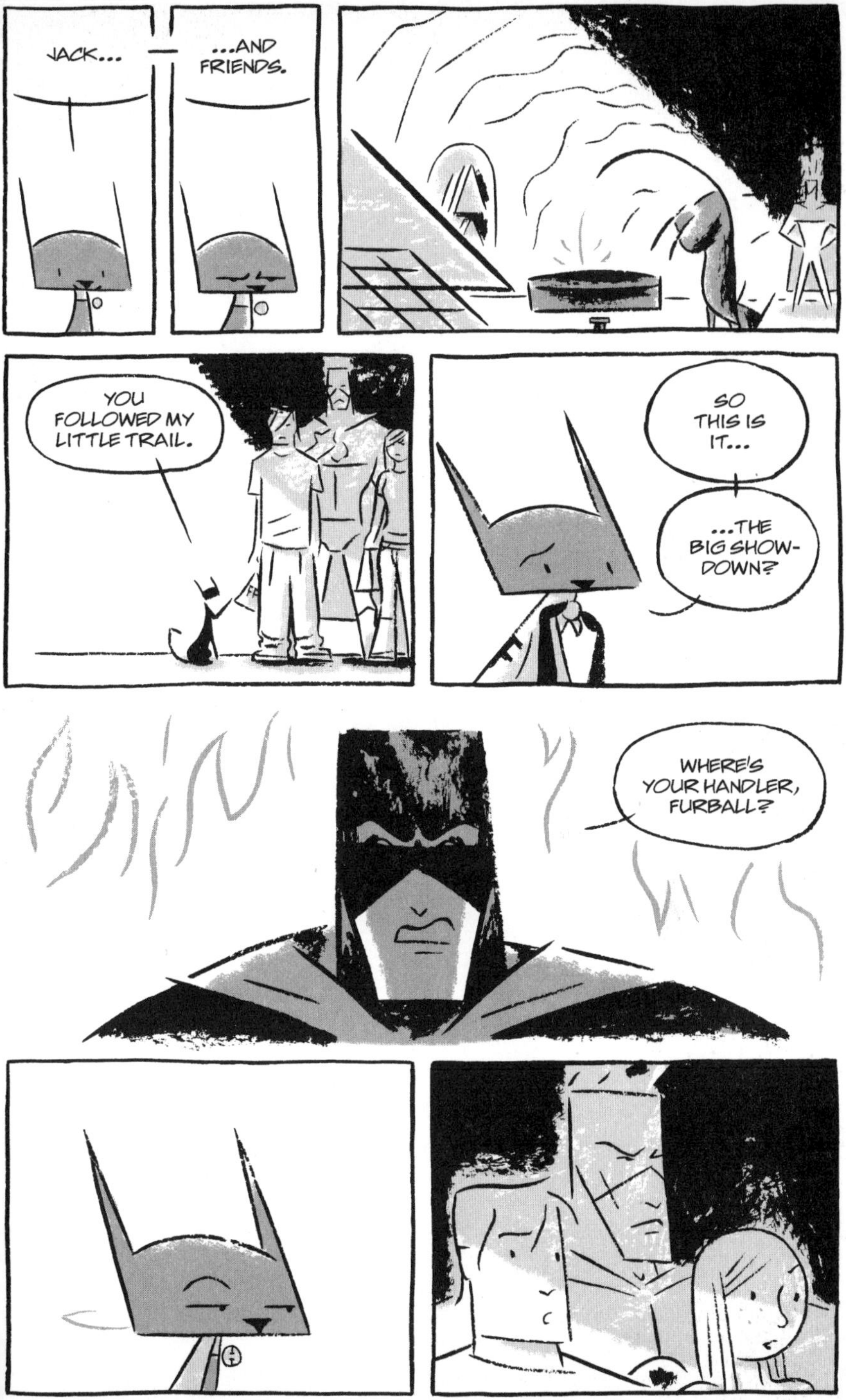
JACK...
...AND FRIENDS.
YOU FOLLOWED MY LITTLE TRAIL.
SO THIS IS IT...
...THE BIG SHOW-DOWN?
WHERE'S YOUR HANDLER, FURBALL?

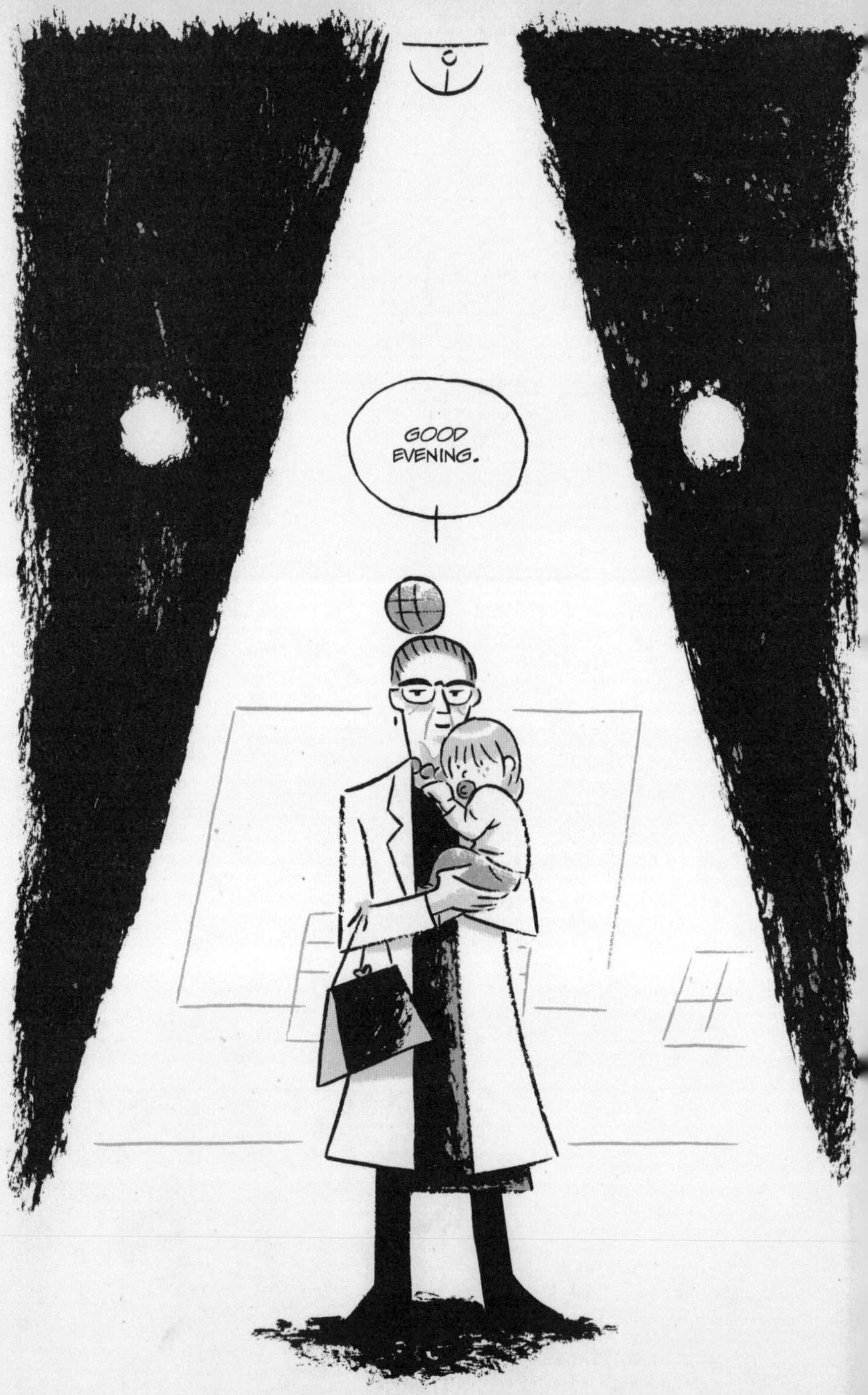
GOOD EVENING.

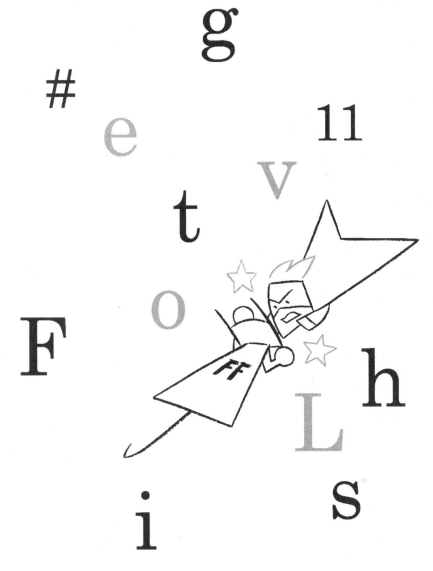

andi watson $2.99 U.S., $4.60 CAN.   ONI PRESS

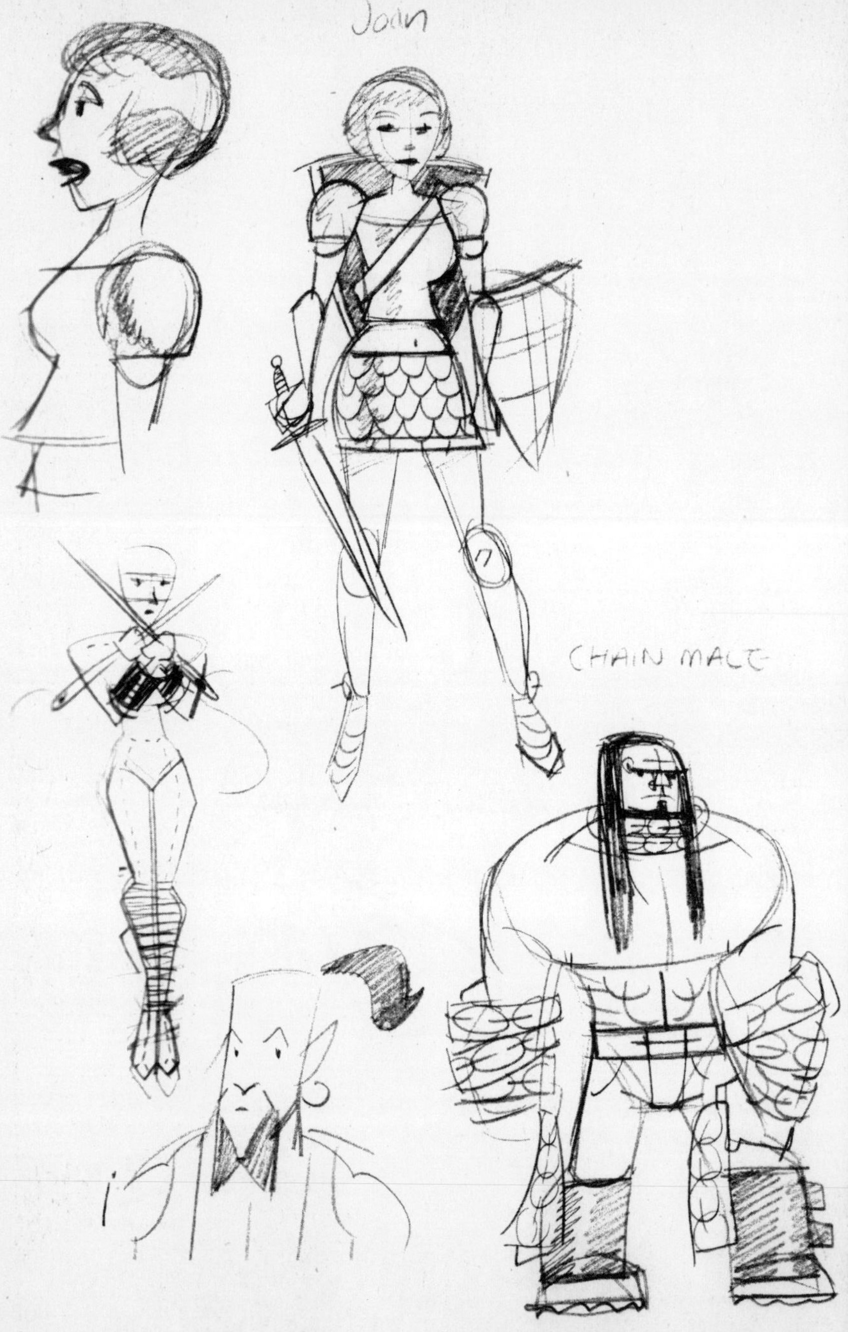
Joan
CHAIN MALE

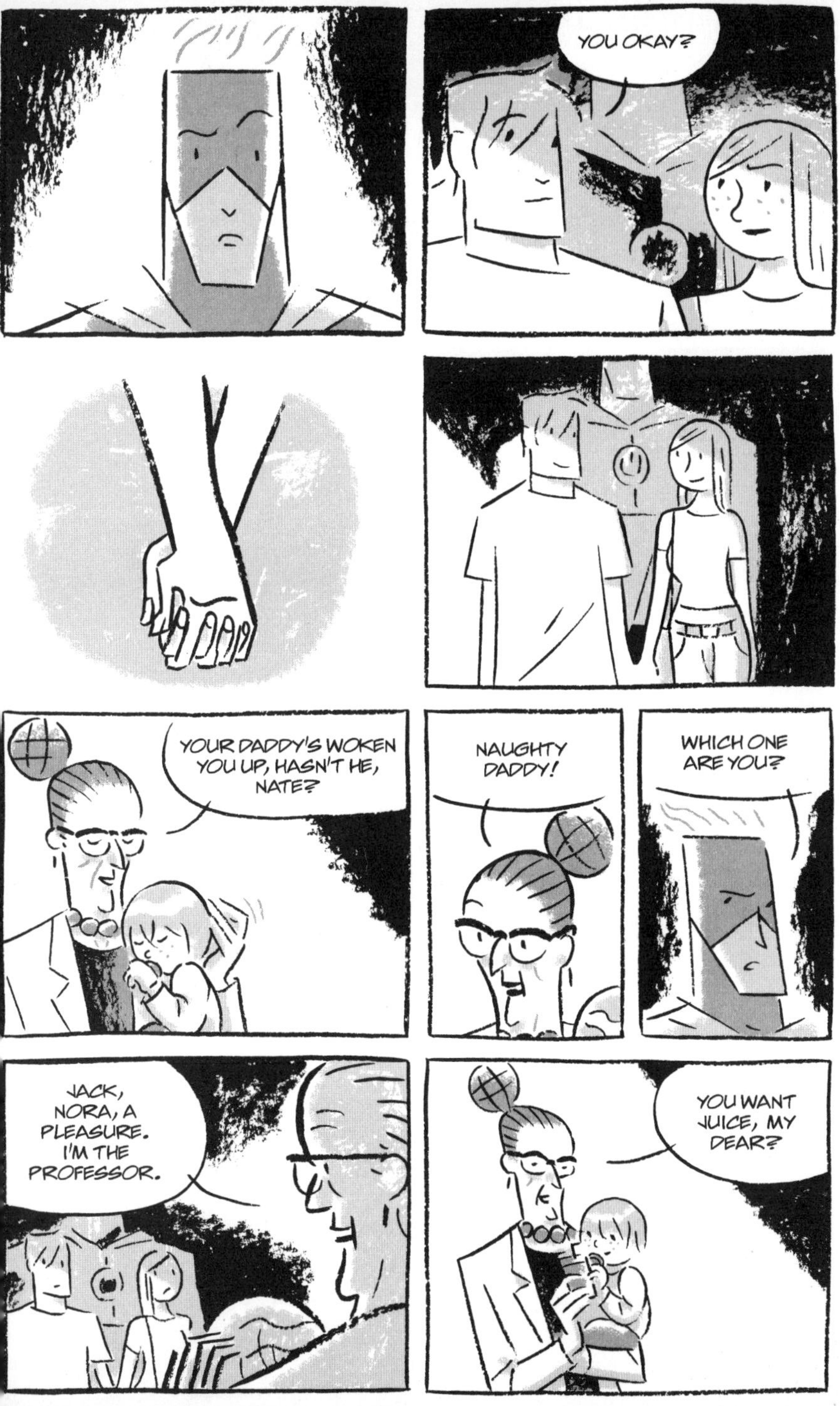
YOU OKAY?
YOUR DADDY'S WOKEN YOU UP, HASN'T HE, NATE?
NAUGHTY DADDY!
WHICH ONE ARE YOU?
JACK, NORA, A PLEASURE. I'M THE PROFESSOR.
YOU WANT JUICE, MY DEAR?

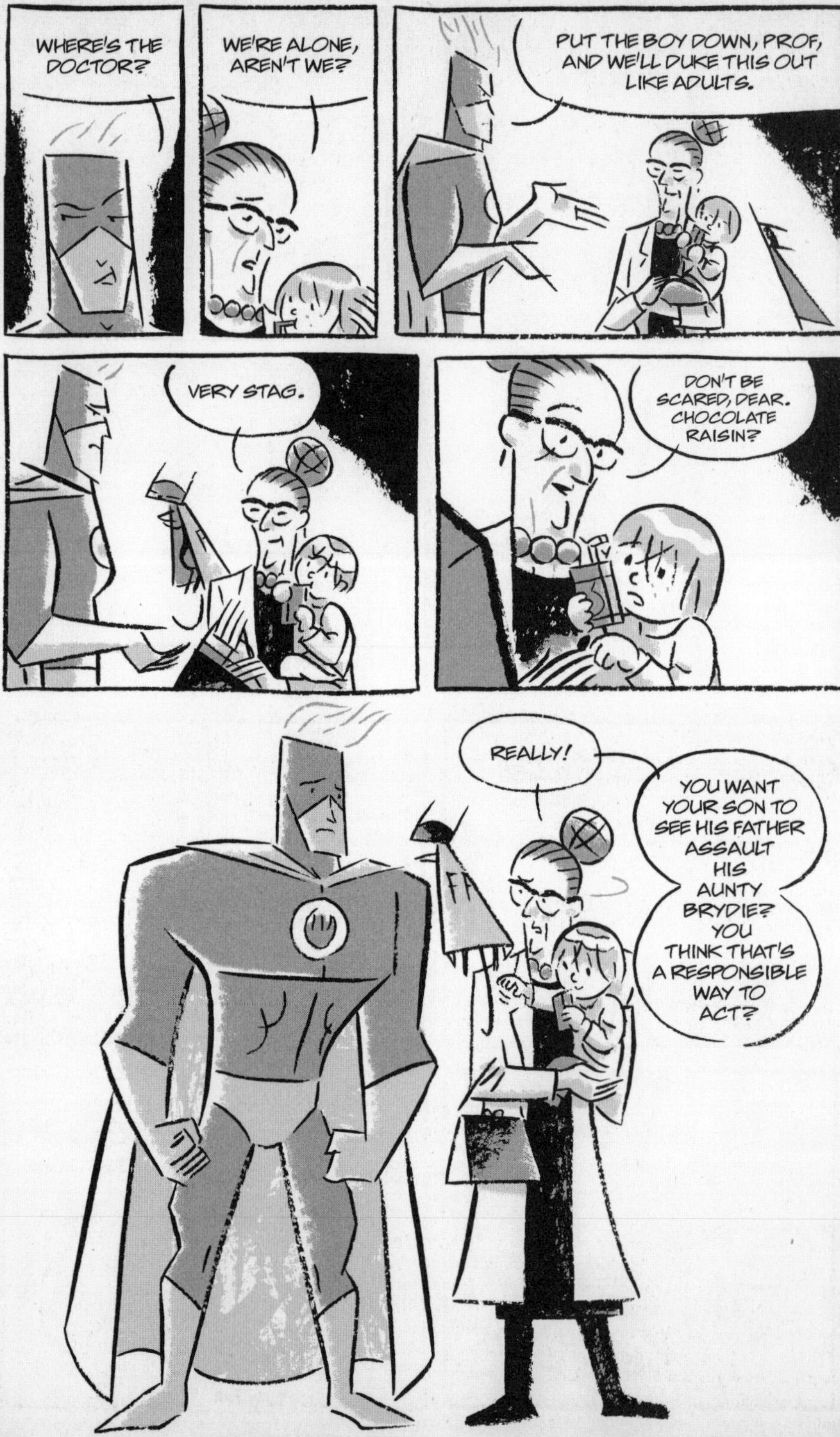
WHERE'S THE DOCTOR?
WE'RE ALONE, AREN'T WE?
PUT THE BOY DOWN, PROF, AND WE'LL DUKE THIS OUT LIKE ADULTS.
VERY STAG.
DON'T BE SCARED, DEAR. CHOCOLATE RAISIN?
REALLY!
YOU WANT YOUR SON TO SEE HIS FATHER ASSAULT HIS AUNTY BRYDIE? YOU THINK THAT'S A RESPONSIBLE WAY TO ACT?

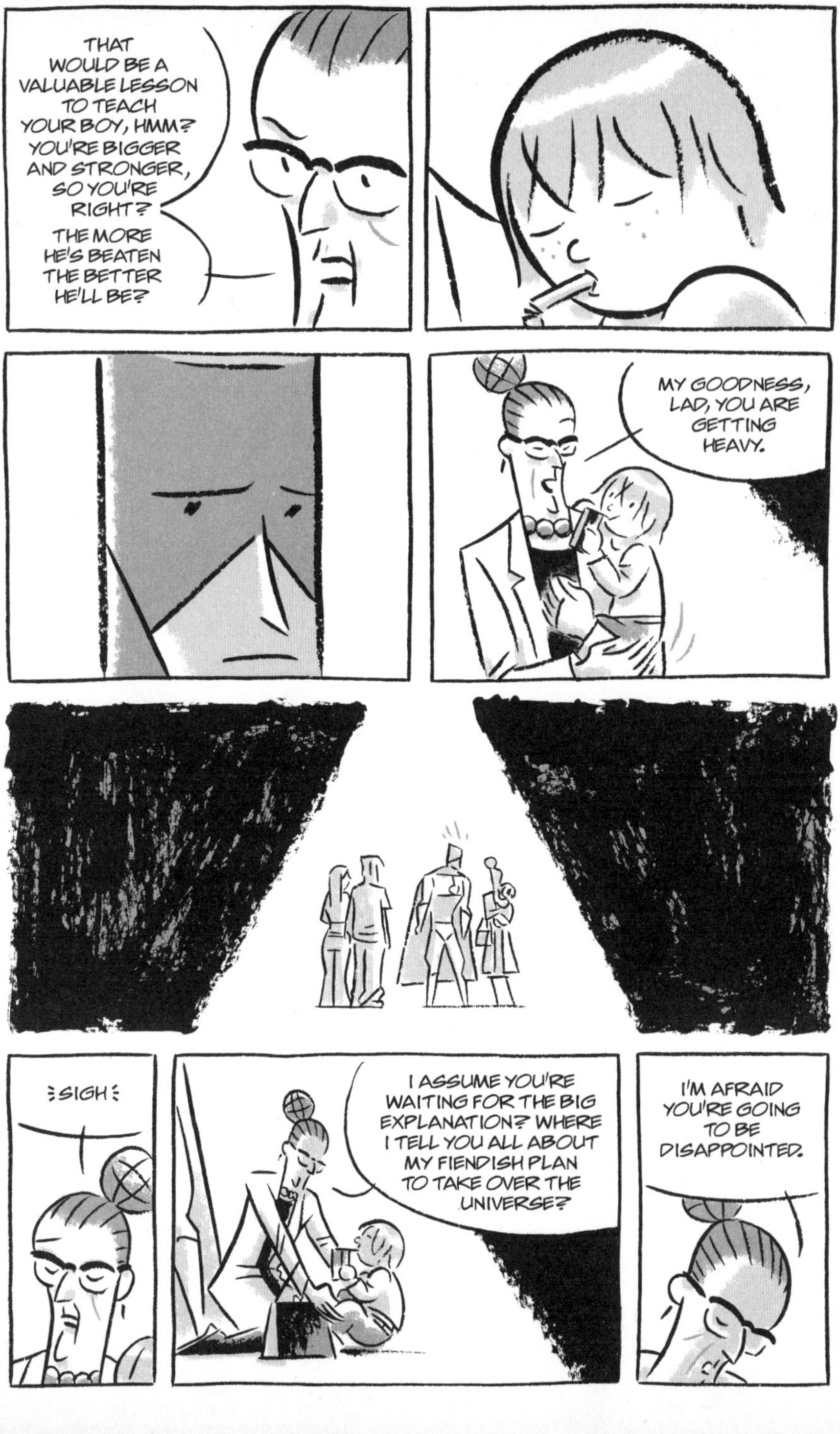
THAT WOULD BE A VALUABLE LESSON TO TEACH YOUR BOY, HMM? YOU'RE BIGGER AND STRONGER, SO YOU'RE RIGHT?
THE MORE HE'S BEATEN THE BETTER HE'LL BE?
MY GOODNESS, LAD, YOU ARE GETTING HEAVY.
SIGH
I ASSUME YOU'RE WAITING FOR THE BIG EXPLANATION? WHERE I TELL YOU ALL ABOUT MY FIENDISH PLAN TO TAKE OVER THE UNIVERSE?
I'M AFRAID YOU'RE GOING TO BE DISAPPOINTED.

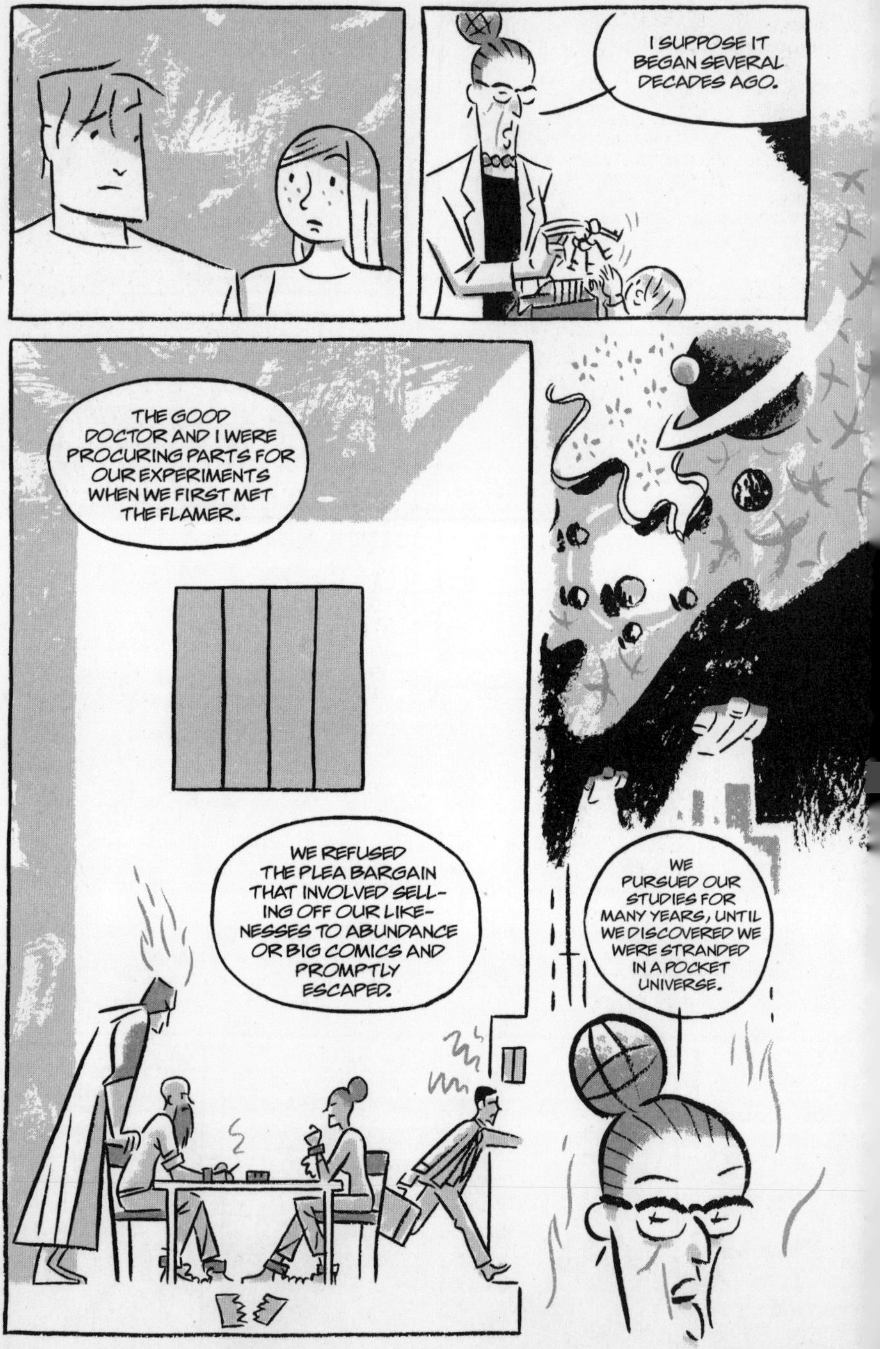
I SUPPOSE IT BEGAN SEVERAL DECADES AGO.
THE GOOD DOCTOR AND I WERE PROCURING PARTS FOR OUR EXPERIMENTS WHEN WE FIRST MET THE FLAMER.
WE REFUSED THE PLEA BARGAIN THAT INVOLVED SELLING OFF OUR LIKENESSES TO ABUNDANCE OR BIG COMICS AND PROMPTLY ESCAPED.
WE PURSUED OUR STUDIES FOR MANY YEARS, UNTIL WE DISCOVERED WE WERE STRANDED IN A POCKET UNIVERSE.

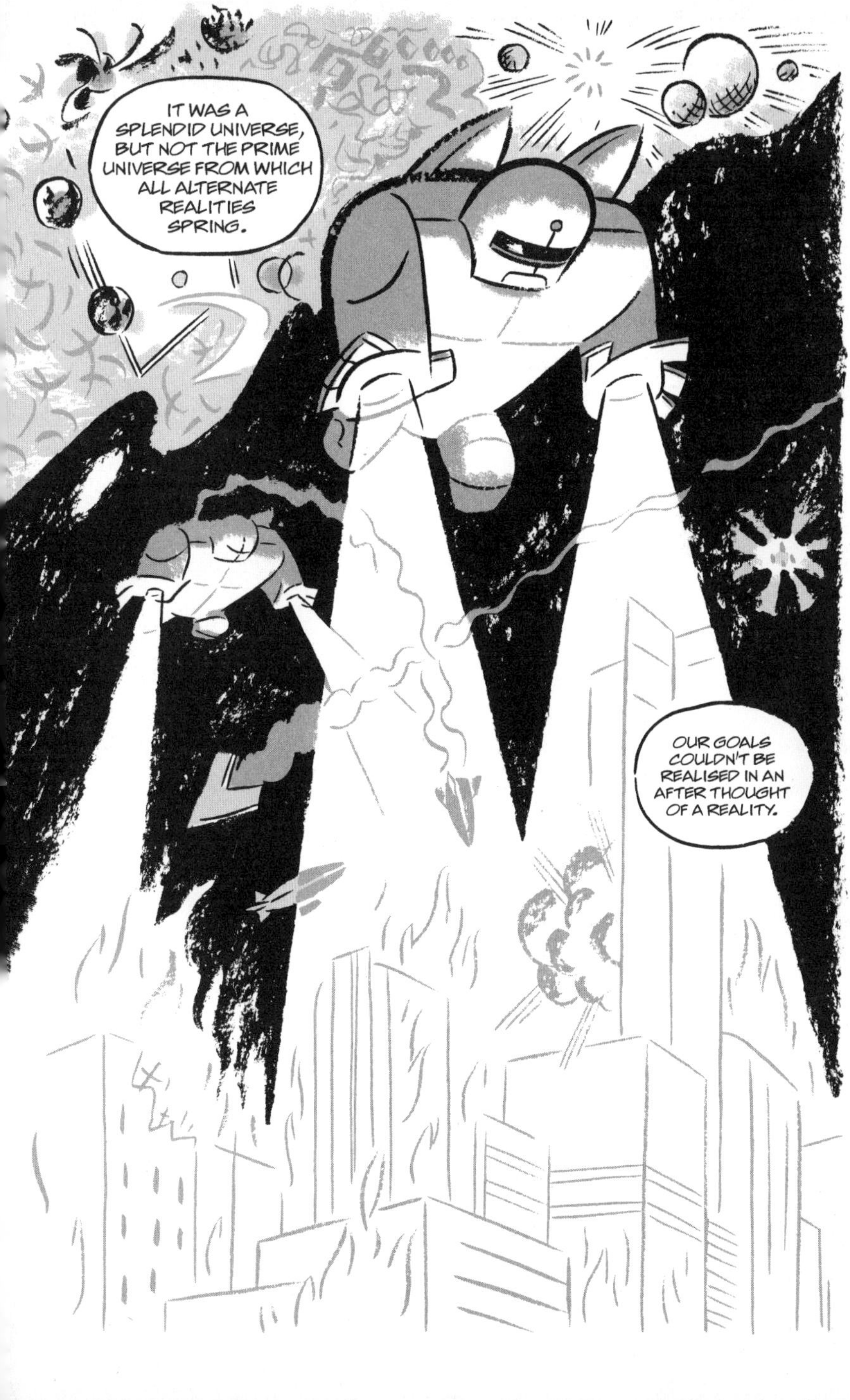
IT WAS A SPLENDID UNIVERSE, BUT NOT THE PRIME UNIVERSE FROM WHICH ALL ALTERNATE REALITIES SPRING.
OUR GOALS COULDN'T BE REALISED IN AN AFTER THOUGHT OF A REALITY.

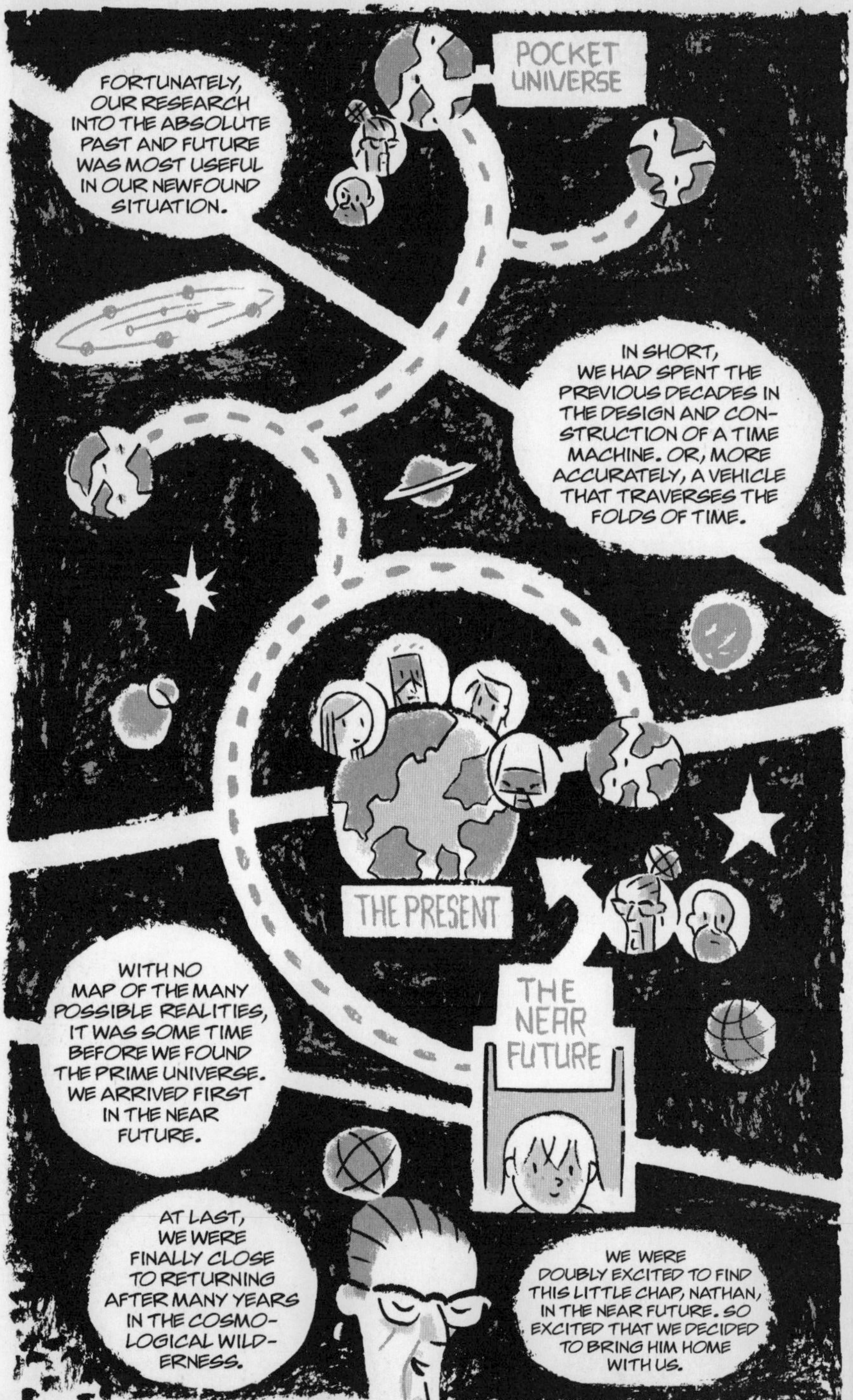
POCKET UNIVERSE
FORTUNATELY, OUR RESEARCH INTO THE ABSOLUTE PAST AND FUTURE WAS MOST USEFUL IN OUR NEWFOUND SITUATION.
IN SHORT, WE HAD SPENT THE PREVIOUS DECADES IN THE DESIGN AND CON- STRUCTION OF A TIME MACHINE. OR, MORE ACCURATELY, A VEHICLE THAT TRAVERSES THE FOLDS OF TIME.
THE PRESENT
THE NEAR FUTURE
WITH NO MAP OF THE MANY POSSIBLE REALITIES, IT WAS SOME TIME BEFORE WE FOUND THE PRIME UNIVERSE. WE ARRIVED FIRST IN THE NEAR FUTURE.
AT LAST, WE WERE FINALLY CLOSE TO RETURNING AFTER MANY YEARS IN THE COSMO- LOGICAL WILD- ERNESS.
WE WERE DOUBLY EXCITED TO FIND THIS LITTLE CHAP, NATHAN, IN THE NEAR FUTURE. SO EXCITED THAT WE DECIDED TO BRING HIM HOME WITH US.

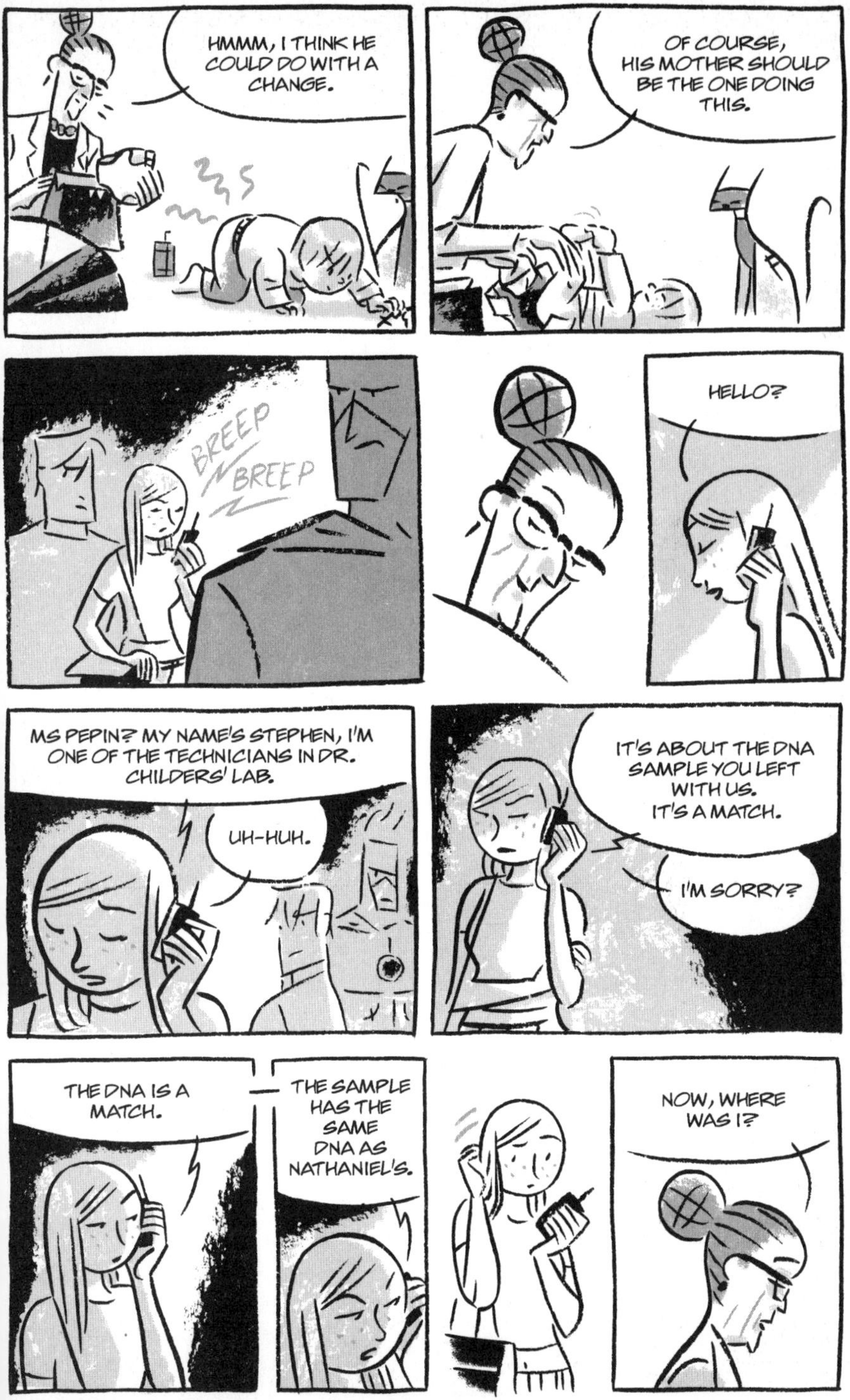
HMMM, I THINK HE COULD DO WITH A CHANGE.
OF COURSE, HIS MOTHER SHOULD BE THE ONE DOING THIS.
BREEP
BREEP
HELLO?
MS PEPIN? MY NAME'S STEPHEN, I'M ONE OF THE TECHNICIANS IN DR. CHILDERS' LAB.
UH-HUH.
IT'S ABOUT THE DNA SAMPLE YOU LEFT WITH US. IT'S A MATCH.
I'M SORRY?
THE DNA IS A MATCH.
THE SAMPLE HAS THE SAME DNA AS NATHANIEL'S.
NOW, WHERE WAS I?

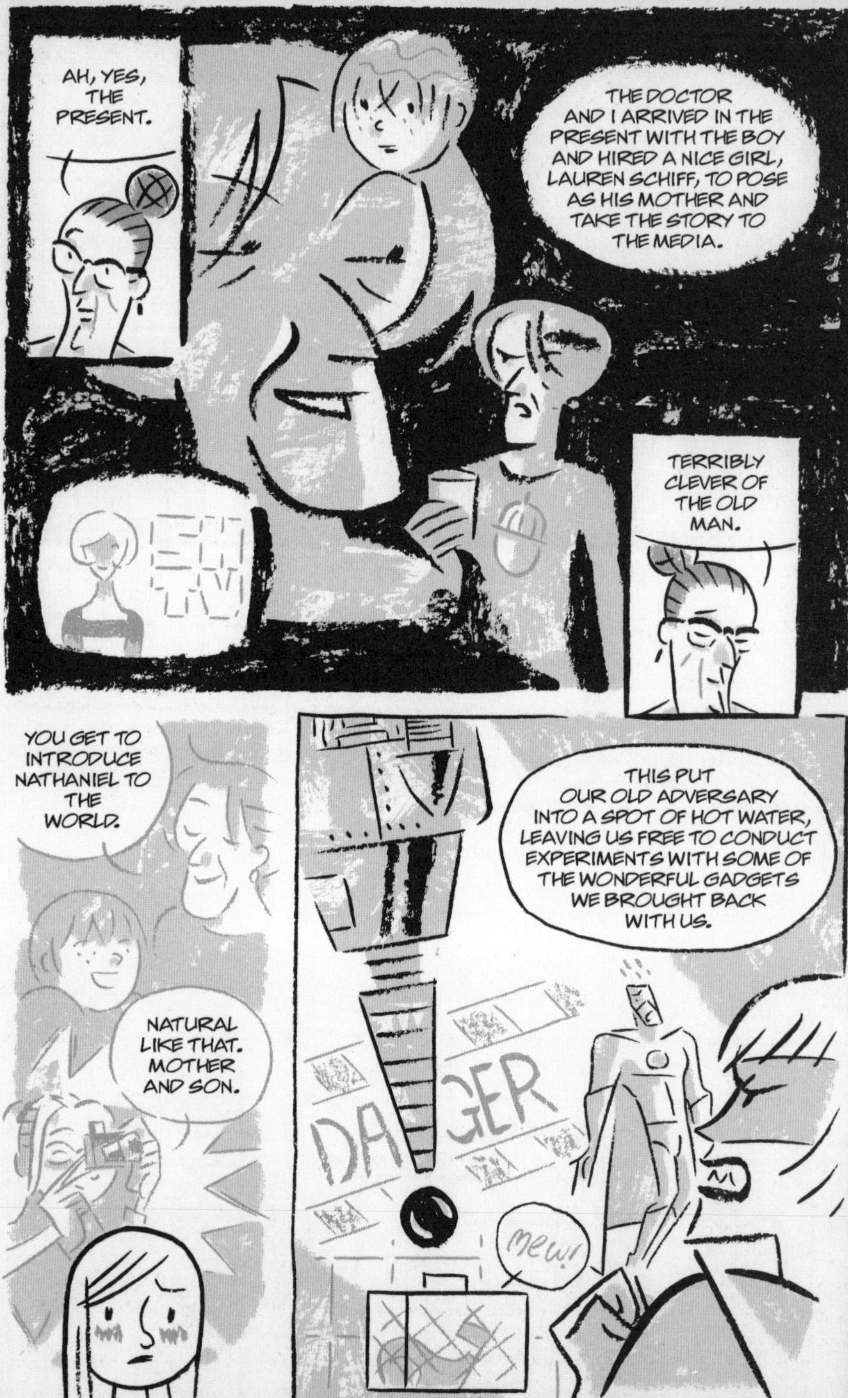
AH, YES, THE PRESENT.
THE DOCTOR AND I ARRIVED IN THE PRESENT WITH THE BOY AND HIRED A NICE GIRL, LAUREN SCHIFF, TO POSE AS HIS MOTHER AND TAKE THE STORY TO THE MEDIA.
TERRIBLY CLEVER OF THE OLD MAN.
YOU GET TO INTRODUCE NATHANIEL TO THE WORLD.
NATURAL LIKE THAT. MOTHER AND SON.
THIS PUT OUR OLD ADVERSARY INTO A SPOT OF HOT WATER, LEAVING US FREE TO CONDUCT EXPERIMENTS WITH SOME OF THE WONDERFUL GADGETS WE BROUGHT BACK WITH US.
DA GER
mew!

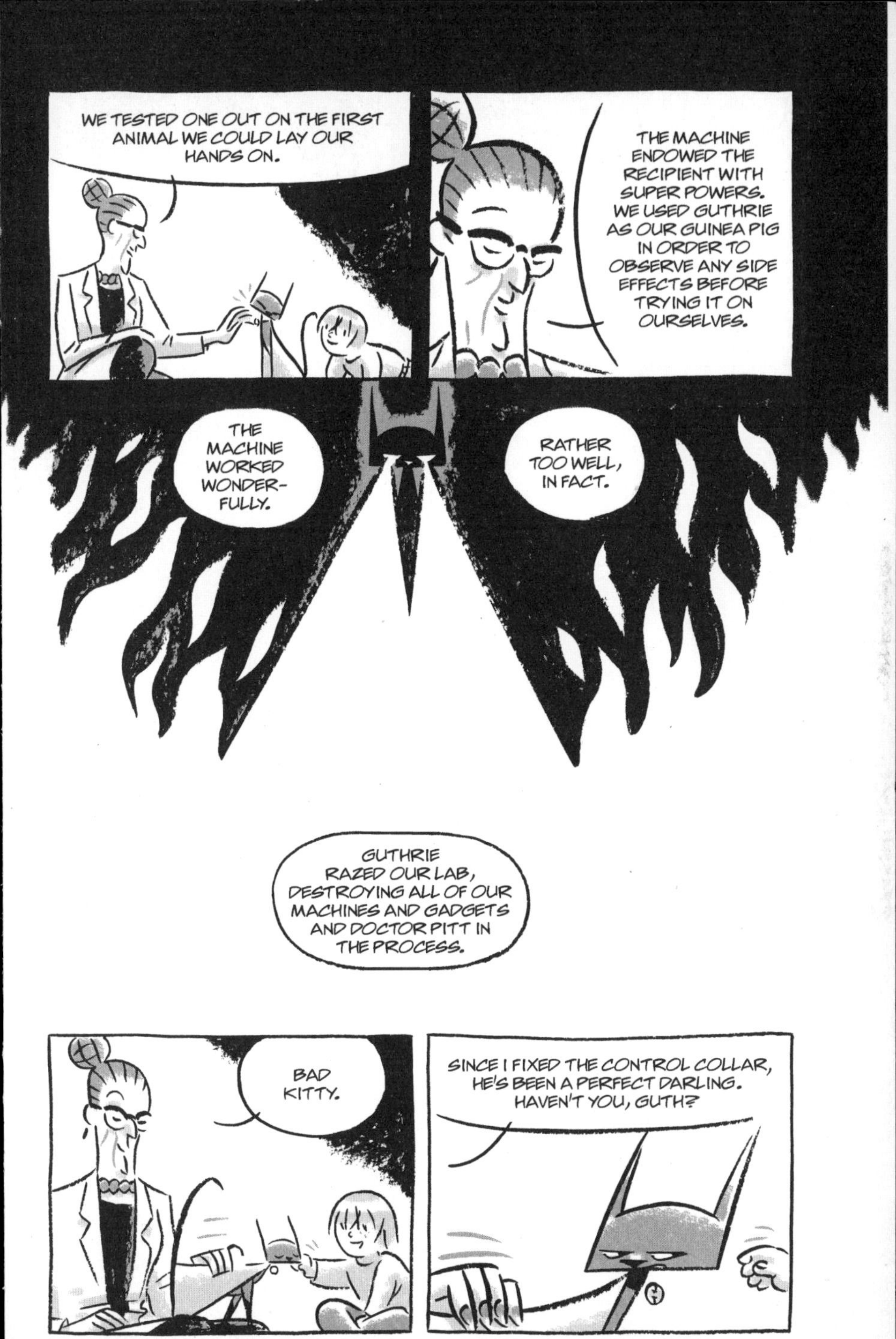
WE TESTED ONE OUT ON THE FIRST ANIMAL WE COULD LAY OUR HANDS ON.
THE MACHINE ENDOWED THE RECIPIENT WITH SUPER POWERS. WE USED GUTHRIE AS OUR GUINEA PIG IN ORDER TO OBSERVE ANY SIDE EFFECTS BEFORE TRYING IT ON OURSELVES.
THE MACHINE WORKED WONDER-FULLY.
RATHER TOO WELL, IN FACT.
GUTHRIE RAZED OUR LAB, DESTROYING ALL OF OUR MACHINES AND GADGETS AND DOCTOR PITT IN THE PROCESS.
BAD KITTY.
SINCE I FIXED THE CONTROL COLLAR, HE'S BEEN A PERFECT DARLING. HAVEN'T YOU, GUTH?

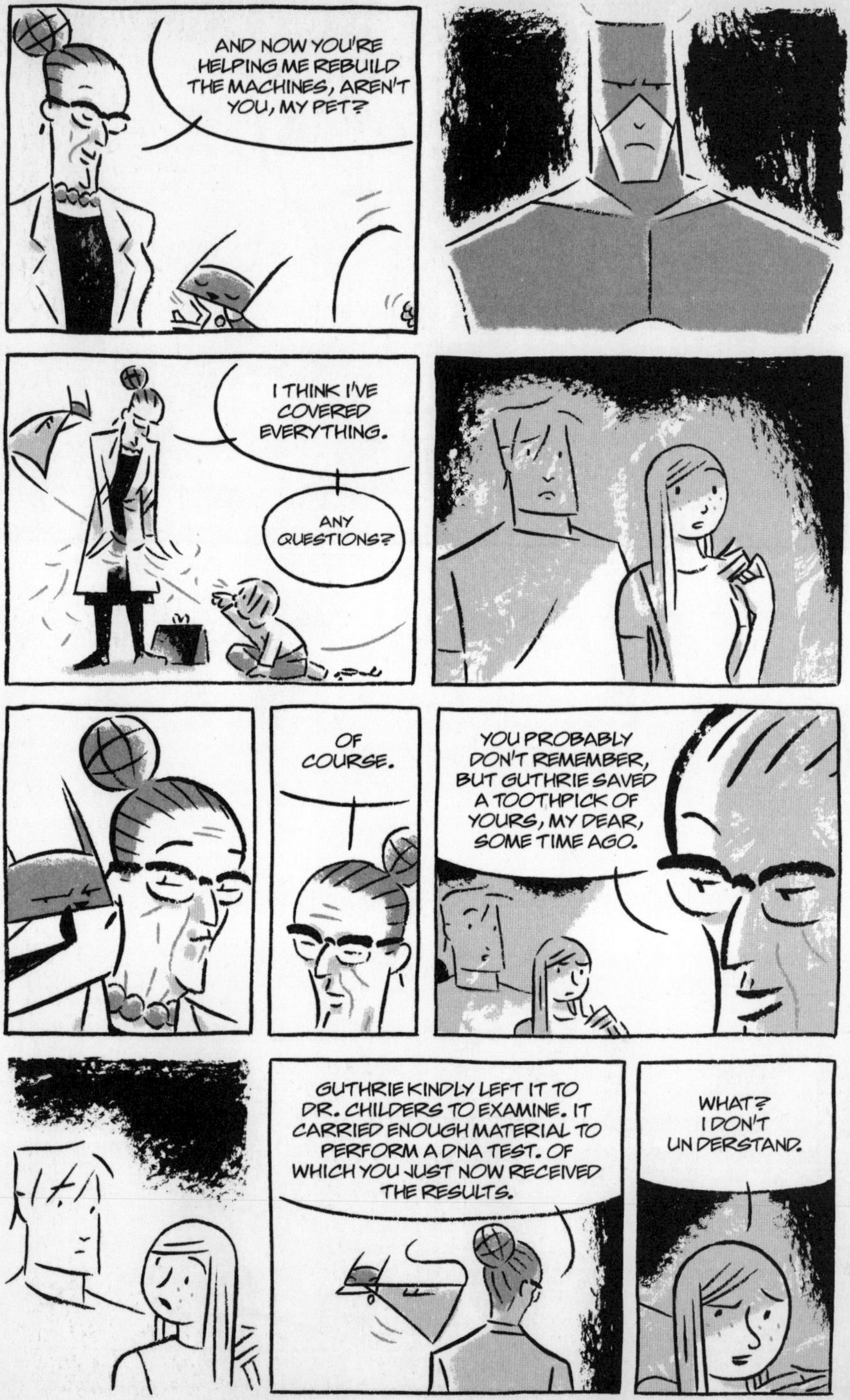
AND NOW YOU'RE HELPING ME REBUILD THE MACHINES, AREN'T YOU, MY PET?
I THINK I'VE COVERED EVERYTHING.
ANY QUESTIONS?
OF COURSE.
YOU PROBABLY DON'T REMEMBER, BUT GUTHRIE SAVED A TOOTHPICK OF YOURS, MY DEAR, SOME TIME AGO.
GUTHRIE KINDLY LEFT IT TO DR. CHILDERS TO EXAMINE. IT CARRIED ENOUGH MATERIAL TO PERFORM A DNA TEST. OF WHICH YOU JUST NOW RECEIVED THE RESULTS.
WHAT? I DON'T UNDERSTAND.

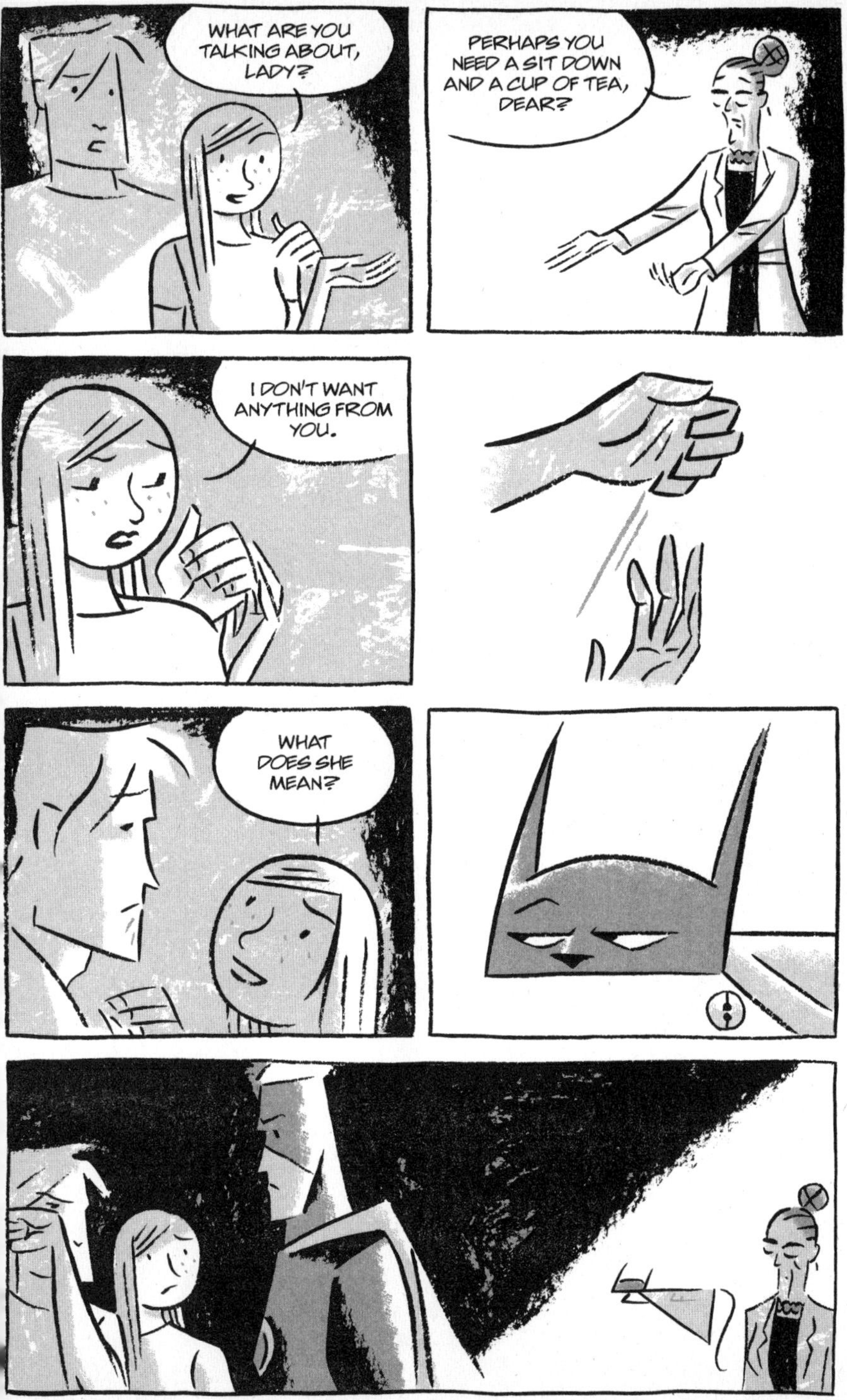
WHAT ARE YOU TALKING ABOUT, LADY?
PERHAPS YOU NEED A SIT DOWN AND A CUP OF TEA, DEAR?
I DON'T WANT ANYTHING FROM YOU.
WHAT DOES SHE MEAN?

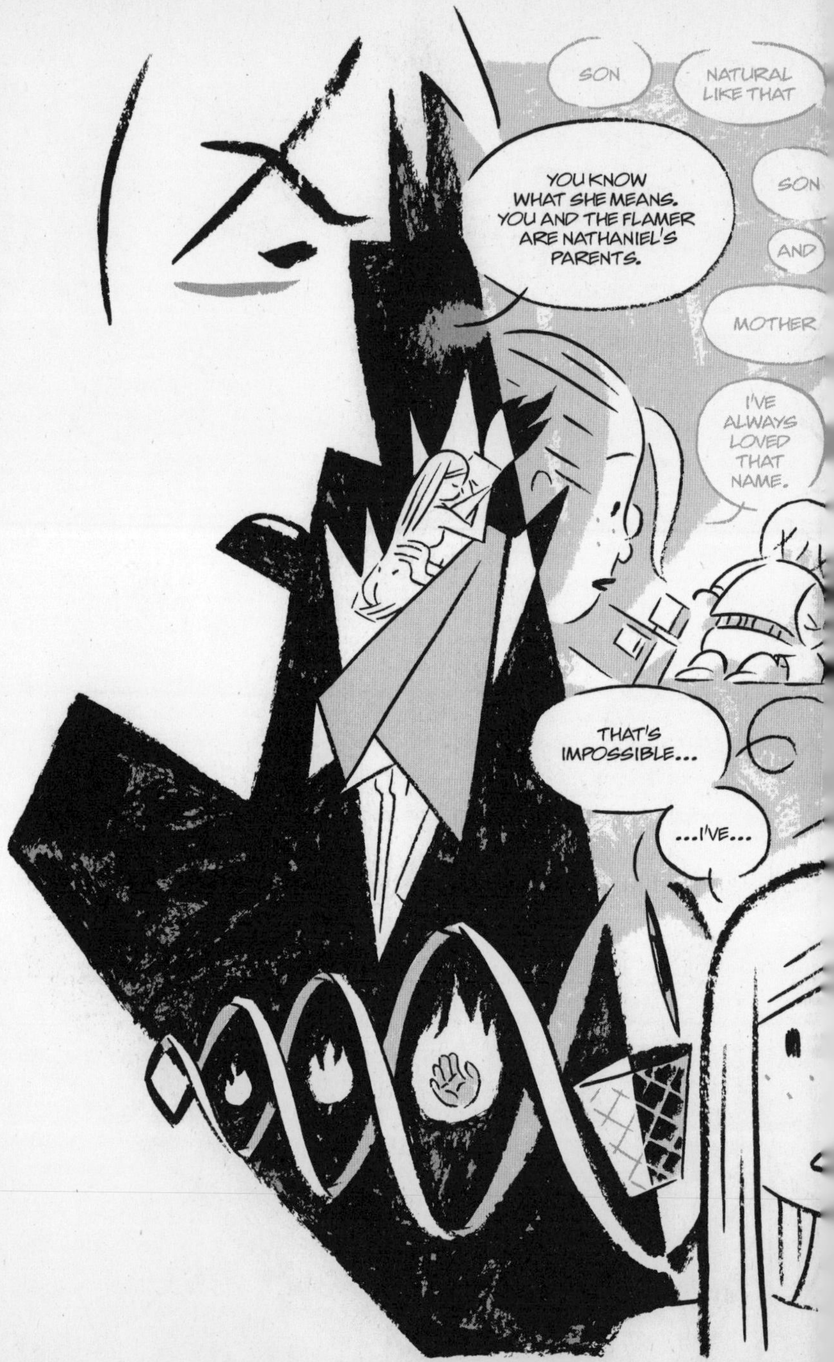
SON
NATURAL LIKE THAT
YOU KNOW WHAT SHE MEANS. YOU AND THE FLAMER ARE NATHANIEL'S PARENTS.
SON
AND
MOTHER
I'VE ALWAYS LOVED THAT NAME.
THAT'S IMPOSSIBLE...
...I'VE...

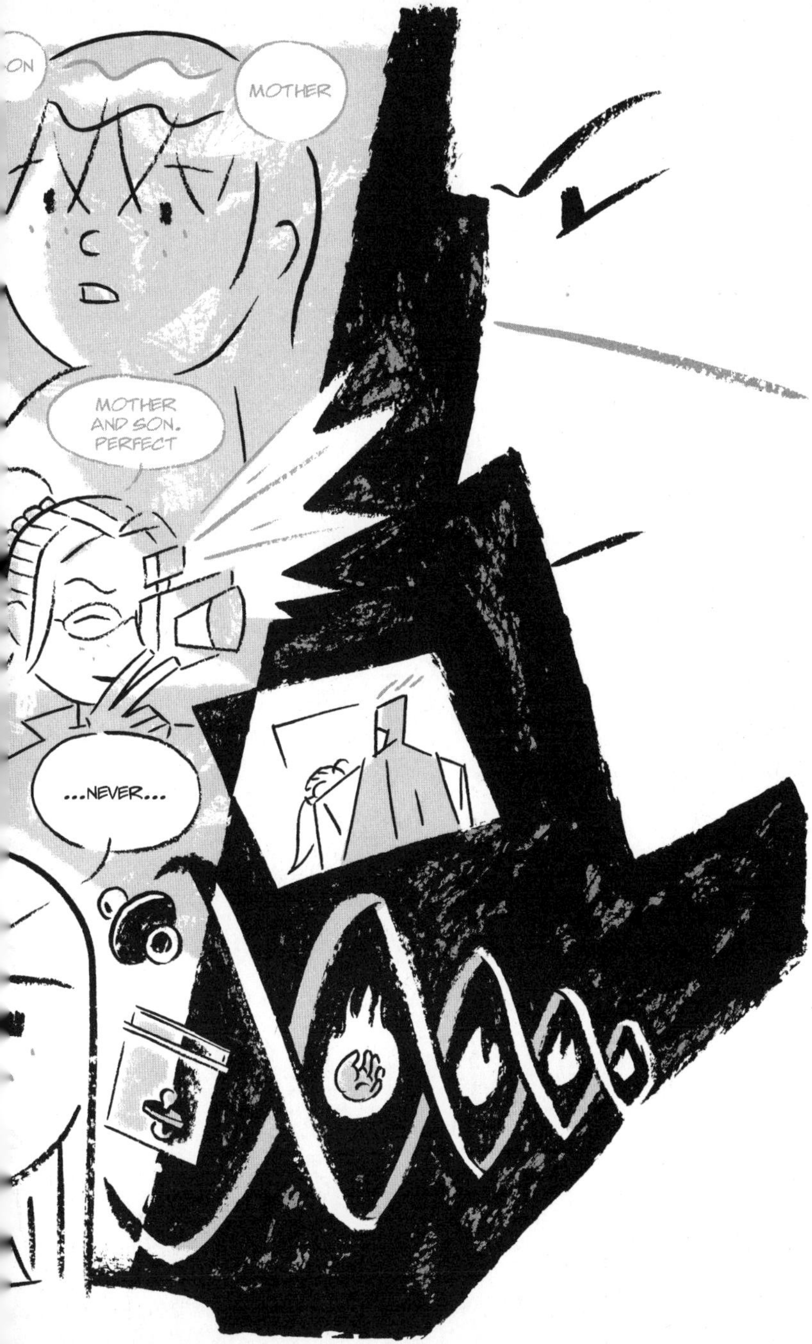
ON
MOTHER
MOTHER AND SON. PERFECT
...NEVER...

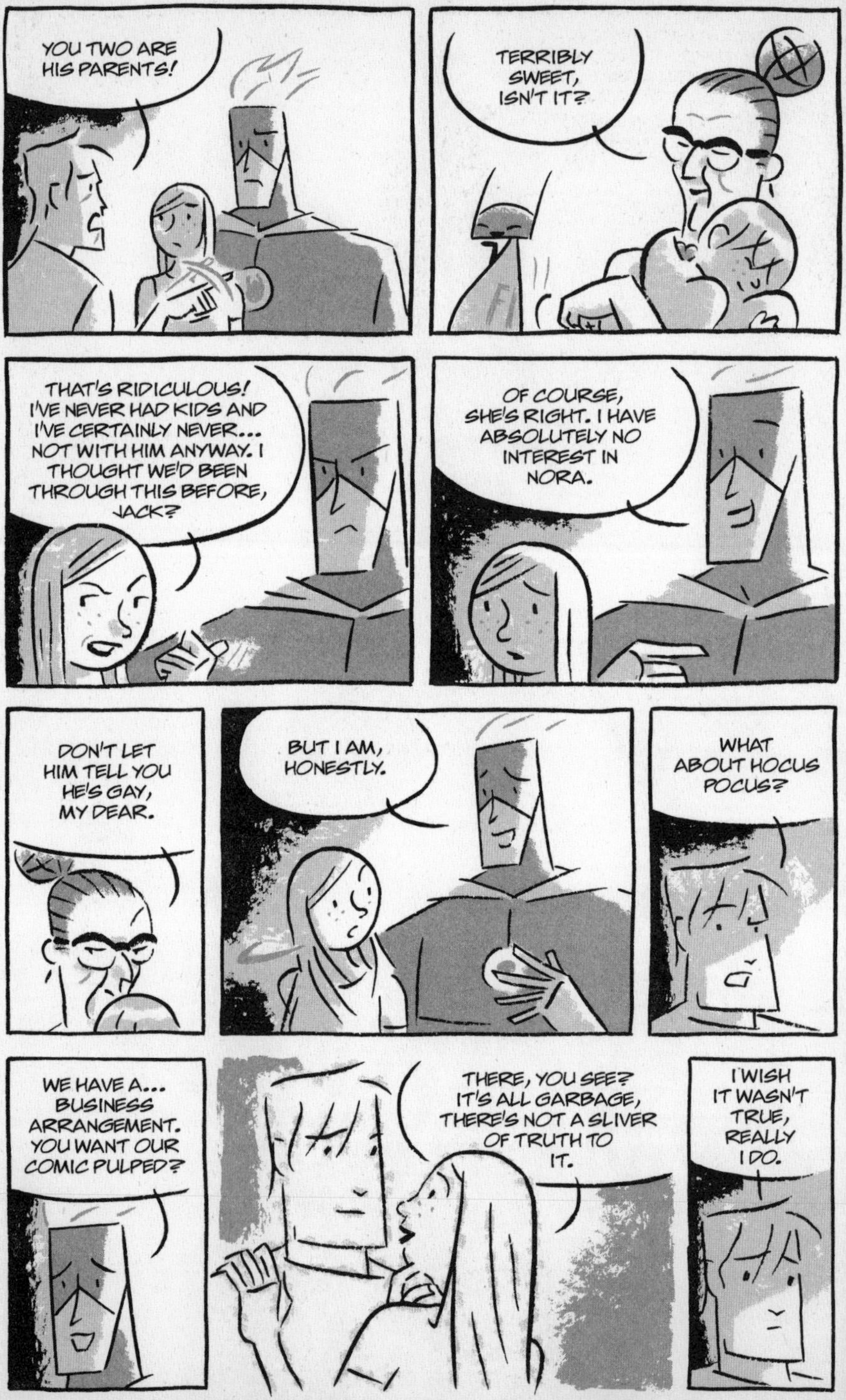
YOU TWO ARE HIS PARENTS!
TERRIBLY SWEET, ISN'T IT?
THAT'S RIDICULOUS! I'VE NEVER HAD KIDS AND I'VE CERTAINLY NEVER... NOT WITH HIM ANYWAY. I THOUGHT WE'D BEEN THROUGH THIS BEFORE, JACK?
OF COURSE, SHE'S RIGHT. I HAVE ABSOLUTELY NO INTEREST IN NORA.
DON'T LET HIM TELL YOU HE'S GAY, MY DEAR.
BUT I AM, HONESTLY.
WHAT ABOUT HOCUS POCUS?
WE HAVE A... BUSINESS ARRANGEMENT. YOU WANT OUR COMIC PULPED?
THERE, YOU SEE? IT'S ALL GARBAGE, THERE'S NOT A SLIVER OF TRUTH TO IT.
I WISH IT WASN'T TRUE, REALLY I DO.

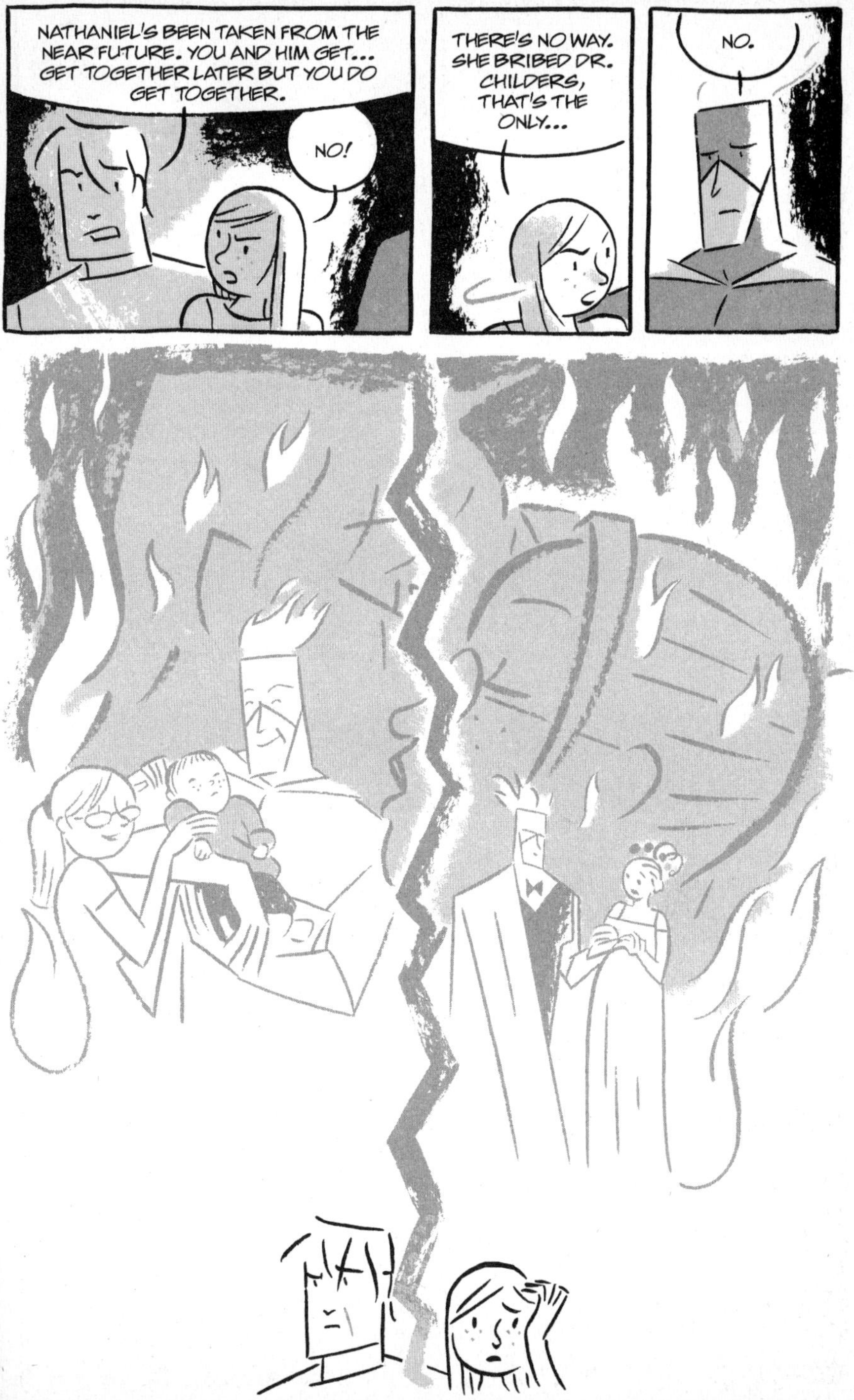
NATHANIEL'S BEEN TAKEN FROM THE NEAR FUTURE. YOU AND HIM GET... GET TOGETHER LATER BUT YOU DO GET TOGETHER.
NO!
THERE'S NO WAY. SHE BRIBED DR. CHILDERS, THAT'S THE ONLY...
NO.

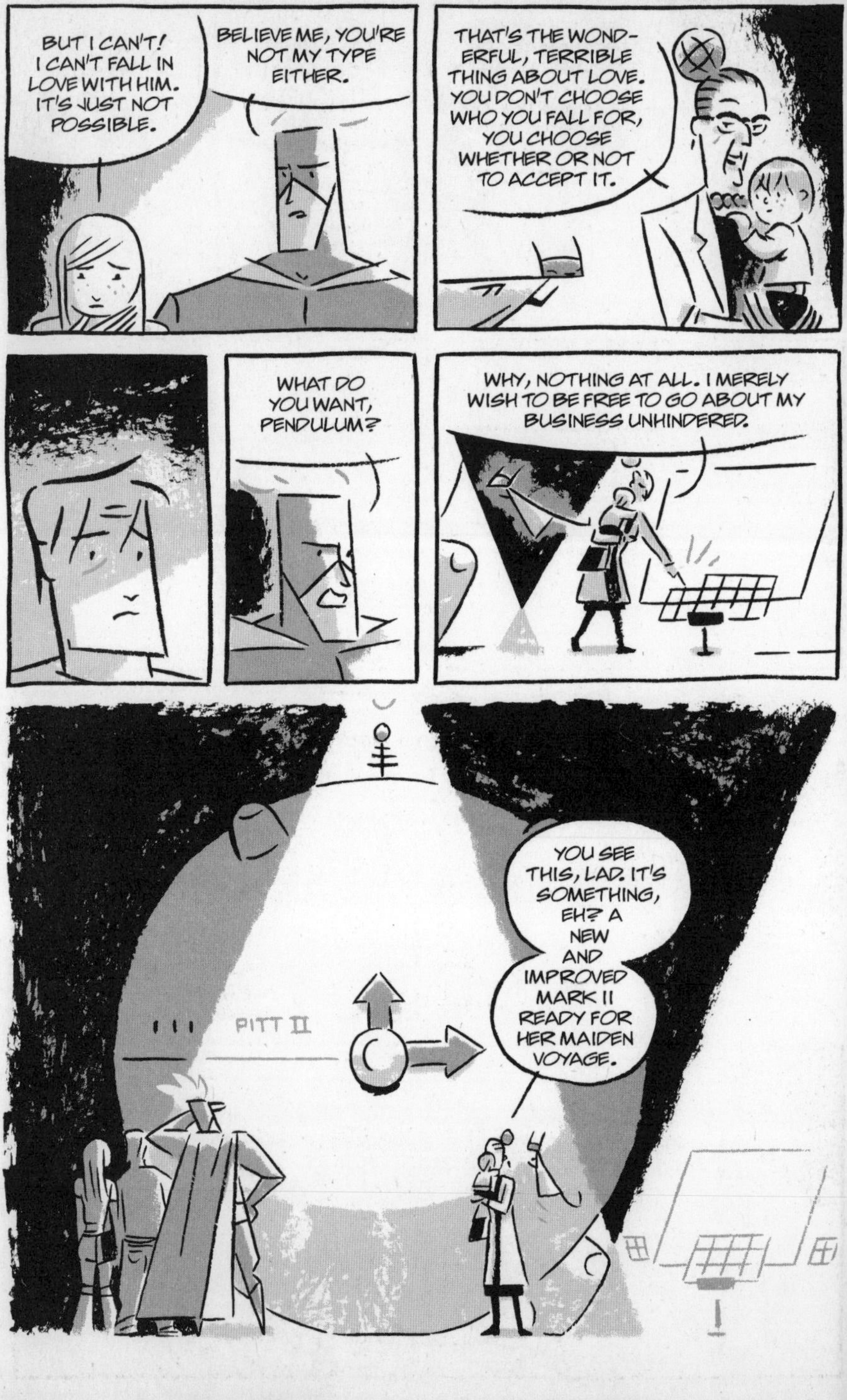
BUT I CAN'T! I CAN'T FALL IN LOVE WITH HIM. IT'S JUST NOT POSSIBLE.
BELIEVE ME, YOU'RE NOT MY TYPE EITHER.
THAT'S THE WONDERFUL, TERRIBLE THING ABOUT LOVE. YOU DON'T CHOOSE WHO YOU FALL FOR, YOU CHOOSE WHETHER OR NOT TO ACCEPT IT.
WHAT DO YOU WANT, PENDULUM?
WHY, NOTHING AT ALL. I MERELY WISH TO BE FREE TO GO ABOUT MY BUSINESS UNHINDERED.
PITT II
YOU SEE THIS, LAD. IT'S SOMETHING, EH? A NEW AND IMPROVED MARK II READY FOR HER MAIDEN VOYAGE.

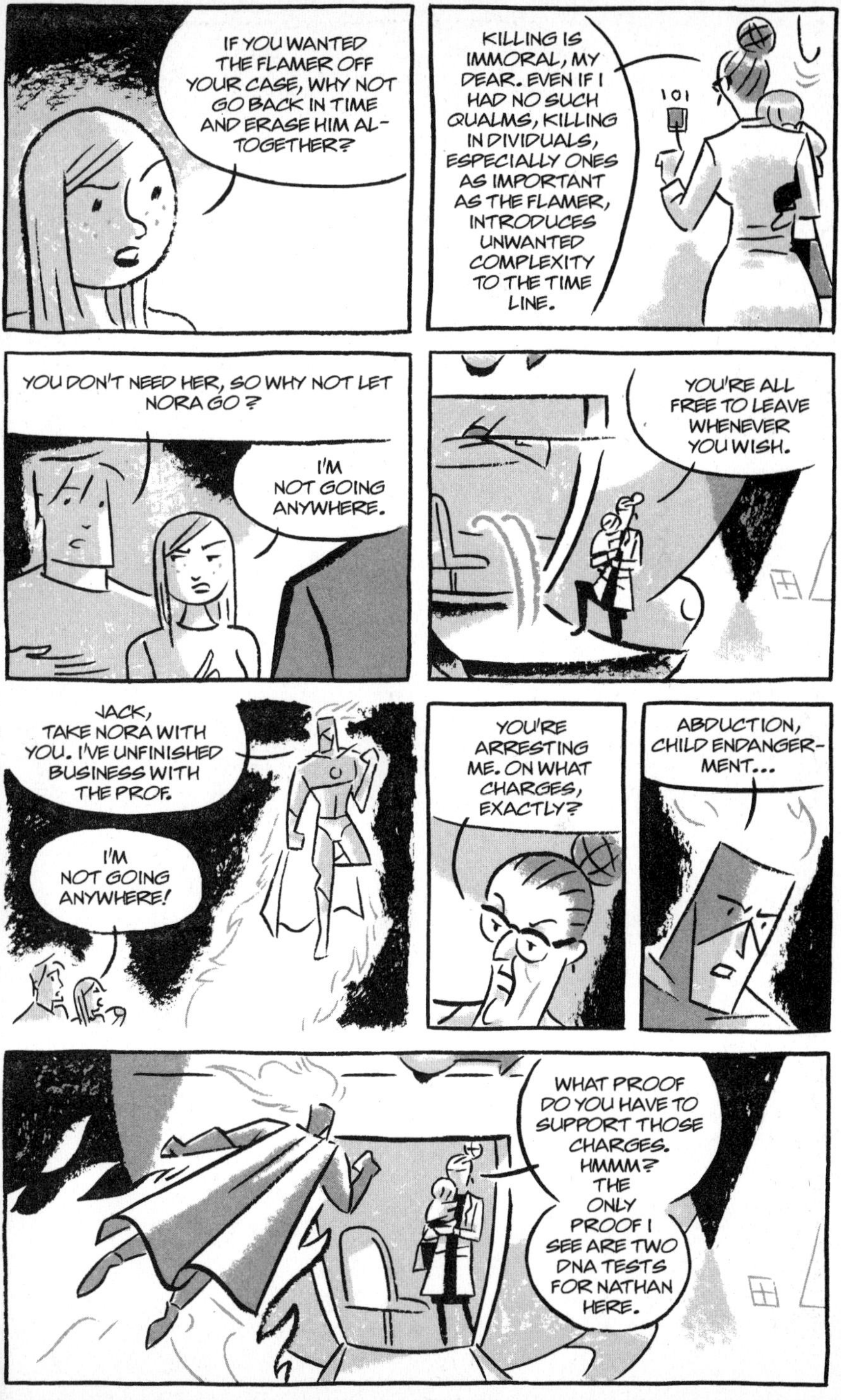
IF YOU WANTED THE FLAMER OFF YOUR CASE, WHY NOT GO BACK IN TIME AND ERASE HIM ALTOGETHER?
KILLING IS IMMORAL, MY DEAR. EVEN IF I HAD NO SUCH QUALMS, KILLING INDIVIDUALS, ESPECIALLY ONES AS IMPORTANT AS THE FLAMER, INTRODUCES UNWANTED COMPLEXITY TO THE TIME LINE.
YOU DON'T NEED HER, SO WHY NOT LET NORA GO?
I'M NOT GOING ANYWHERE.
YOU'RE ALL FREE TO LEAVE WHENEVER YOU WISH.
JACK, TAKE NORA WITH YOU. I'VE UNFINISHED BUSINESS WITH THE PROF.
I'M NOT GOING ANYWHERE!
YOU'RE ARRESTING ME. ON WHAT CHARGES, EXACTLY?
ABDUCTION, CHILD ENDANGERMENT...
WHAT PROOF DO YOU HAVE TO SUPPORT THOSE CHARGES. HMMM? THE ONLY PROOF I SEE ARE TWO DNA TESTS FOR NATHAN HERE.

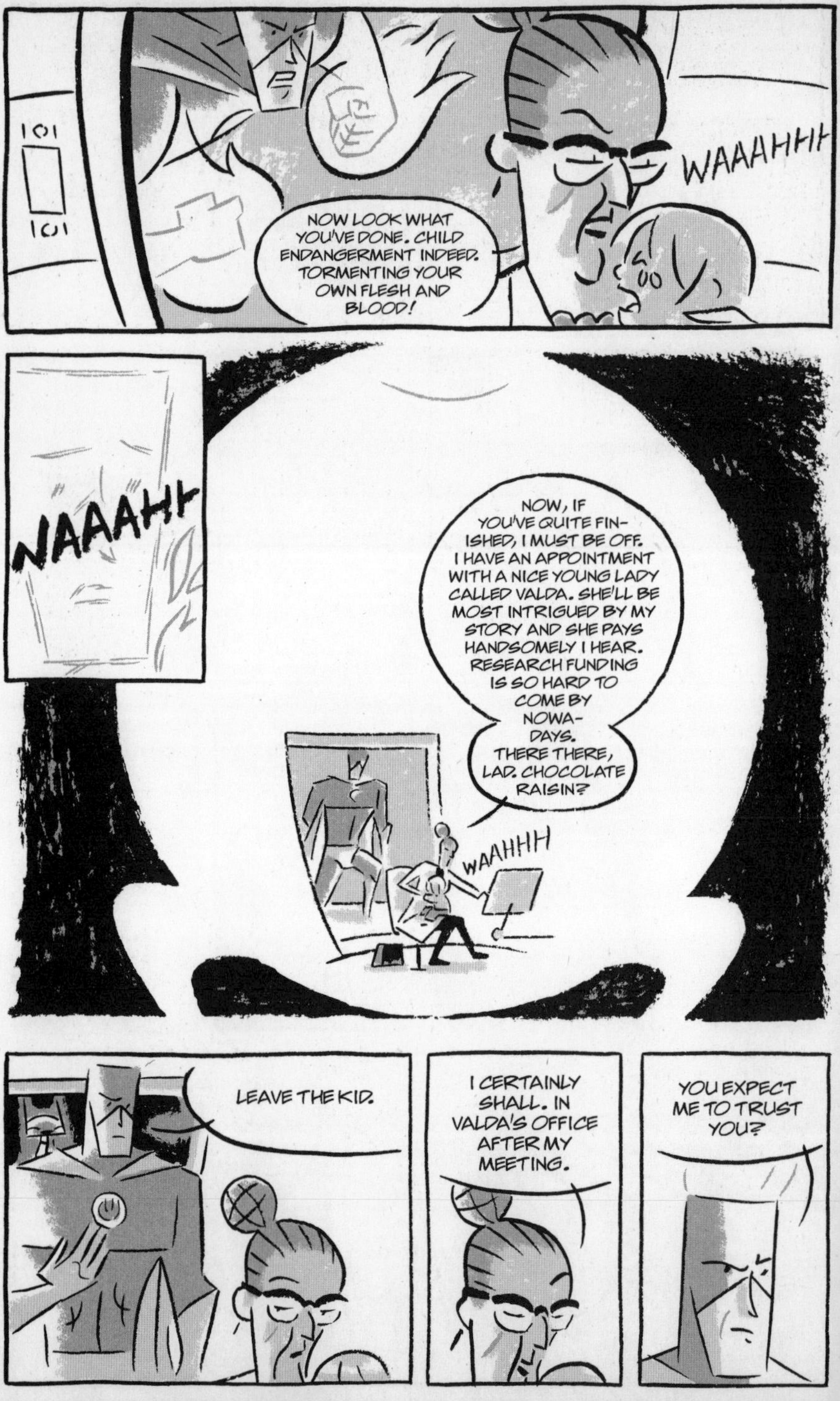
WAAAHHH
NOW LOOK WHAT YOU'VE DONE. CHILD ENDANGERMENT INDEED. TORMENTING YOUR OWN FLESH AND BLOOD!
NAAAHH
NOW, IF YOU'VE QUITE FIN-ISHED, I MUST BE OFF. I HAVE AN APPOINTMENT WITH A NICE YOUNG LADY CALLED VALDA. SHE'LL BE MOST INTRIGUED BY MY STORY AND SHE PAYS HANDSOMELY I HEAR. RESEARCH FUNDING IS SO HARD TO COME BY NOWA-DAYS. THERE THERE, LAD. CHOCOLATE RAISIN?
WAAHHH
LEAVE THE KID.
I CERTAINLY SHALL. IN VALDA'S OFFICE AFTER MY MEETING.
YOU EXPECT ME TO TRUST YOU?

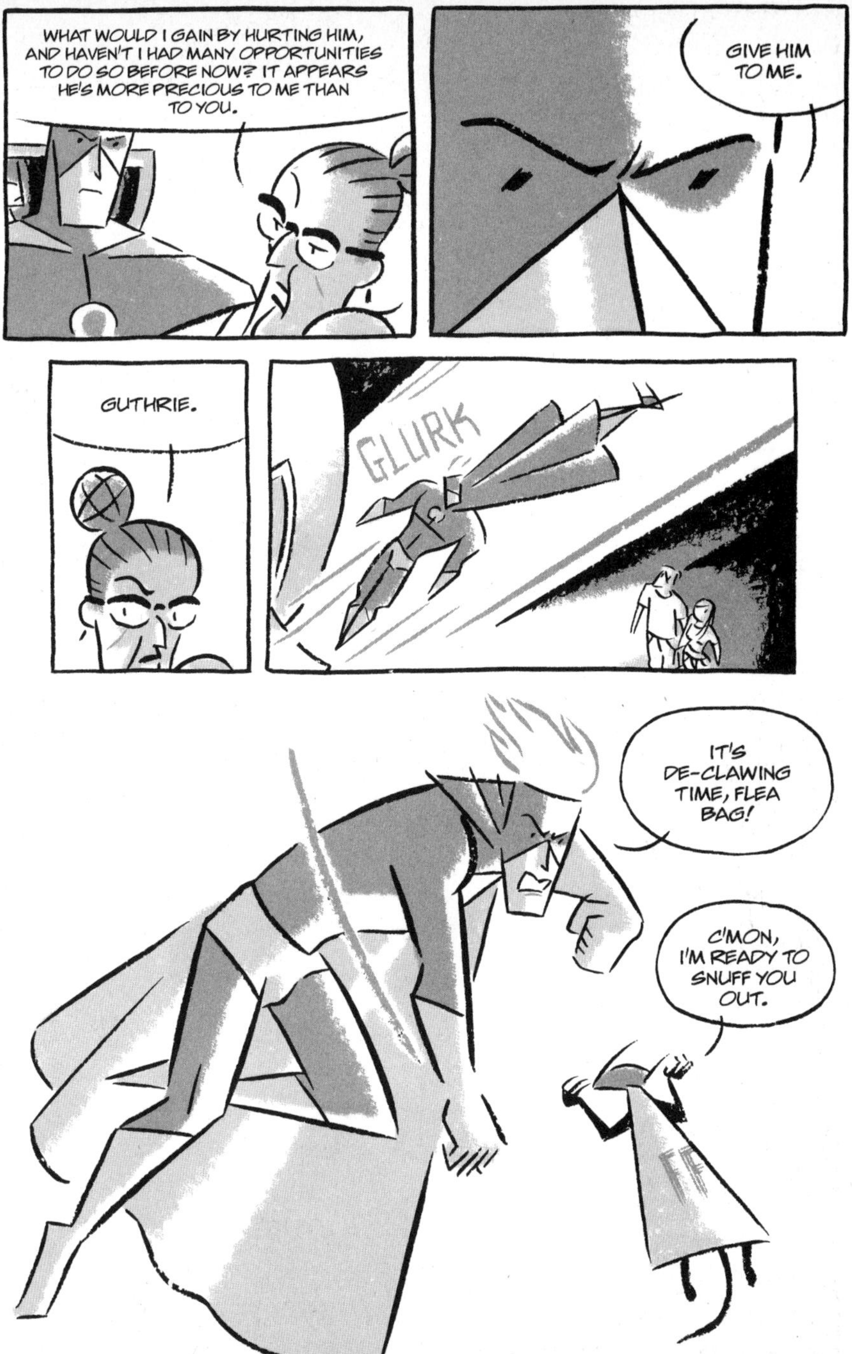
WHAT WOULD I GAIN BY HURTING HIM, AND HAVEN'T I HAD MANY OPPORTUNITIES TO DO SO BEFORE NOW? IT APPEARS HE'S MORE PRECIOUS TO ME THAN TO YOU.
GIVE HIM TO ME.
GUTHRIE.
GLURK
IT'S DE-CLAWING TIME, FLEA BAG!
C'MON, I'M READY TO SNUFF YOU OUT.

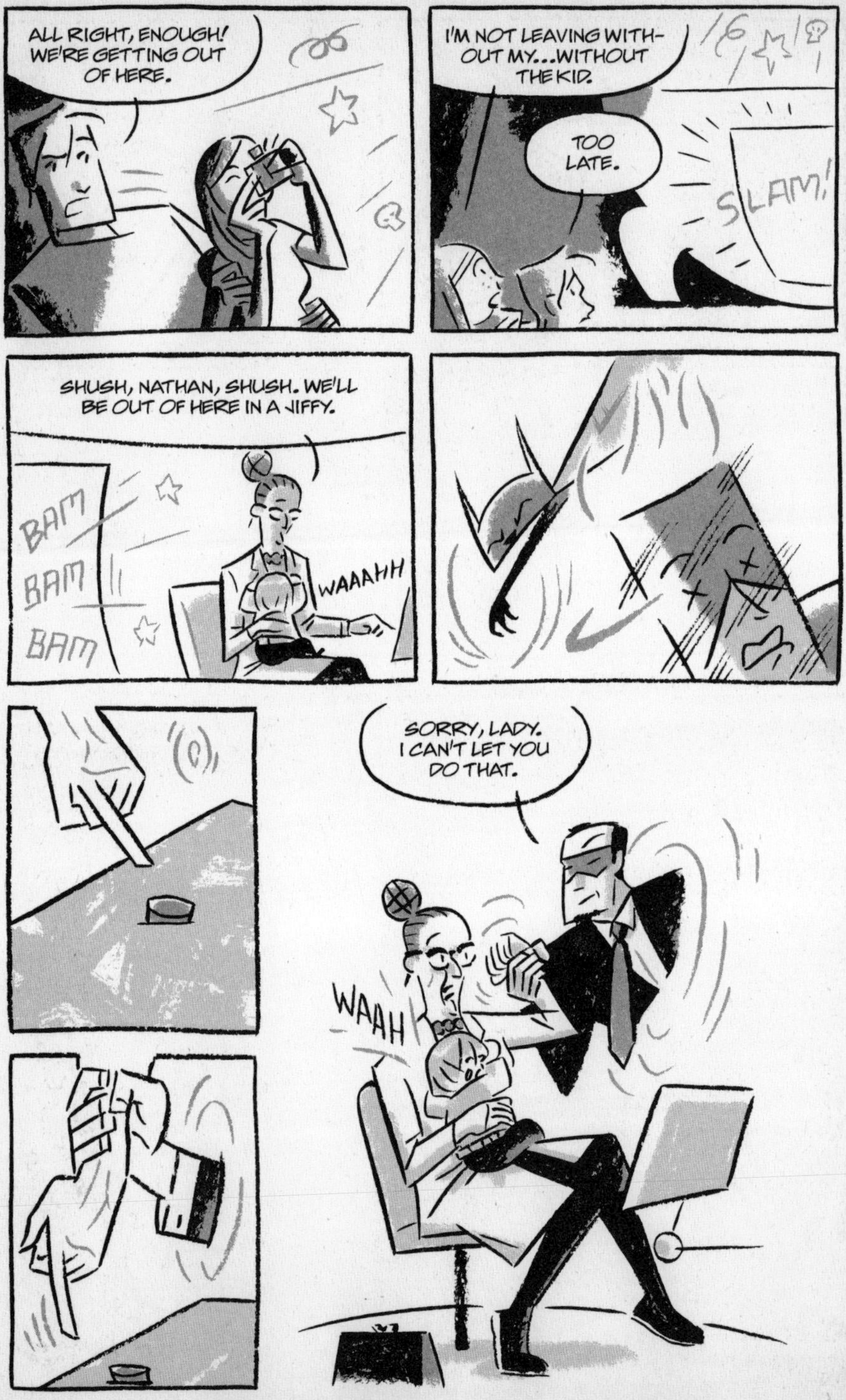
ALL RIGHT, ENOUGH! WE'RE GETTING OUT OF HERE.
I'M NOT LEAVING WITH-OUT MY...WITHOUT THE KID.
TOO LATE.
SLAM!
SHUSH, NATHAN, SHUSH. WE'LL BE OUT OF HERE IN A JIFFY.
BAM
BAM
BAM
WAAAHH
SORRY, LADY. I CAN'T LET YOU DO THAT.
WAAH

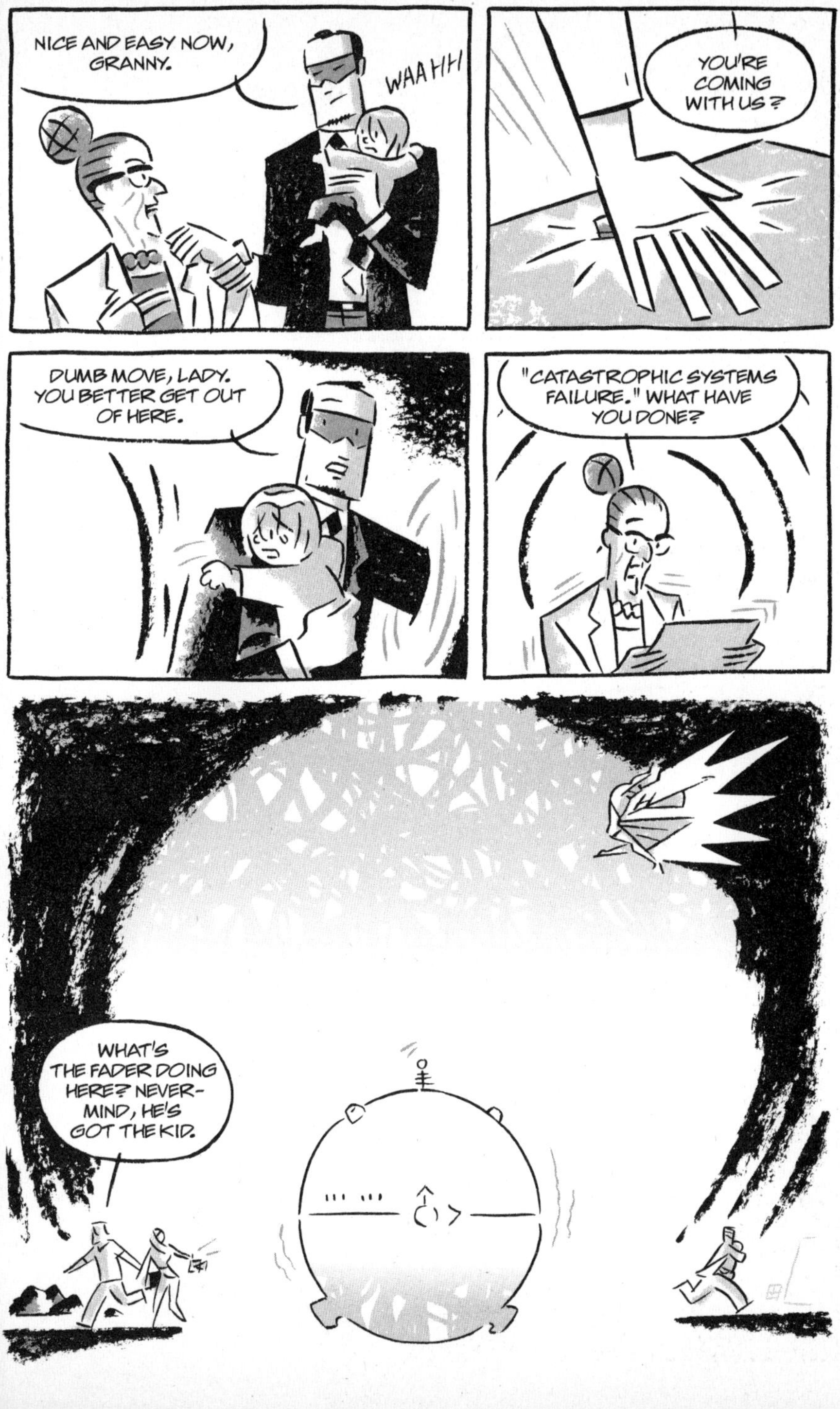
NICE AND EASY NOW, GRANNY.
WAAHH
YOU'RE COMING WITH US?
DUMB MOVE, LADY. YOU BETTER GET OUT OF HERE.
"CATASTROPHIC SYSTEMS FAILURE." WHAT HAVE YOU DONE?
WHAT'S THE FADER DOING HERE? NEVER-MIND, HE'S GOT THE KID.

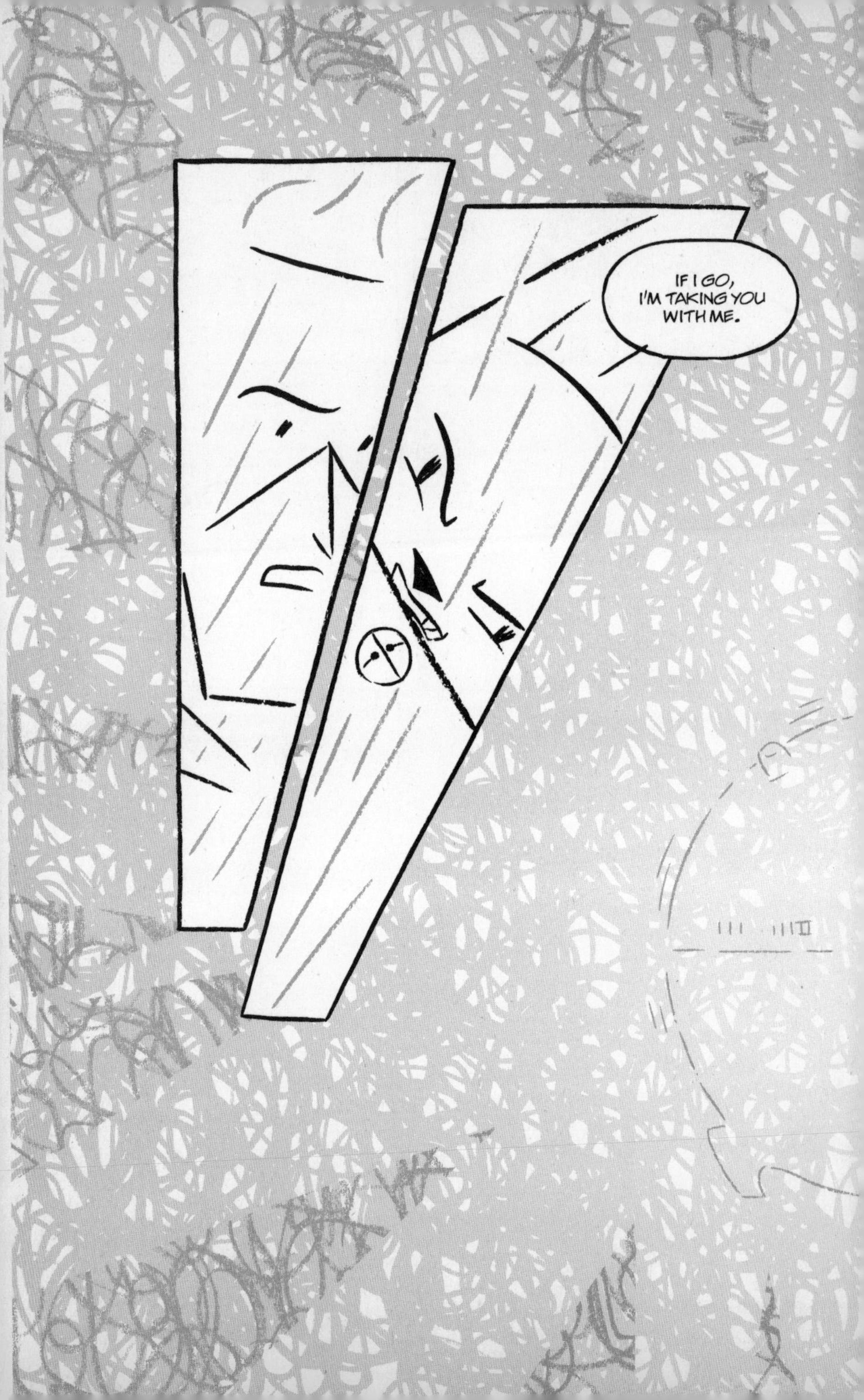
IF I GO, I'M TAKING YOU WITH ME.

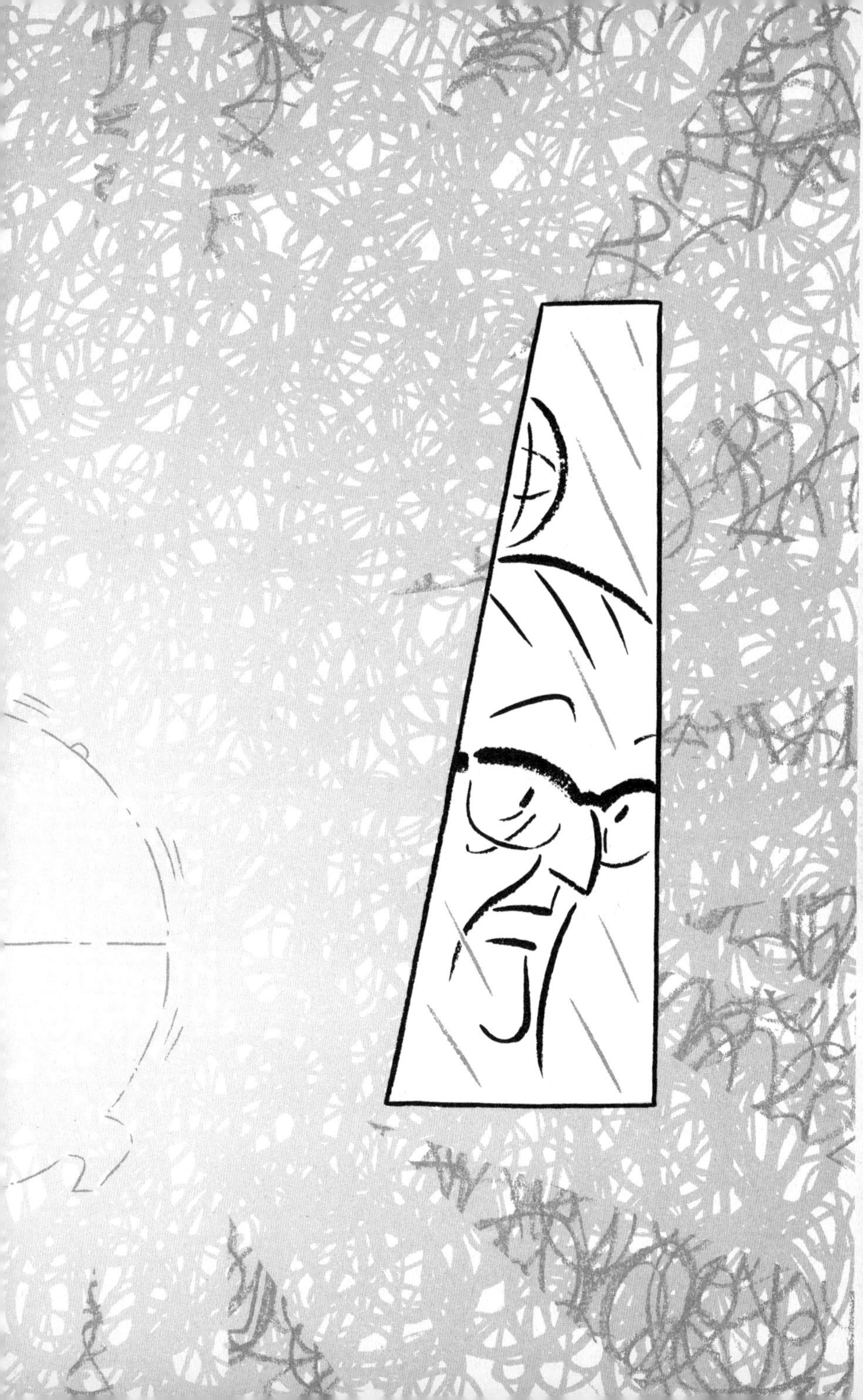

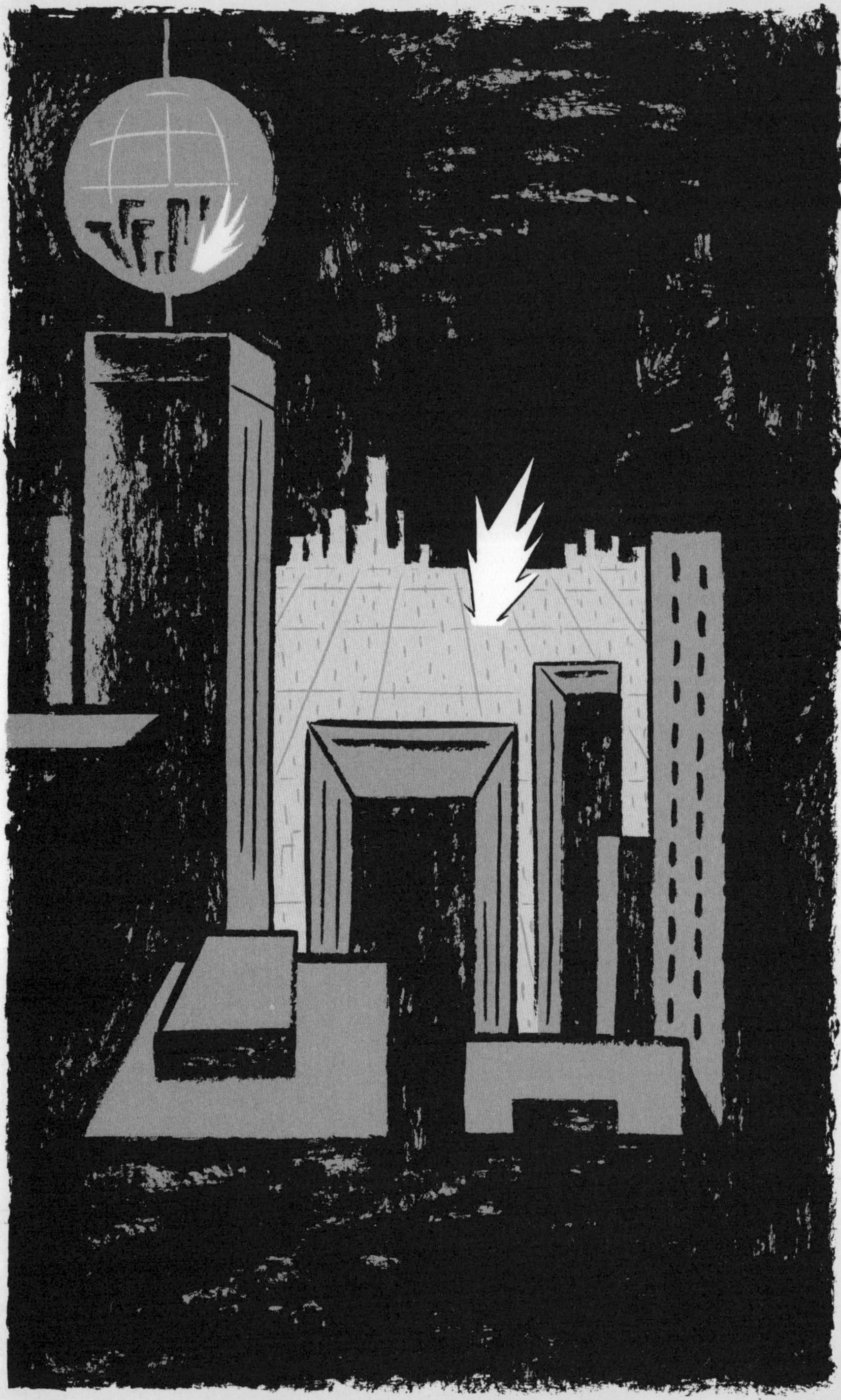

Love Fights™   number twelve   andi watson

ONI PRESS
$2.99 U.S., $4.60 CAN.

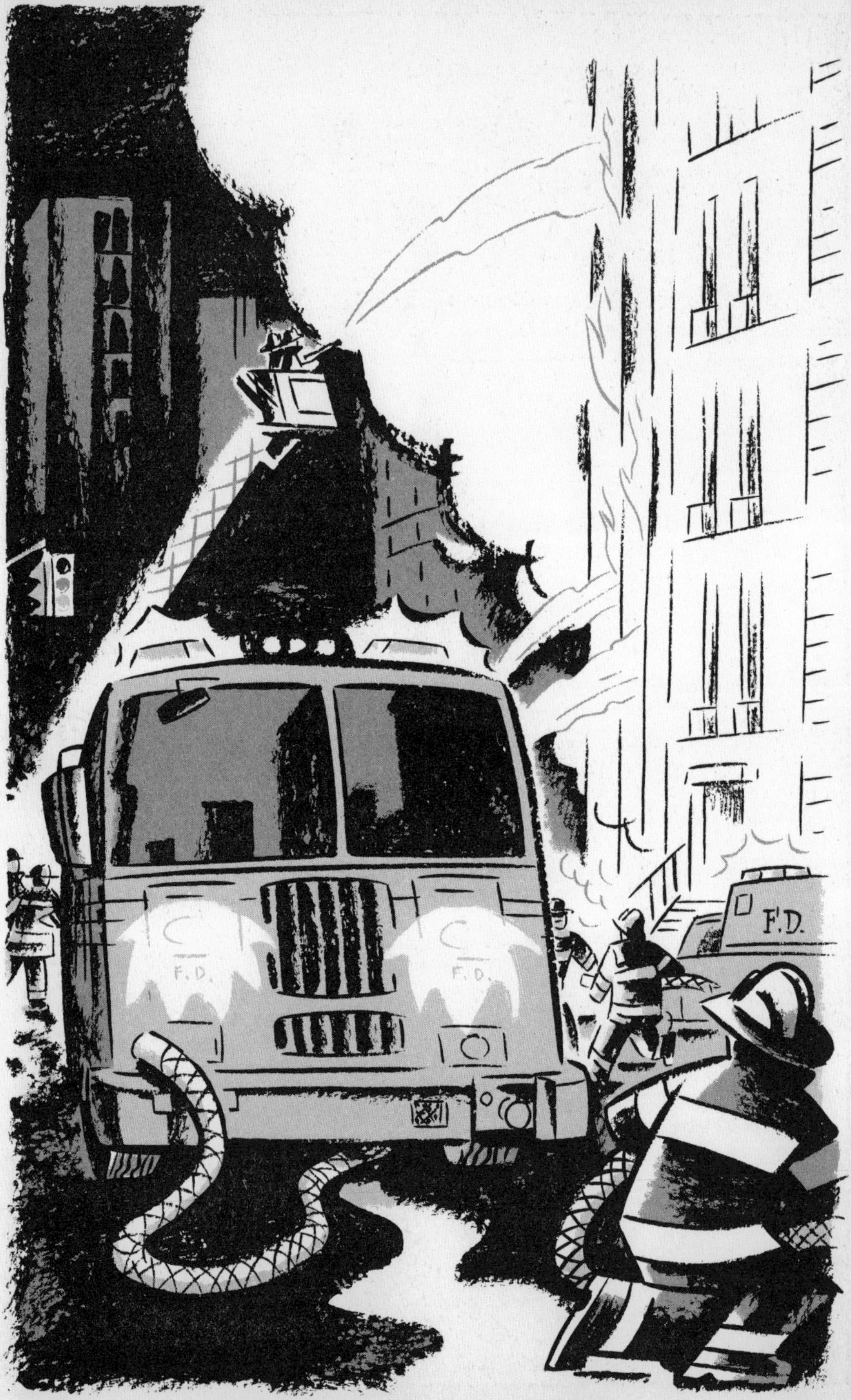
F.D.
F.D.
F.D.

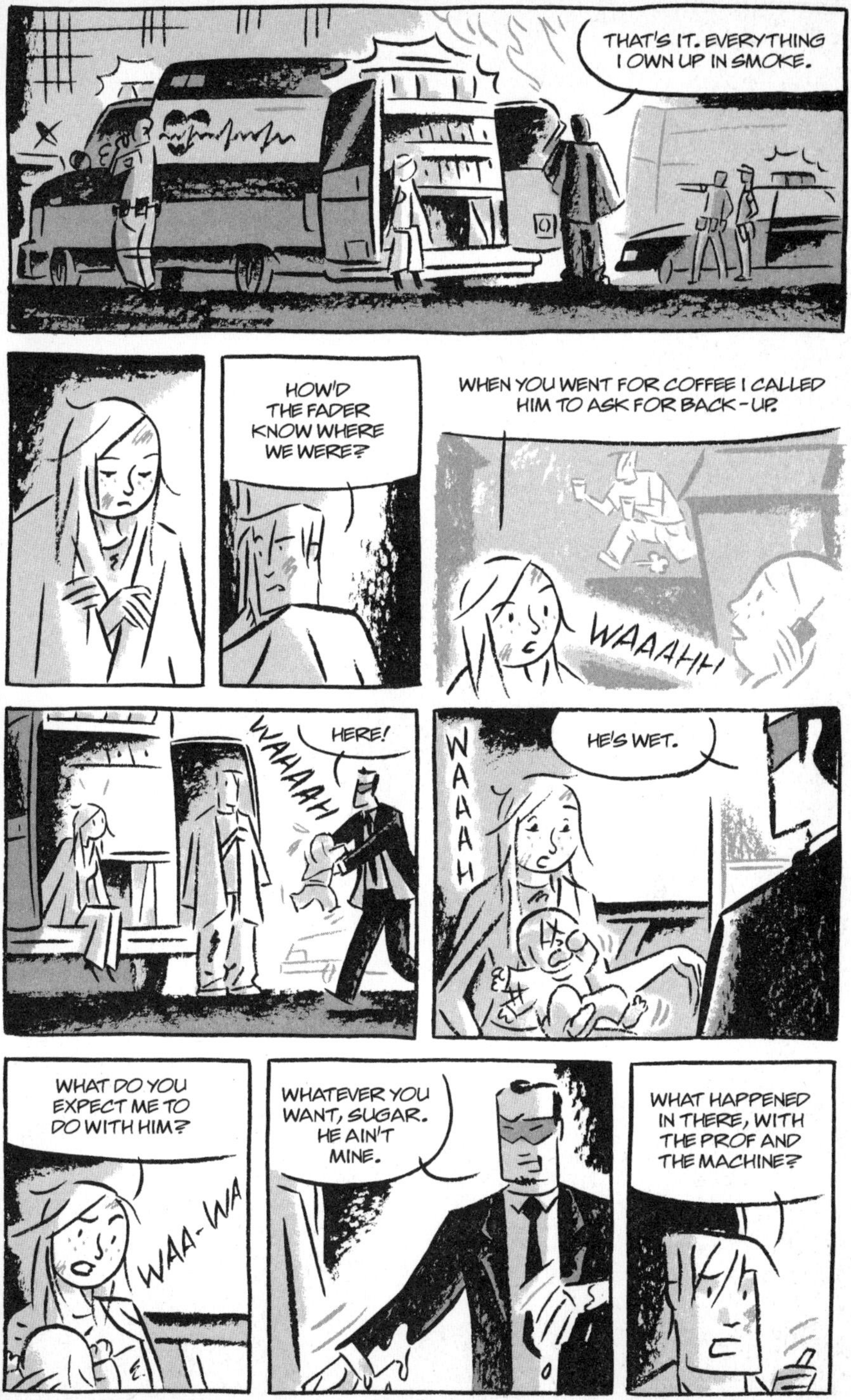
THAT'S IT. EVERYTHING I OWN UP IN SMOKE.
HOW'D THE FADER KNOW WHERE WE WERE?
WHEN YOU WENT FOR COFFEE I CALLED HIM TO ASK FOR BACK-UP.
WAAAHH
WAAAAH
HERE!
WAAAAH
HE'S WET.
WHAT DO YOU EXPECT ME TO DO WITH HIM?
WAA-WA
WHATEVER YOU WANT, SUGAR. HE AIN'T MINE.
WHAT HAPPENED IN THERE, WITH THE PROF AND THE MACHINE?

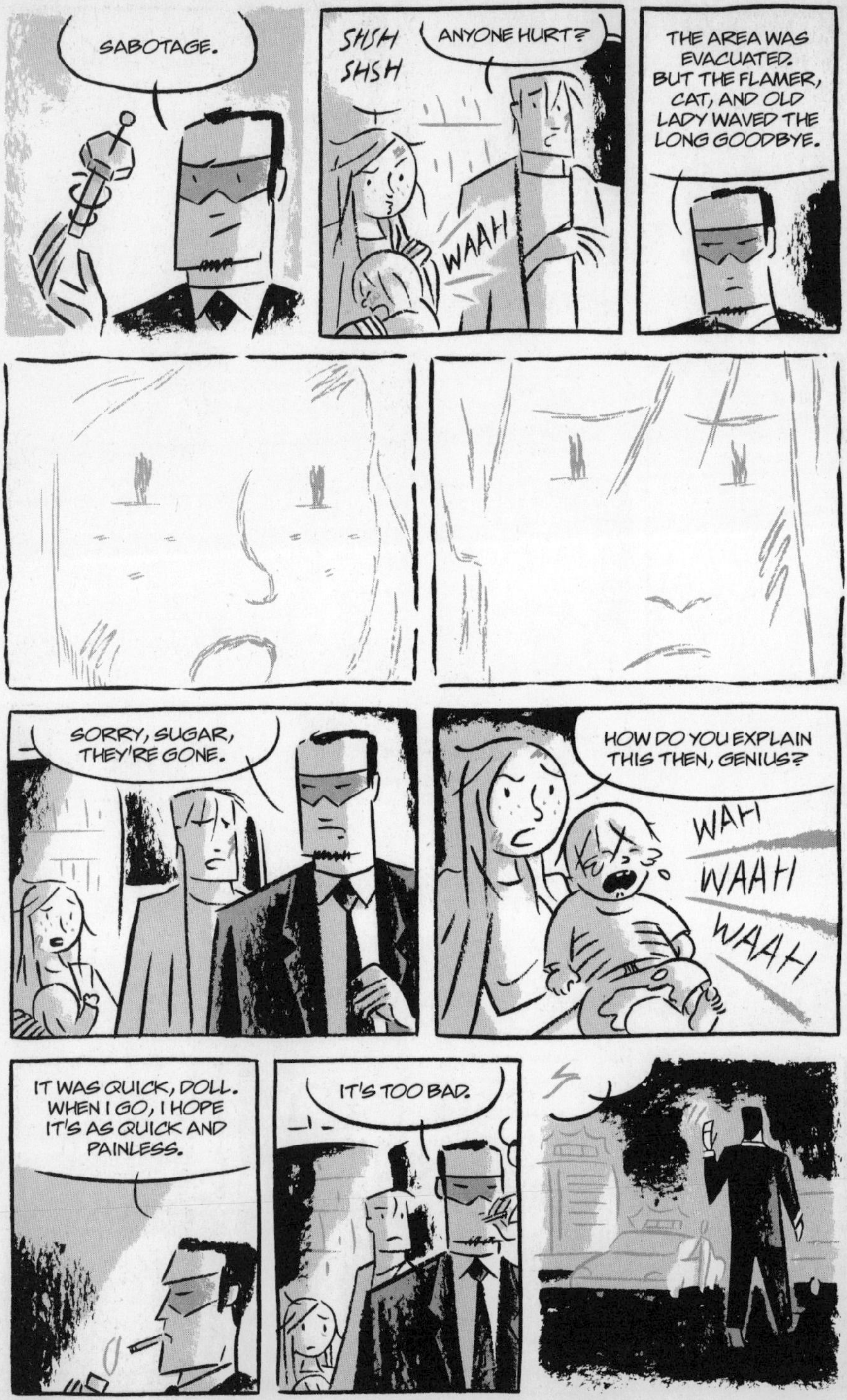
SABOTAGE.
SHSH SHSH
ANYONE HURT?
WAAH
THE AREA WAS EVACUATED. BUT THE FLAMER, CAT, AND OLD LADY WAVED THE LONG GOODBYE.
SORRY, SUGAR, THEY'RE GONE.
HOW DO YOU EXPLAIN THIS THEN, GENIUS?
WAH
WAAH
WAAH
IT WAS QUICK, DOLL. WHEN I GO, I HOPE IT'S AS QUICK AND PAINLESS.
IT'S TOO BAD.

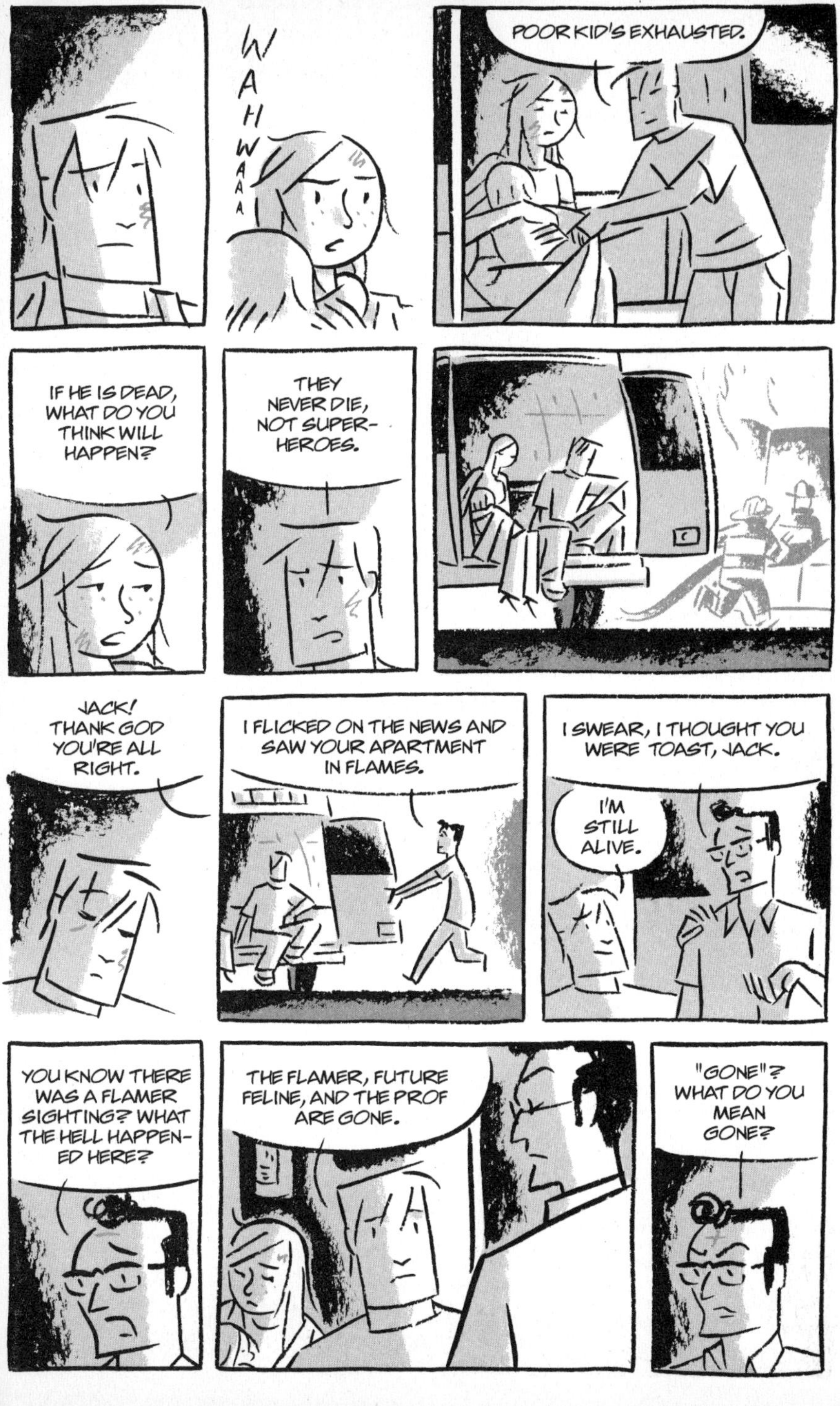
WAHWAAAA
POOR KID'S EXHAUSTED.
IF HE IS DEAD, WHAT DO YOU THINK WILL HAPPEN?
THEY NEVER DIE, NOT SUPER-HEROES.
JACK! THANK GOD YOU'RE ALL RIGHT.
I FLICKED ON THE NEWS AND SAW YOUR APARTMENT IN FLAMES.
I SWEAR, I THOUGHT YOU WERE TOAST, JACK.
I'M STILL ALIVE.
YOU KNOW THERE WAS A FLAMER SIGHTING? WHAT THE HELL HAPPEN-ED HERE?
THE FLAMER, FUTURE FELINE, AND THE PROF ARE GONE.
"GONE"? WHAT DO YOU MEAN GONE?

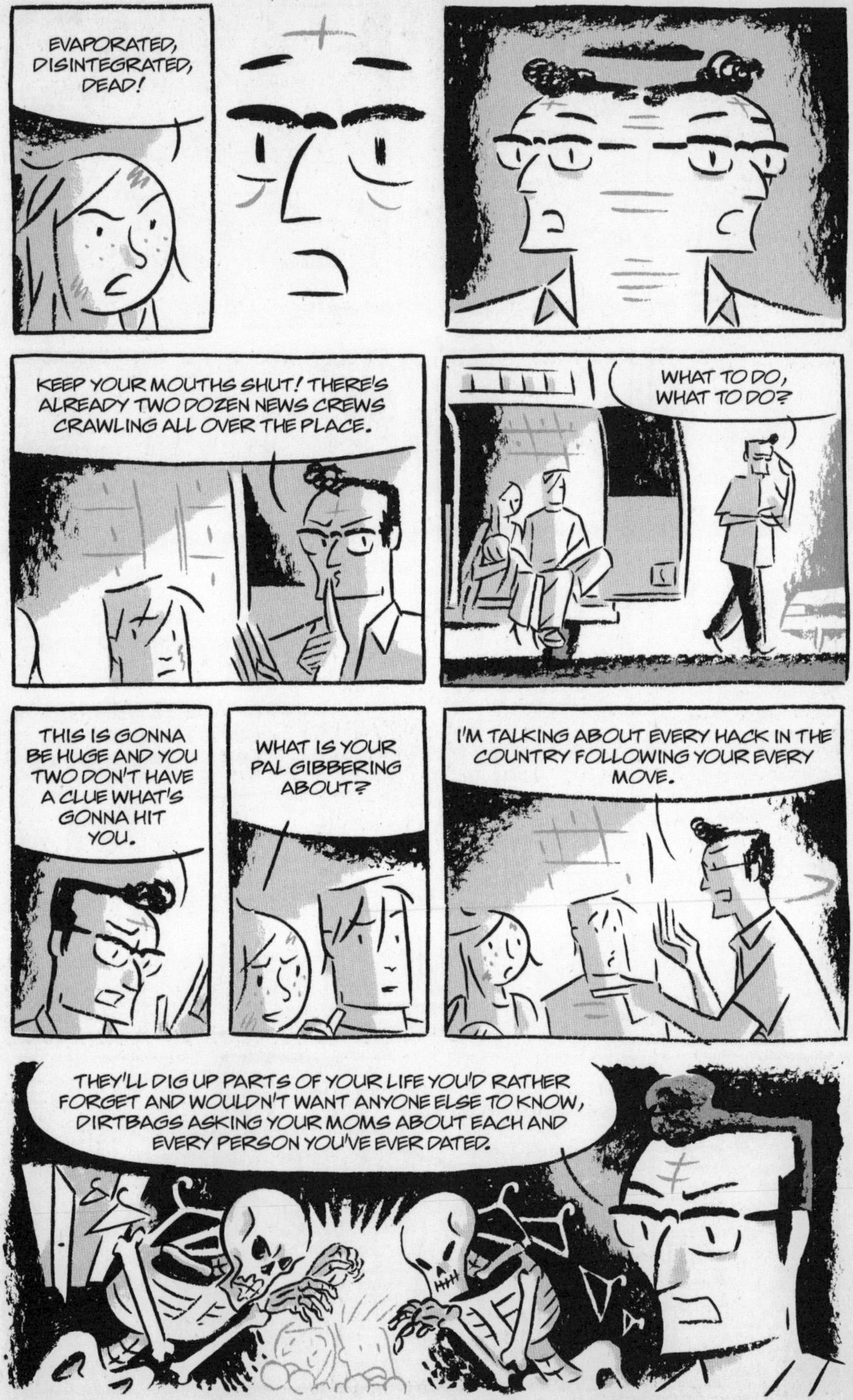
EVAPORATED, DISINTEGRATED, DEAD!
KEEP YOUR MOUTHS SHUT! THERE'S ALREADY TWO DOZEN NEWS CREWS CRAWLING ALL OVER THE PLACE.
WHAT TO DO, WHAT TO DO?
THIS IS GONNA BE HUGE AND YOU TWO DON'T HAVE A CLUE WHAT'S GONNA HIT YOU.
WHAT IS YOUR PAL GIBBERING ABOUT?
I'M TALKING ABOUT EVERY HACK IN THE COUNTRY FOLLOWING YOUR EVERY MOVE.
THEY'LL DIG UP PARTS OF YOUR LIFE YOU'D RATHER FORGET AND WOULDN'T WANT ANYONE ELSE TO KNOW, DIRTBAGS ASKING YOUR MOMS ABOUT EACH AND EVERY PERSON YOU'VE EVER DATED.

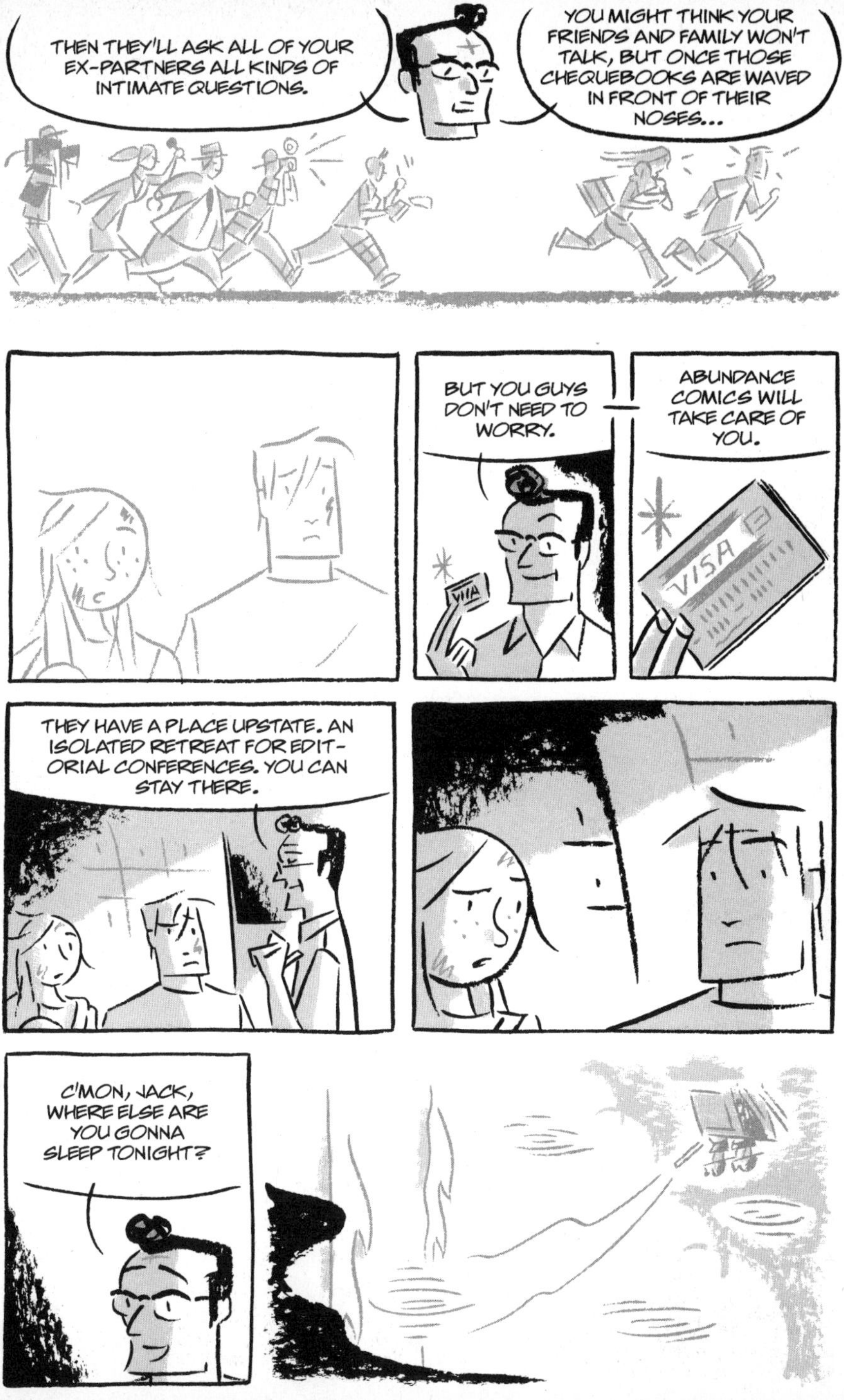
THEN THEY'LL ASK ALL OF YOUR EX-PARTNERS ALL KINDS OF INTIMATE QUESTIONS.
YOU MIGHT THINK YOUR FRIENDS AND FAMILY WON'T TALK, BUT ONCE THOSE CHEQUEBOOKS ARE WAVED IN FRONT OF THEIR NOSES...
BUT YOU GUYS DON'T NEED TO WORRY.
ABUNDANCE COMICS WILL TAKE CARE OF YOU.
VISA
VISA
THEY HAVE A PLACE UPSTATE. AN ISOLATED RETREAT FOR EDIT-ORIAL CONFERENCES. YOU CAN STAY THERE.
C'MON, JACK, WHERE ELSE ARE YOU GONNA SLEEP TONIGHT?

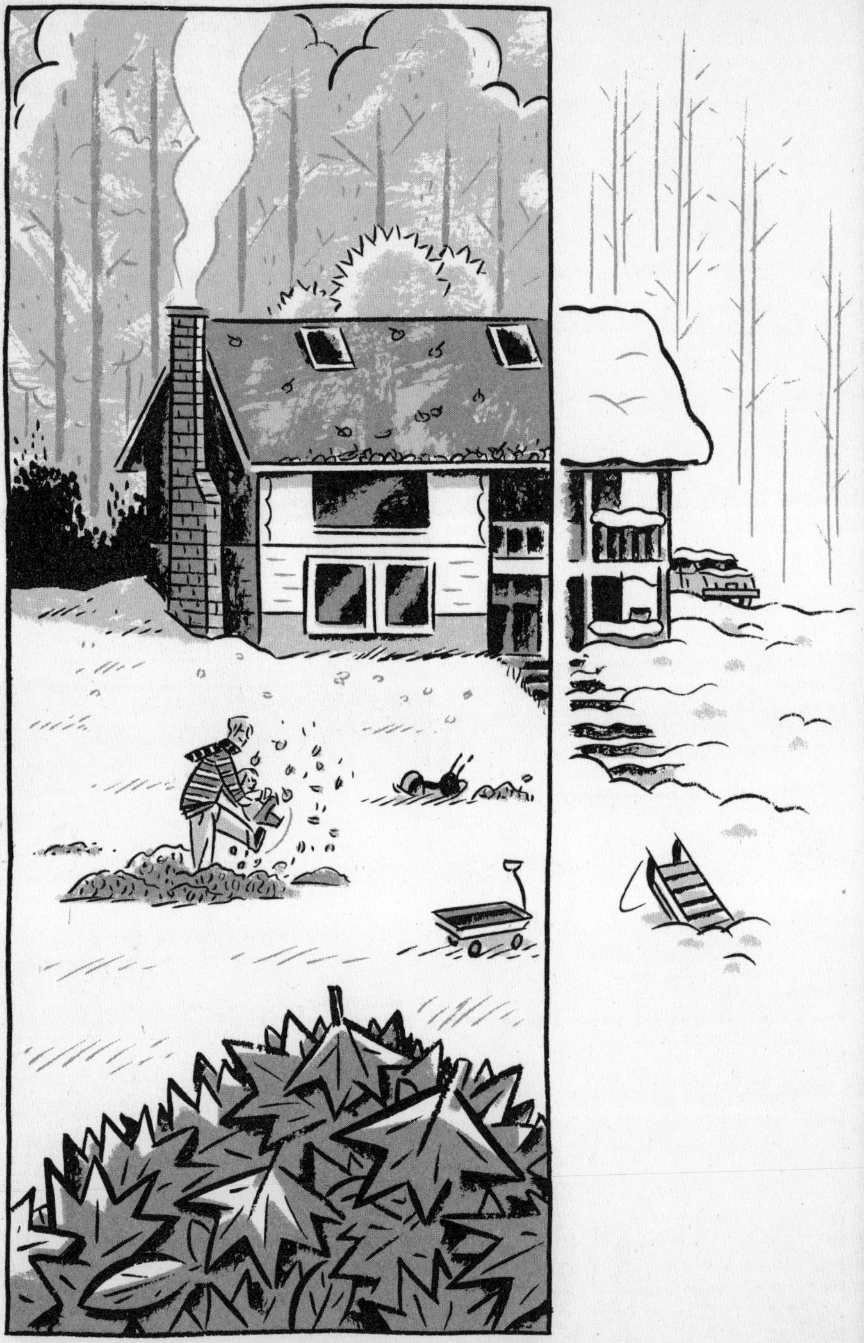

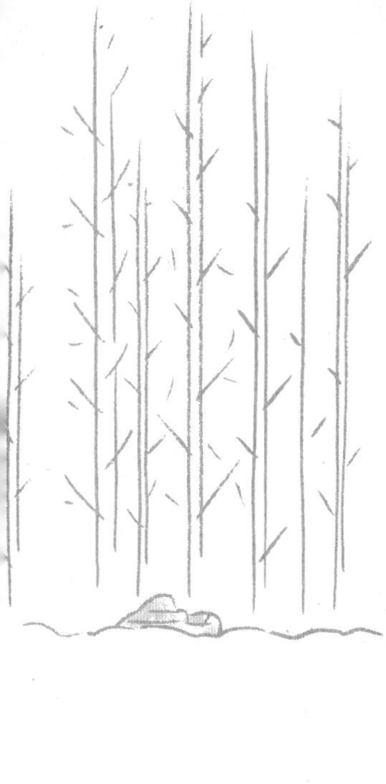

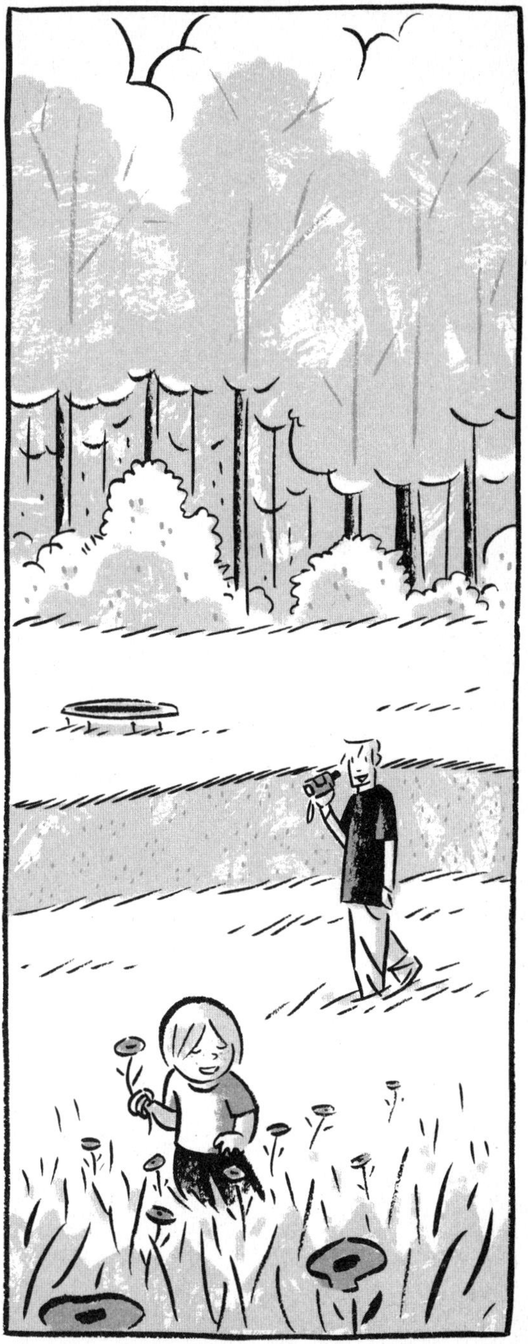

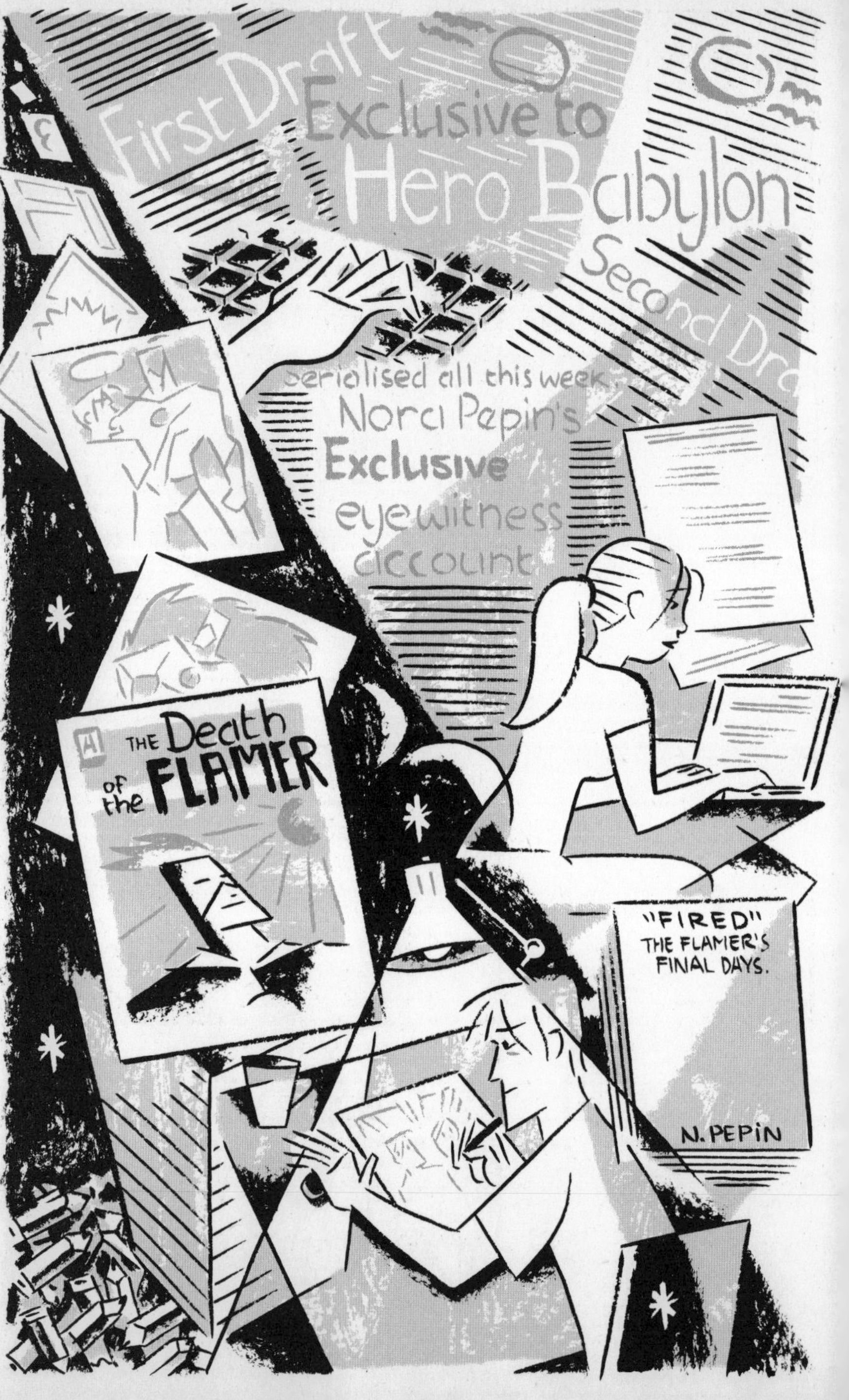

First Draft
Exclusive to
Hero Babylon
Second Dra
serialised all this week
Nora Pepin's
Exclusive
eyewitness
account
THE Death of the FLAMER
"FIRED"
THE FLAMER'S
FINAL DAYS.
N. PEPIN

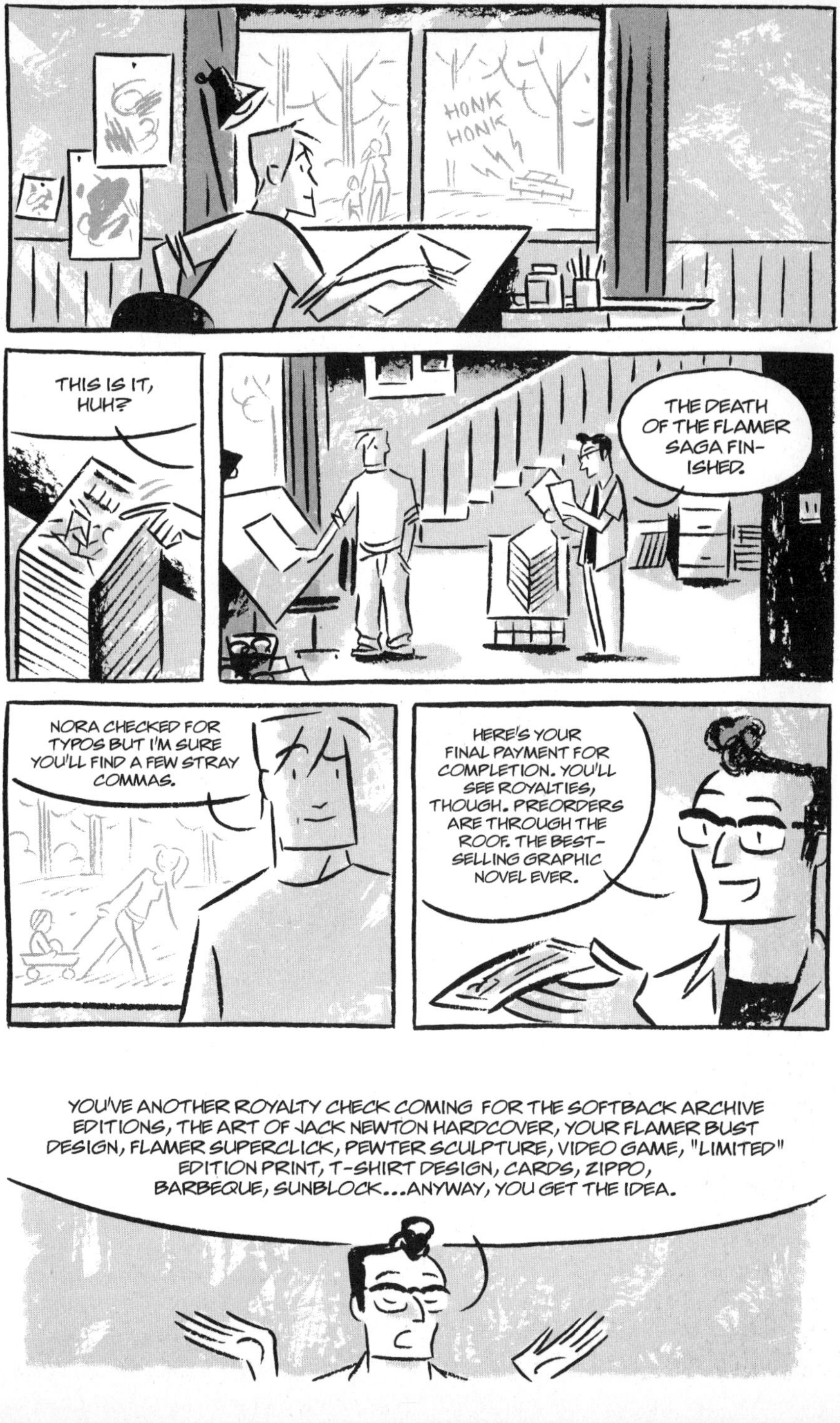
HONK HONK
THIS IS IT, HUH?
THE DEATH OF THE FLAMER SAGA FIN-ISHED.
NORA CHECKED FOR TYPOS BUT I'M SURE YOU'LL FIND A FEW STRAY COMMAS.
HERE'S YOUR FINAL PAYMENT FOR COMPLETION. YOU'LL SEE ROYALTIES, THOUGH. PREORDERS ARE THROUGH THE ROOF. THE BEST-SELLING GRAPHIC NOVEL EVER.
YOU'VE ANOTHER ROYALTY CHECK COMING FOR THE SOFTBACK ARCHIVE EDITIONS, THE ART OF JACK NEWTON HARDCOVER, YOUR FLAMER BUST DESIGN, FLAMER SUPERCLICK, PEWTER SCULPTURE, VIDEO GAME, "LIMITED" EDITION PRINT, T-SHIRT DESIGN, CARDS, ZIPPO, BARBEQUE, SUNBLOCK...ANYWAY, YOU GET THE IDEA.

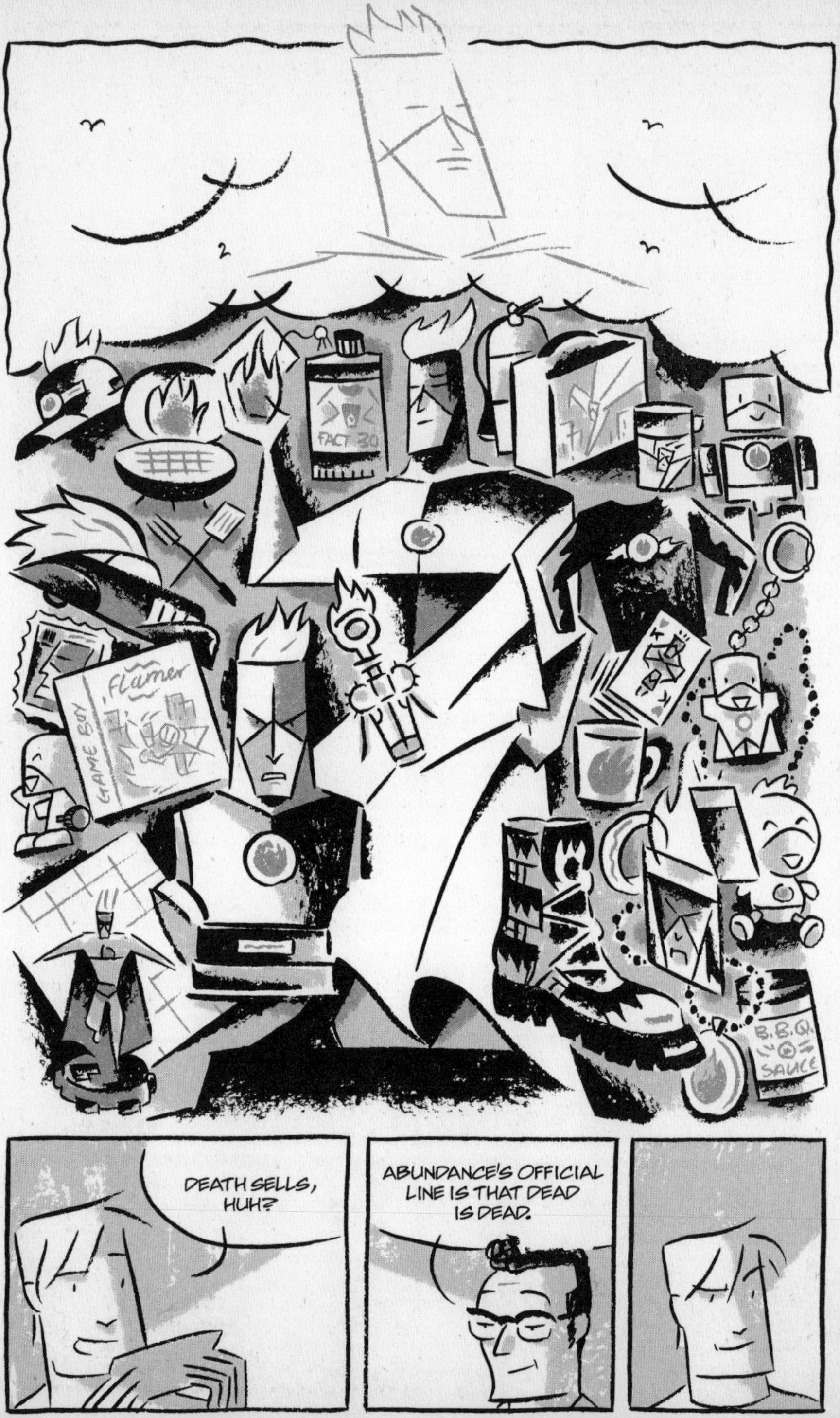
FACT 30
Flamer
GAME BOY
B.B.Q. SAUCE
DEATH SELLS, HUH?
ABUNDANCE'S OFFICIAL LINE IS THAT DEAD IS DEAD.

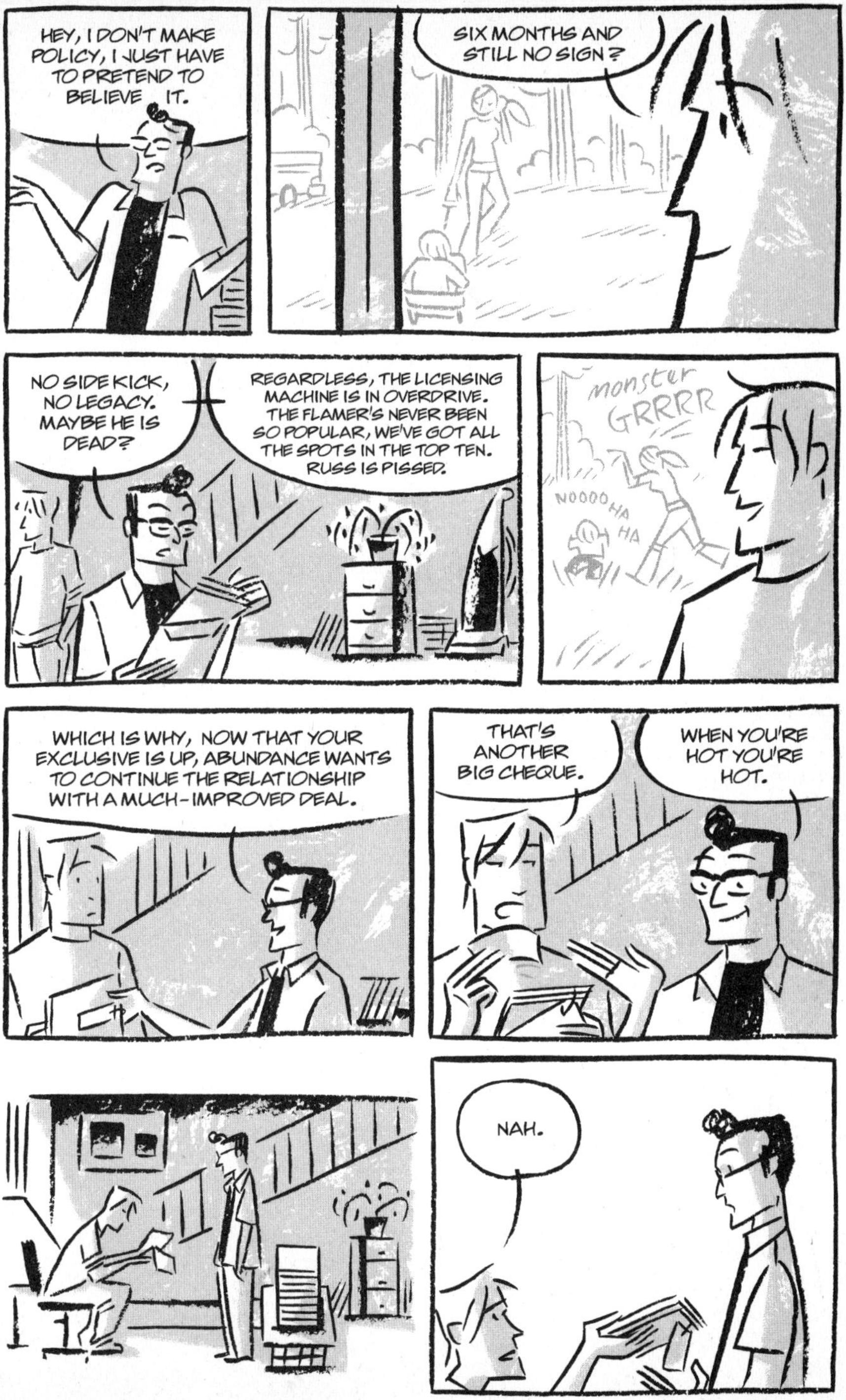
HEY, I DON'T MAKE POLICY, I JUST HAVE TO PRETEND TO BELIEVE IT.
SIX MONTHS AND STILL NO SIGN?
NO SIDEKICK, NO LEGACY. MAYBE HE IS DEAD?
REGARDLESS, THE LICENSING MACHINE IS IN OVERDRIVE. THE FLAMER'S NEVER BEEN SO POPULAR, WE'VE GOT ALL THE SPOTS IN THE TOP TEN. RUSS IS PISSED.
monster
GRRRR
NOOOO
HA
HA
WHICH IS WHY, NOW THAT YOUR EXCLUSIVE IS UP, ABUNDANCE WANTS TO CONTINUE THE RELATIONSHIP WITH A MUCH-IMPROVED DEAL.
THAT'S ANOTHER BIG CHEQUE.
WHEN YOU'RE HOT YOU'RE HOT.
NAH.

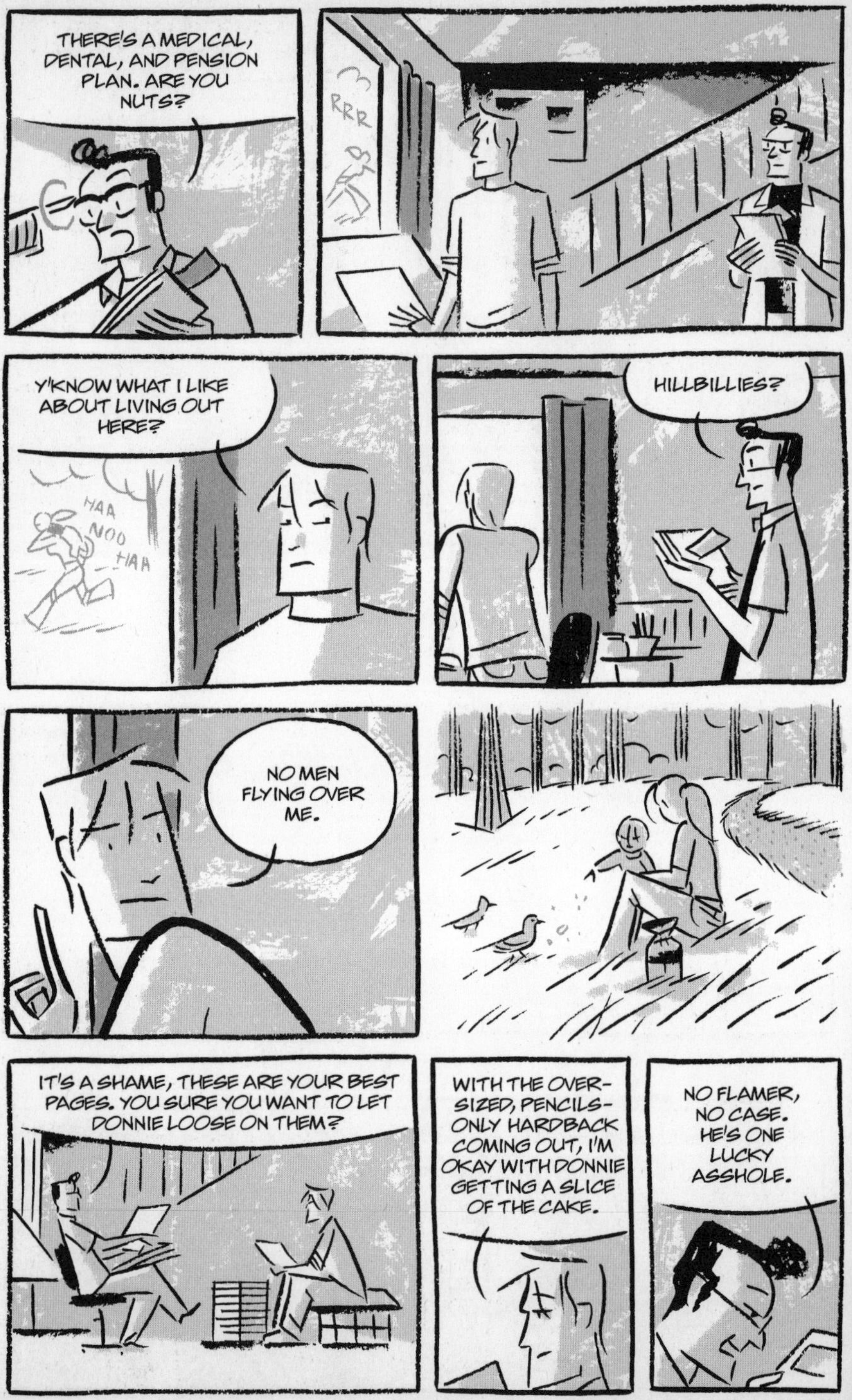
THERE'S A MEDICAL, DENTAL, AND PENSION PLAN. ARE YOU NUTS?
RRR
Y'KNOW WHAT I LIKE ABOUT LIVING OUT HERE?
HAA NOO HAH
HILLBILLIES?
NO MEN FLYING OVER ME.
IT'S A SHAME, THESE ARE YOUR BEST PAGES. YOU SURE YOU WANT TO LET DONNIE LOOSE ON THEM?
WITH THE OVER-SIZED, PENCILS-ONLY HARDBACK COMING OUT, I'M OKAY WITH DONNIE GETTING A SLICE OF THE CAKE.
NO FLAMER, NO CASE. HE'S ONE LUCKY ASSHOLE.

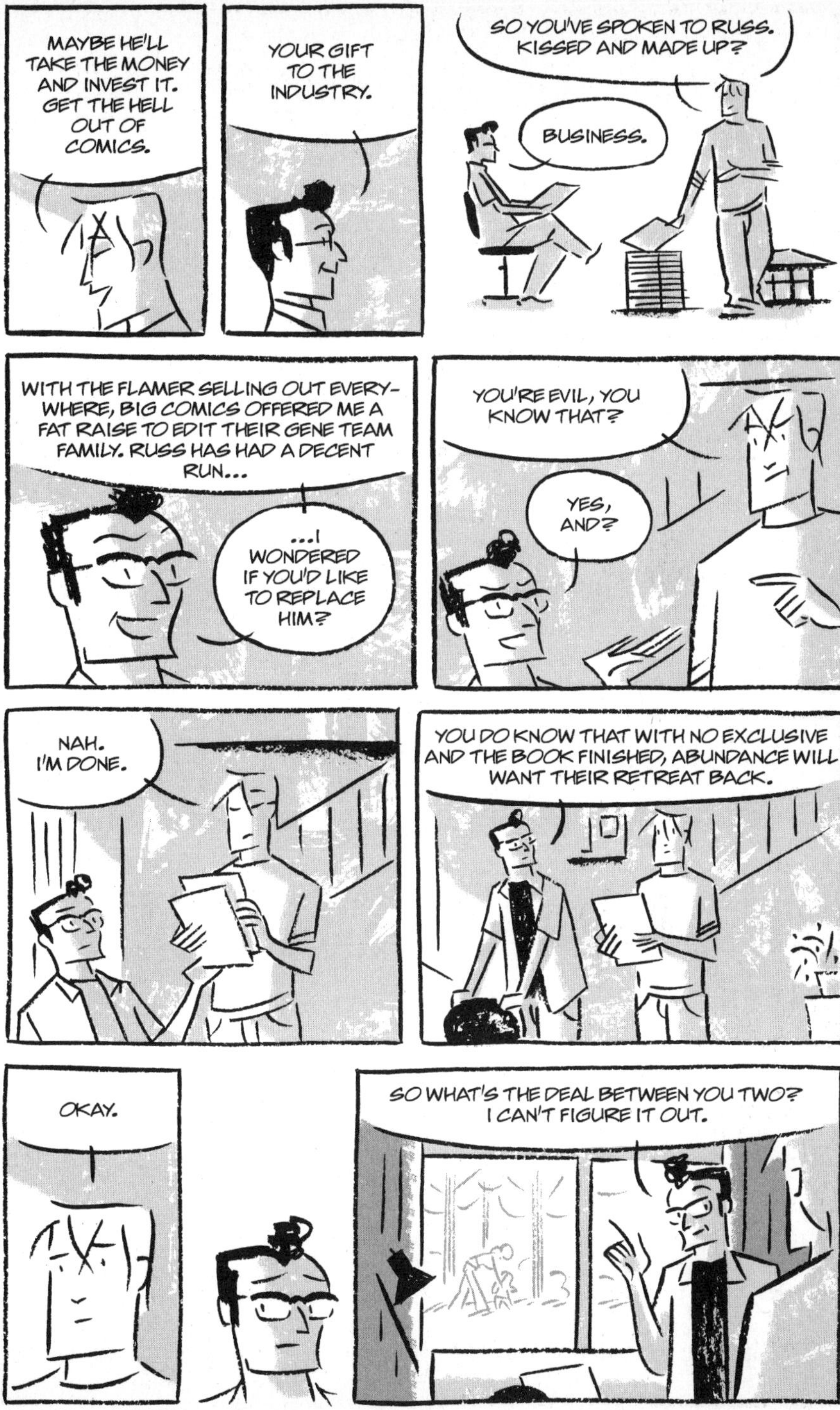
MAYBE HE'LL TAKE THE MONEY AND INVEST IT. GET THE HELL OUT OF COMICS.
YOUR GIFT TO THE INDUSTRY.
SO YOU'VE SPOKEN TO RUSS. KISSED AND MADE UP?
BUSINESS.
WITH THE FLAMER SELLING OUT EVERY-WHERE, BIG COMICS OFFERED ME A FAT RAISE TO EDIT THEIR GENE TEAM FAMILY. RUSS HAS HAD A DECENT RUN...
...I WONDERED IF YOU'D LIKE TO REPLACE HIM?
YOU'RE EVIL, YOU KNOW THAT?
YES, AND?
NAH. I'M DONE.
YOU DO KNOW THAT WITH NO EXCLUSIVE AND THE BOOK FINISHED, ABUNDANCE WILL WANT THEIR RETREAT BACK.
OKAY.
SO WHAT'S THE DEAL BETWEEN YOU TWO? I CAN'T FIGURE IT OUT.

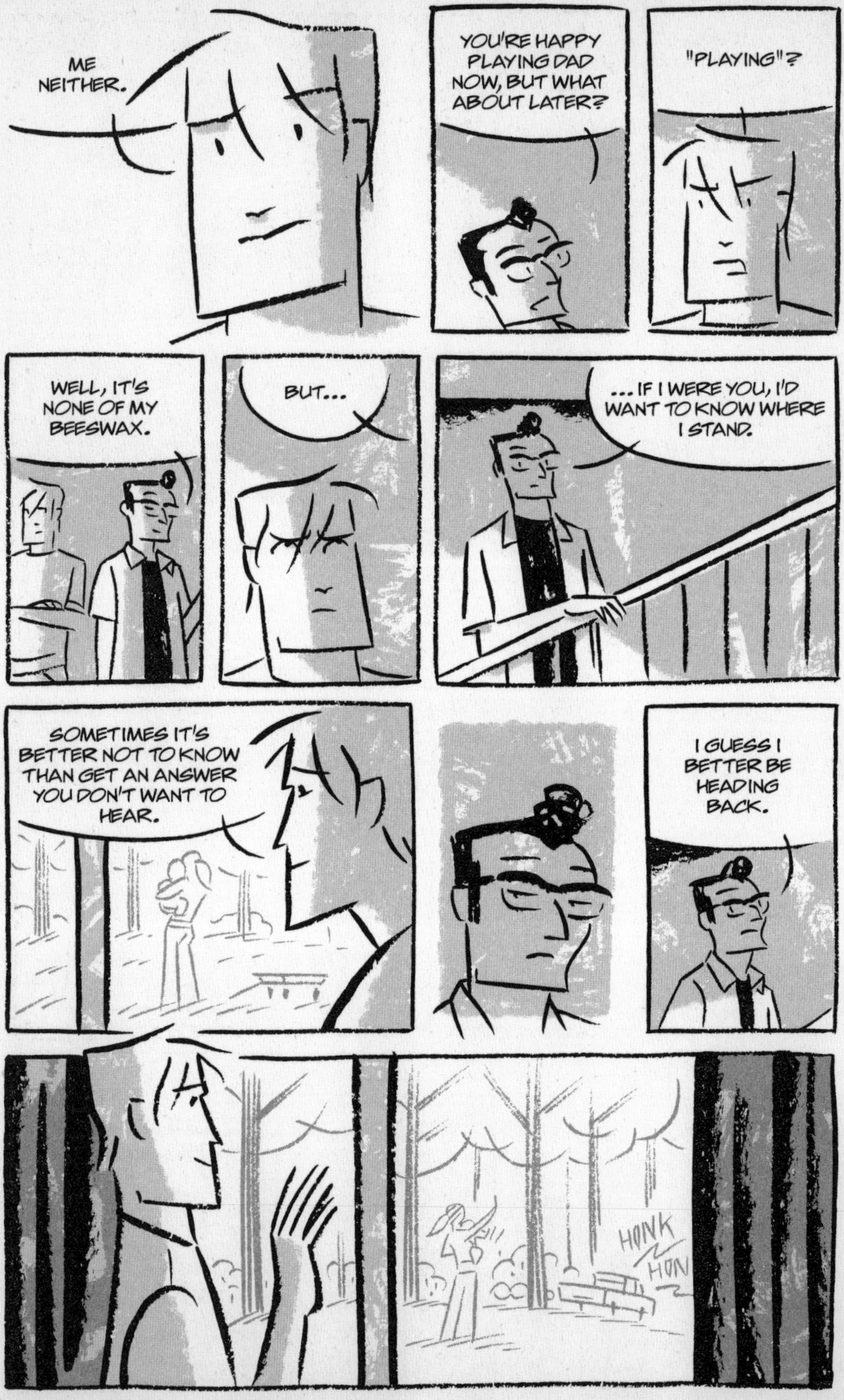
ME NEITHER.
YOU'RE HAPPY PLAYING DAD NOW, BUT WHAT ABOUT LATER?
"PLAYING"?
WELL, IT'S NONE OF MY BEESWAX.
BUT...
...IF I WERE YOU, I'D WANT TO KNOW WHERE I STAND.
SOMETIMES IT'S BETTER NOT TO KNOW THAN GET AN ANSWER YOU DON'T WANT TO HEAR.
I GUESS I BETTER BE HEADING BACK.
HONK
HON

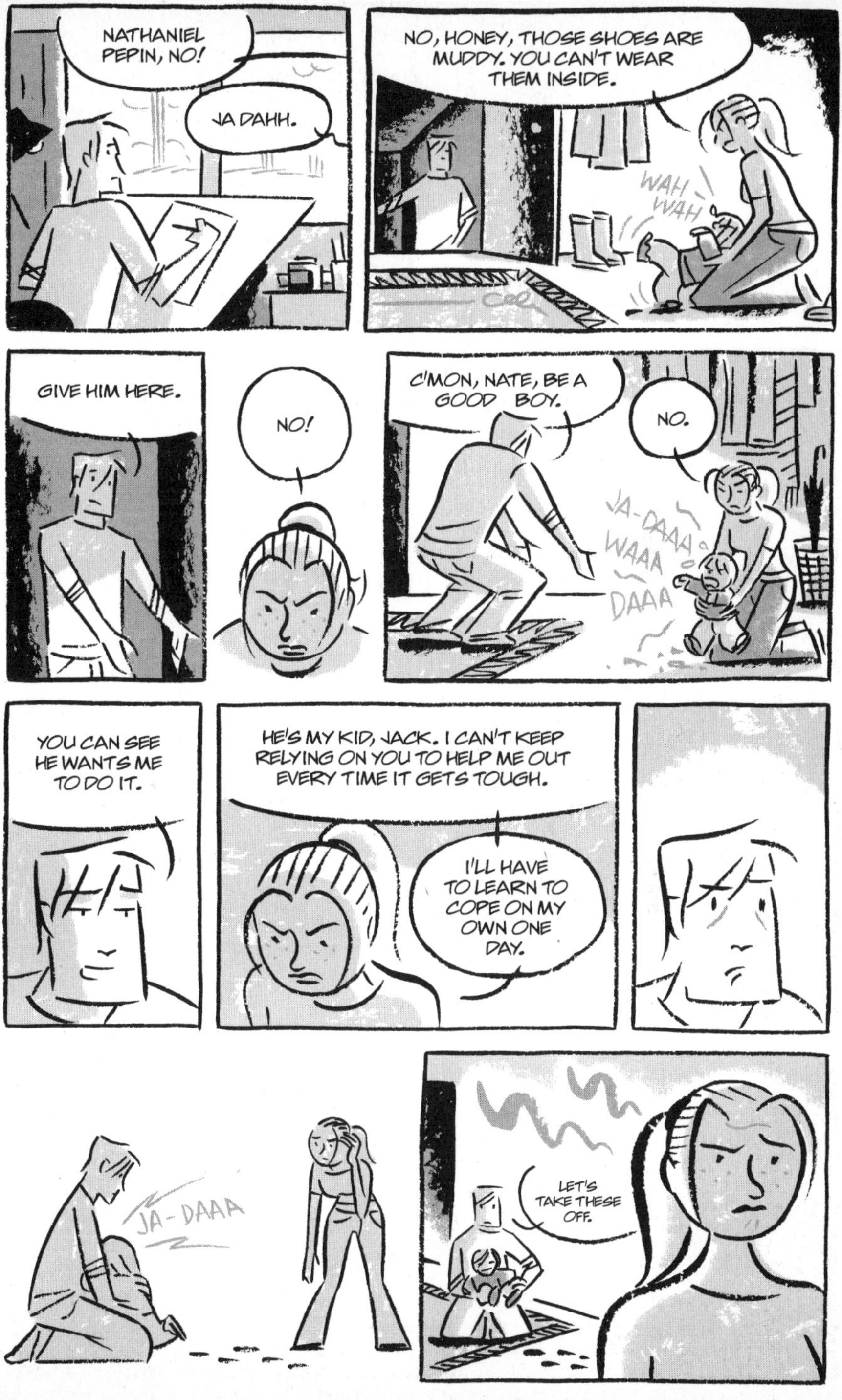
NATHANIEL PEPIN, NO!
JA DAHH.
NO, HONEY, THOSE SHOES ARE MUDDY. YOU CAN'T WEAR THEM INSIDE.
WAH WAH
GIVE HIM HERE.
NO!
C'MON, NATE, BE A GOOD BOY.
NO.
JA-DAAA WAAA DAAA
YOU CAN SEE HE WANTS ME TO DO IT.
HE'S MY KID, JACK. I CAN'T KEEP RELYING ON YOU TO HELP ME OUT EVERY TIME IT GETS TOUGH.
I'LL HAVE TO LEARN TO COPE ON MY OWN ONE DAY.
JA-DAAA
LET'S TAKE THESE OFF.

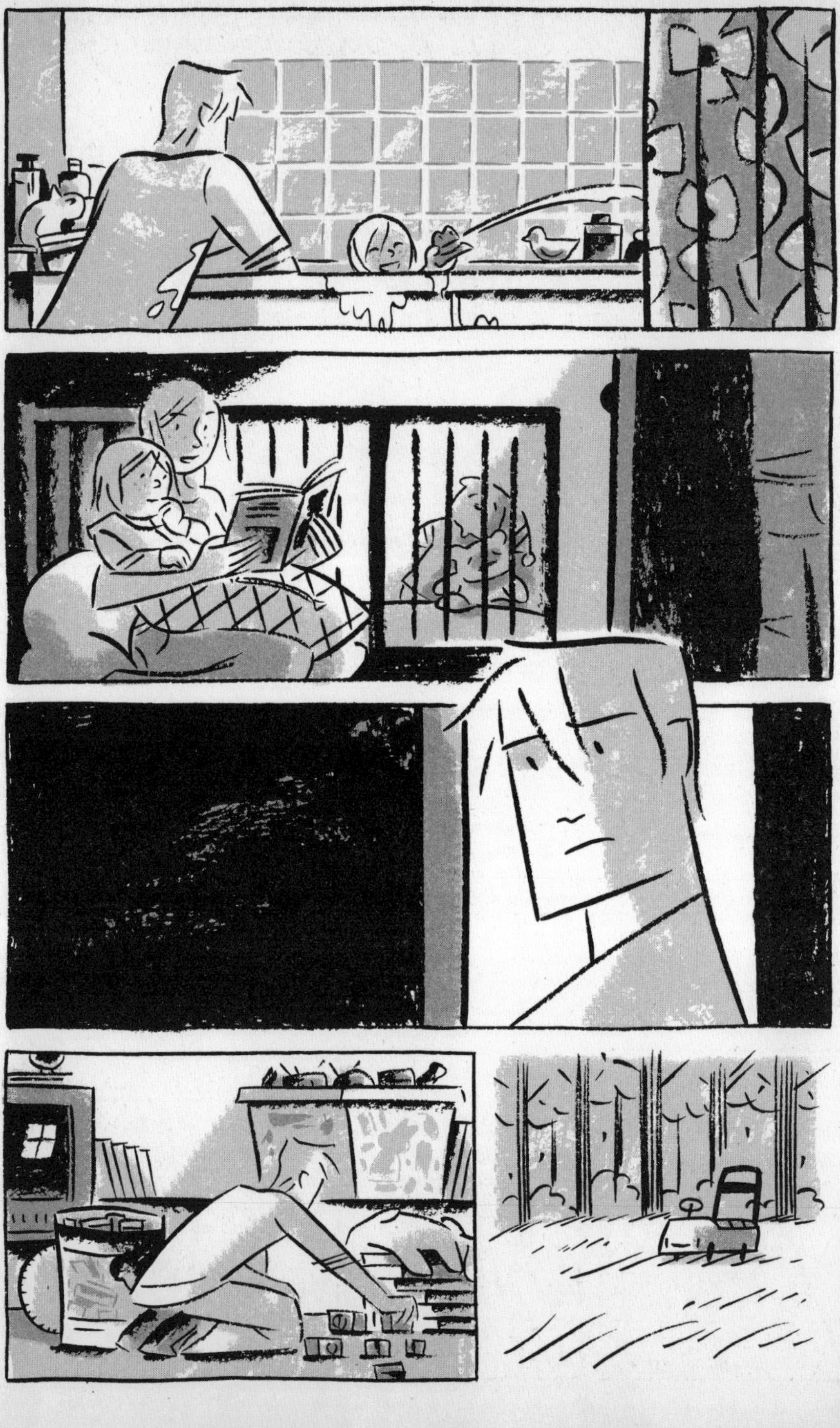

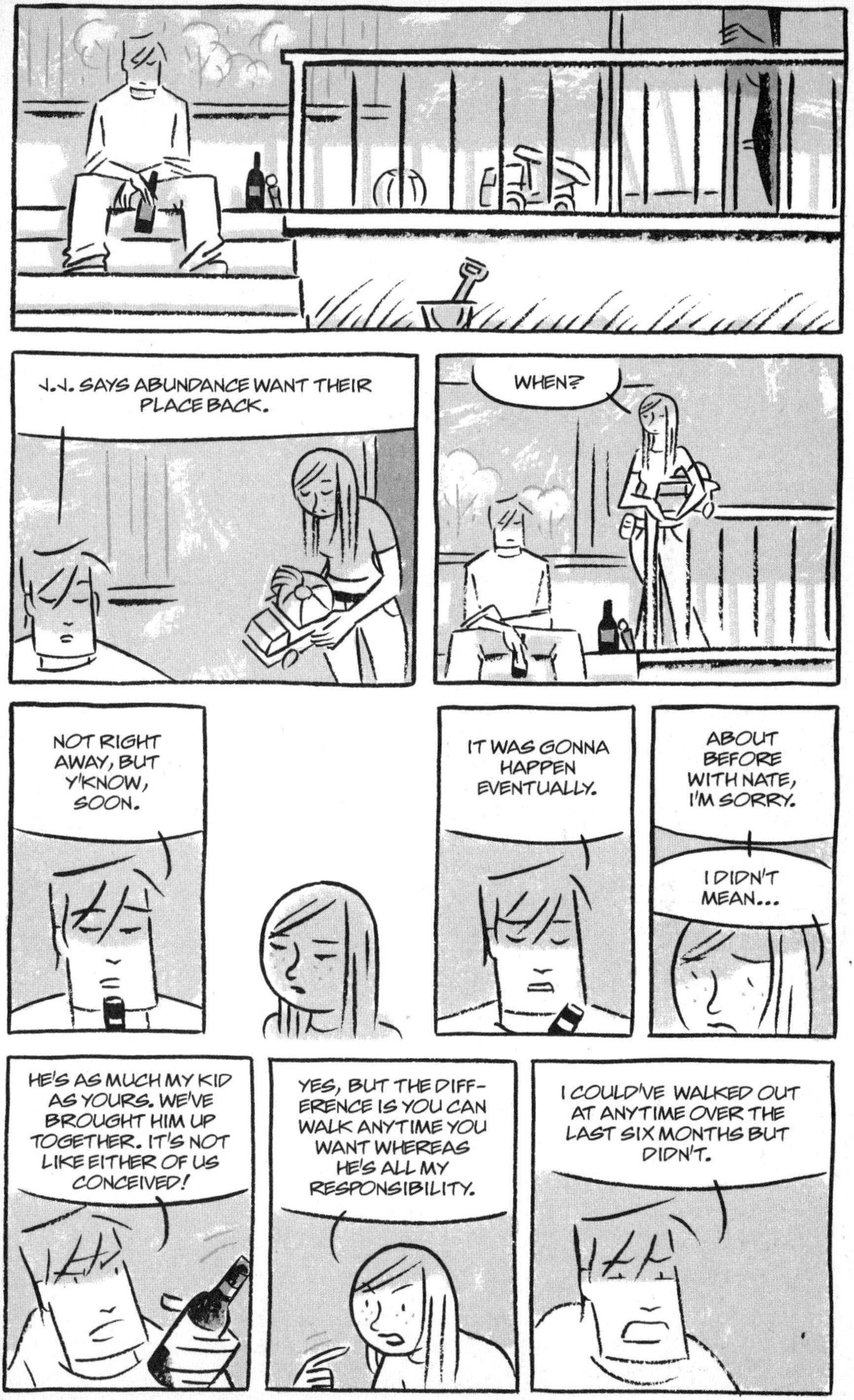
J.J. SAYS ABUNDANCE WANT THEIR PLACE BACK.
WHEN?
NOT RIGHT AWAY, BUT Y'KNOW, SOON.
IT WAS GONNA HAPPEN EVENTUALLY.
ABOUT BEFORE WITH NATE, I'M SORRY.
I DIDN'T MEAN...
HE'S AS MUCH MY KID AS YOURS. WE'VE BROUGHT HIM UP TOGETHER. IT'S NOT LIKE EITHER OF US CONCEIVED!
YES, BUT THE DIFF-ERENCE IS YOU CAN WALK ANYTIME YOU WANT WHEREAS HE'S ALL MY RESPONSIBILITY.
I COULD'VE WALKED OUT AT ANYTIME OVER THE LAST SIX MONTHS BUT DIDN'T.

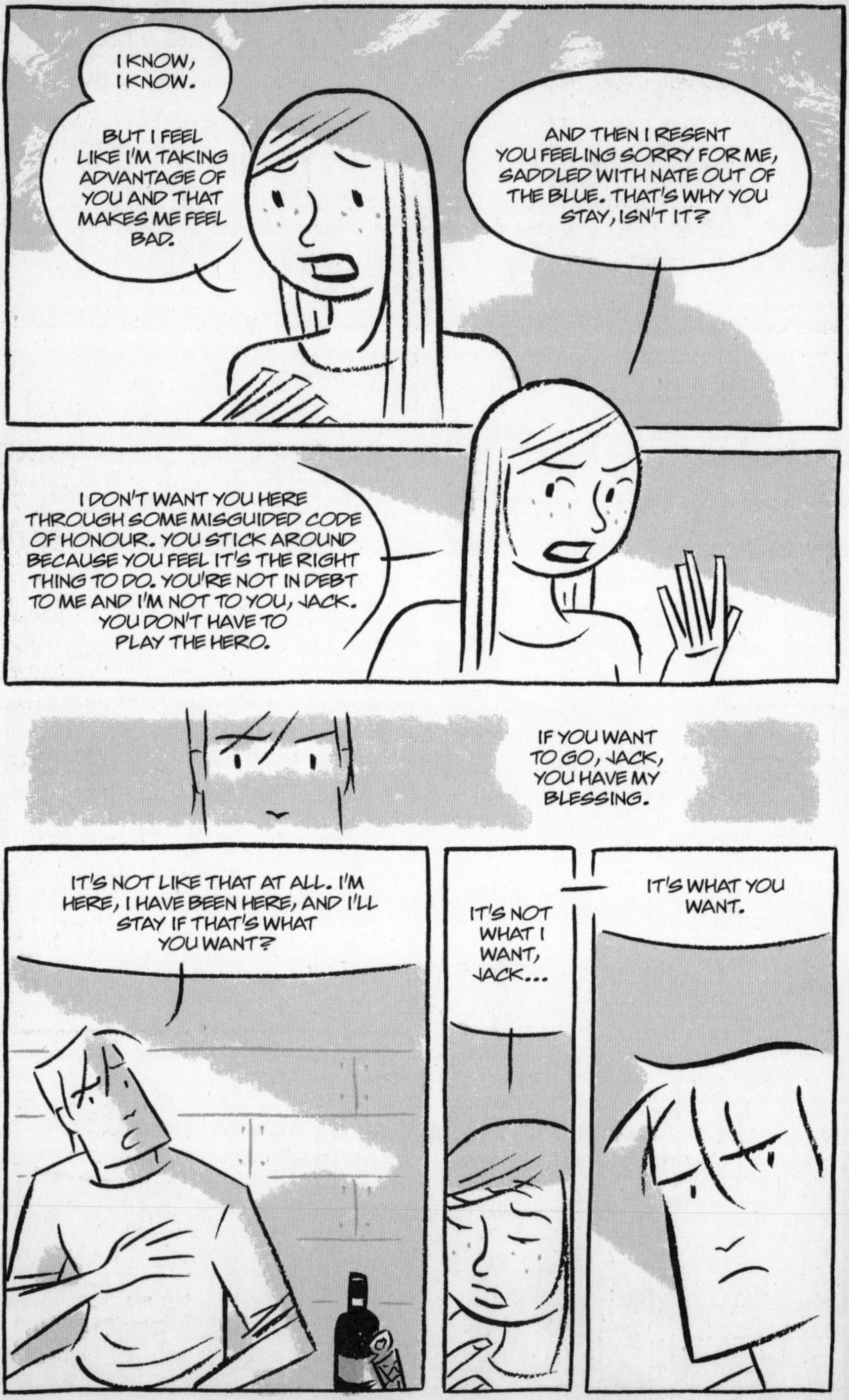
I KNOW, I KNOW.
BUT I FEEL LIKE I'M TAKING ADVANTAGE OF YOU AND THAT MAKES ME FEEL BAD.
AND THEN I RESENT YOU FEELING SORRY FOR ME, SADDLED WITH NATE OUT OF THE BLUE. THAT'S WHY YOU STAY, ISN'T IT?
I DON'T WANT YOU HERE THROUGH SOME MISGUIDED CODE OF HONOUR. YOU STICK AROUND BECAUSE YOU FEEL IT'S THE RIGHT THING TO DO. YOU'RE NOT IN DEBT TO ME AND I'M NOT TO YOU, JACK. YOU DON'T HAVE TO PLAY THE HERO.
IF YOU WANT TO GO, JACK, YOU HAVE MY BLESSING.
IT'S NOT LIKE THAT AT ALL. I'M HERE, I HAVE BEEN HERE, AND I'LL STAY IF THAT'S WHAT YOU WANT?
IT'S NOT WHAT I WANT, JACK...
IT'S WHAT YOU WANT.

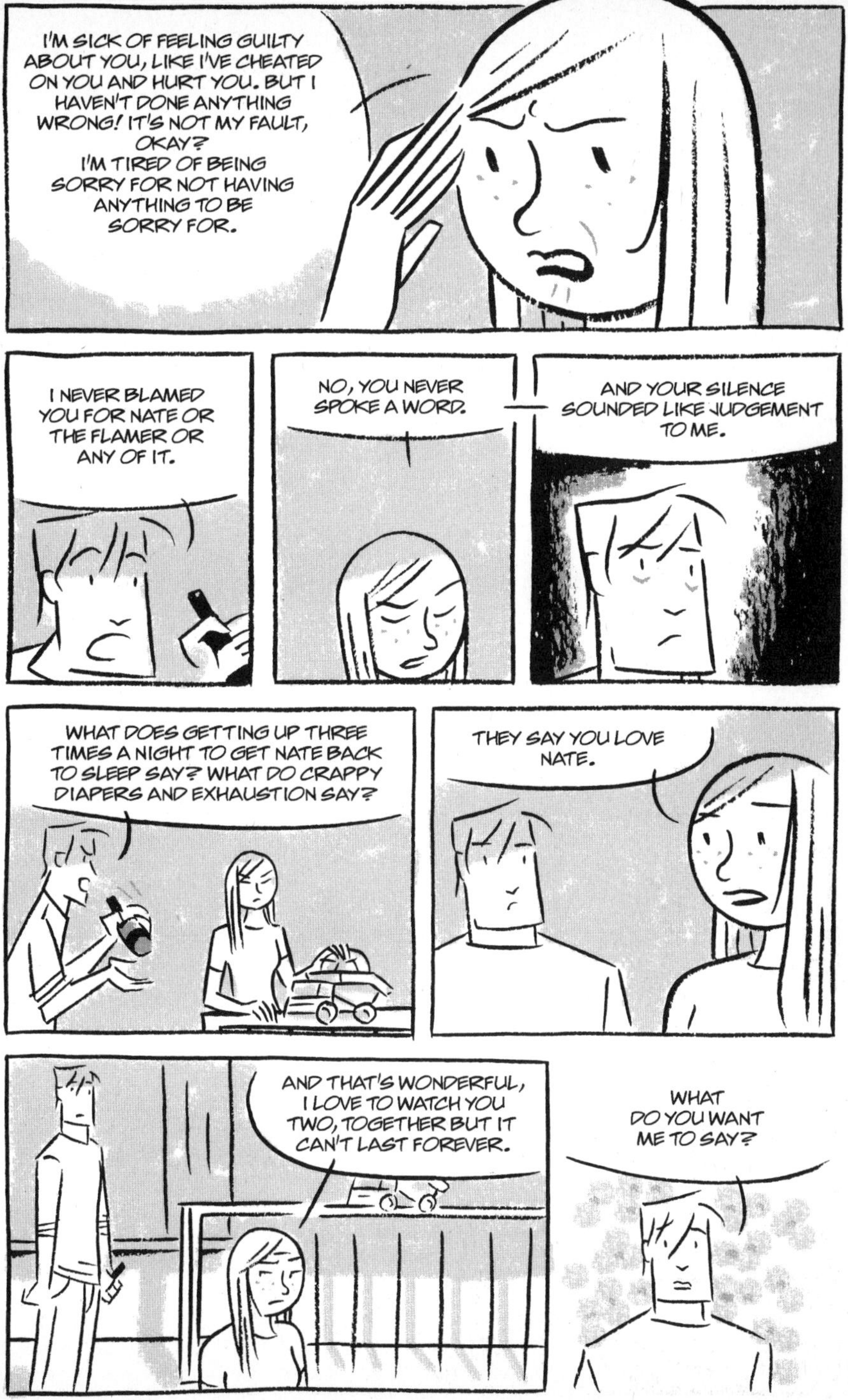
I'M SICK OF FEELING GUILTY ABOUT YOU, LIKE I'VE CHEATED ON YOU AND HURT YOU. BUT I HAVEN'T DONE ANYTHING WRONG! IT'S NOT MY FAULT, OKAY? I'M TIRED OF BEING SORRY FOR NOT HAVING ANYTHING TO BE SORRY FOR.
I NEVER BLAMED YOU FOR NATE OR THE FLAMER OR ANY OF IT.
NO, YOU NEVER SPOKE A WORD.
AND YOUR SILENCE SOUNDED LIKE JUDGEMENT TO ME.
WHAT DOES GETTING UP THREE TIMES A NIGHT TO GET NATE BACK TO SLEEP SAY? WHAT DO CRAPPY DIAPERS AND EXHAUSTION SAY?
THEY SAY YOU LOVE NATE.
AND THAT'S WONDERFUL, I LOVE TO WATCH YOU TWO, TOGETHER BUT IT CAN'T LAST FOREVER.
WHAT DO YOU WANT ME TO SAY?

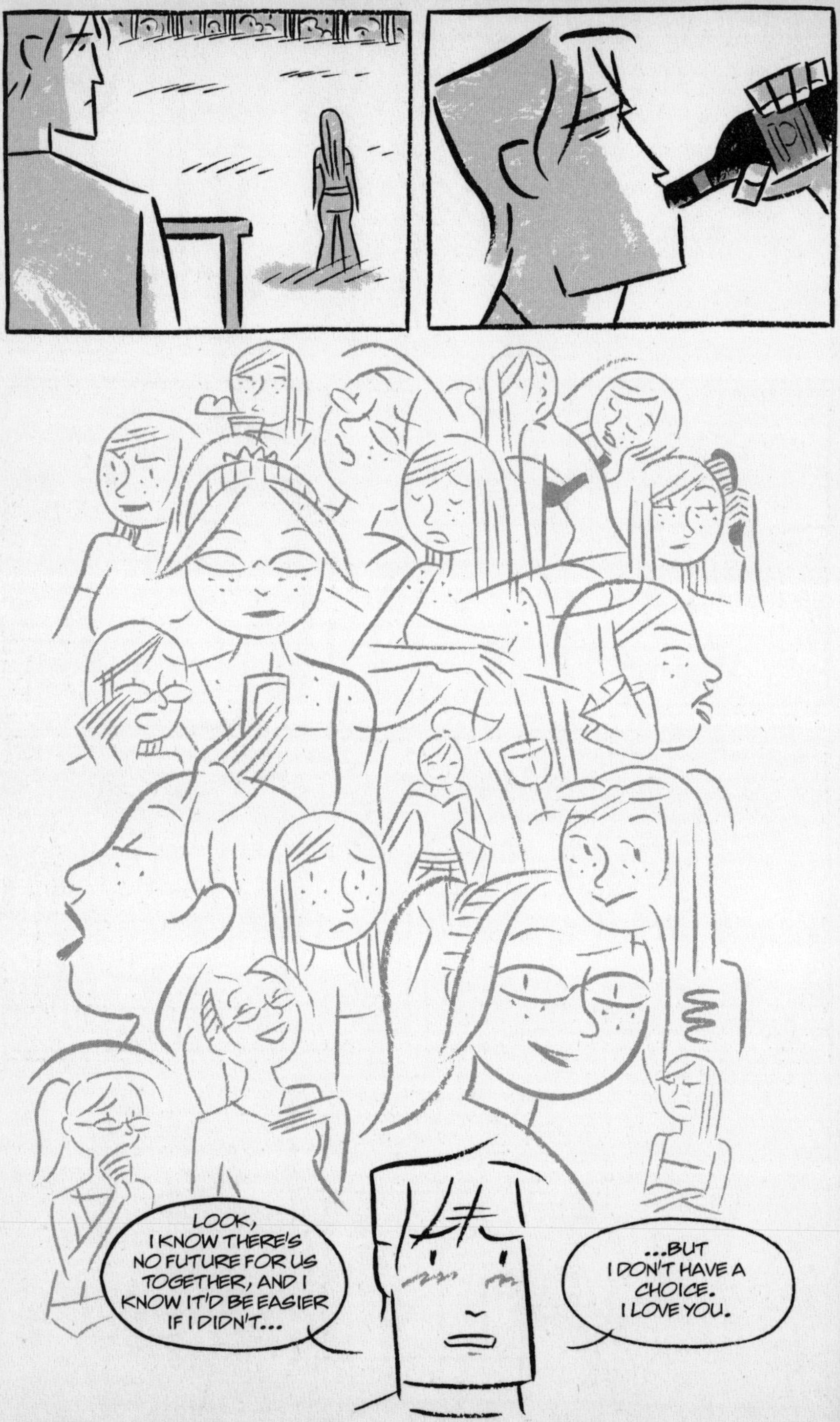
LOOK, I KNOW THERE'S NO FUTURE FOR US TOGETHER, AND I KNOW IT'D BE EASIER IF I DIDN'T...
...BUT I DON'T HAVE A CHOICE. I LOVE YOU.

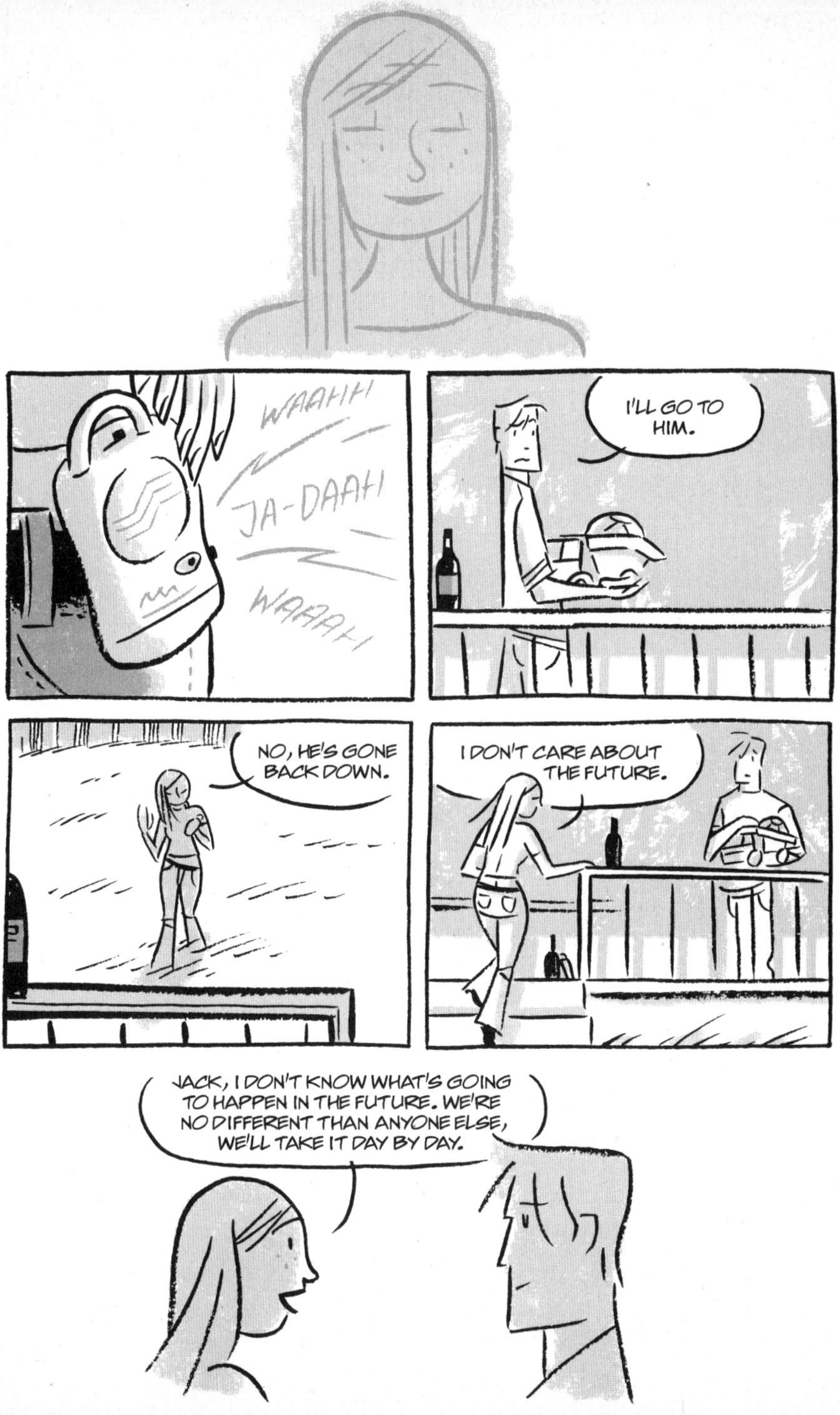
WAAHH
JA-DAAH
WAAAAH
I'LL GO TO HIM.
NO, HE'S GONE BACK DOWN.
I DON'T CARE ABOUT THE FUTURE.
JACK, I DON'T KNOW WHAT'S GOING TO HAPPEN IN THE FUTURE. WE'RE NO DIFFERENT THAN ANYONE ELSE, WE'LL TAKE IT DAY BY DAY.

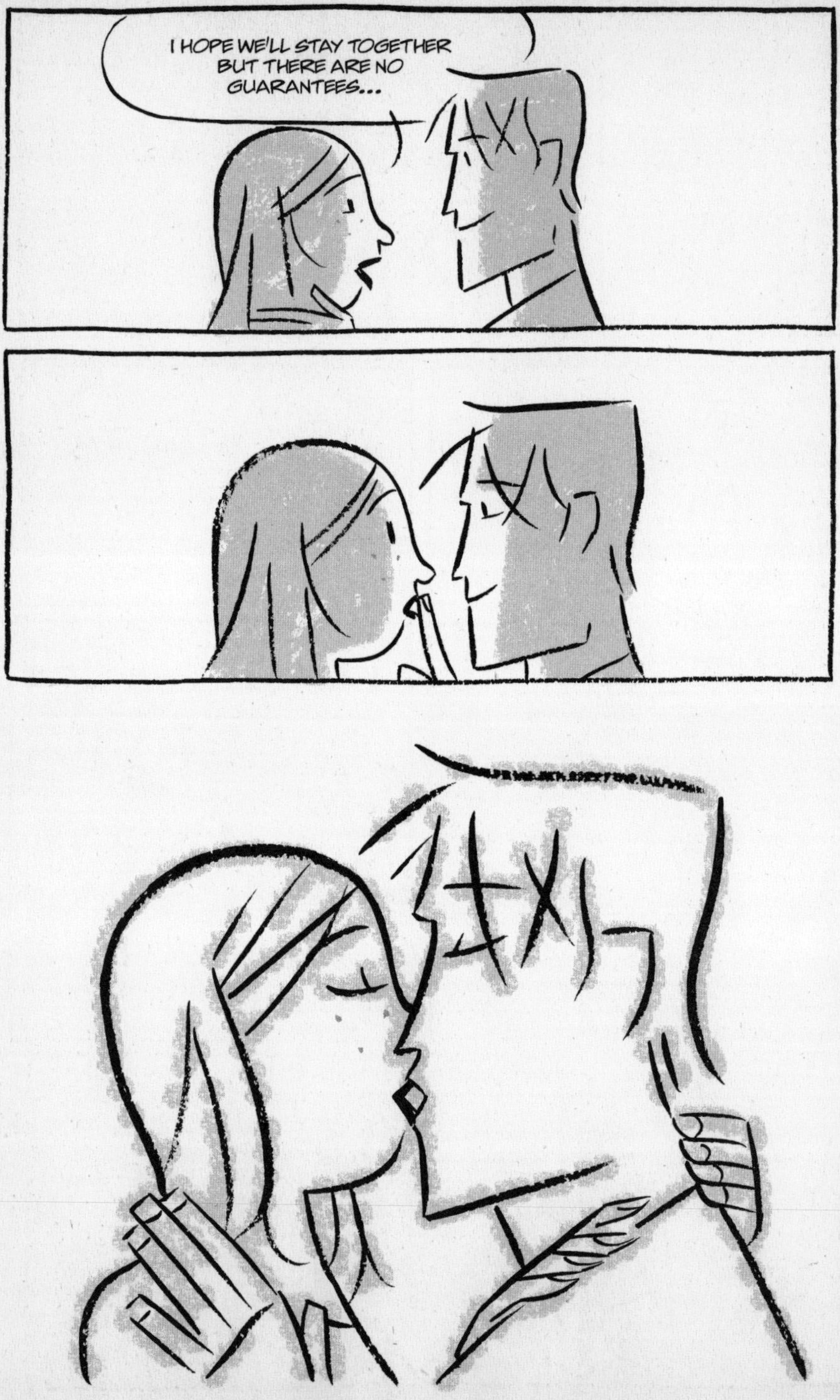
I HOPE WE'LL STAY TOGETHER BUT THERE ARE NO GUARANTEES...

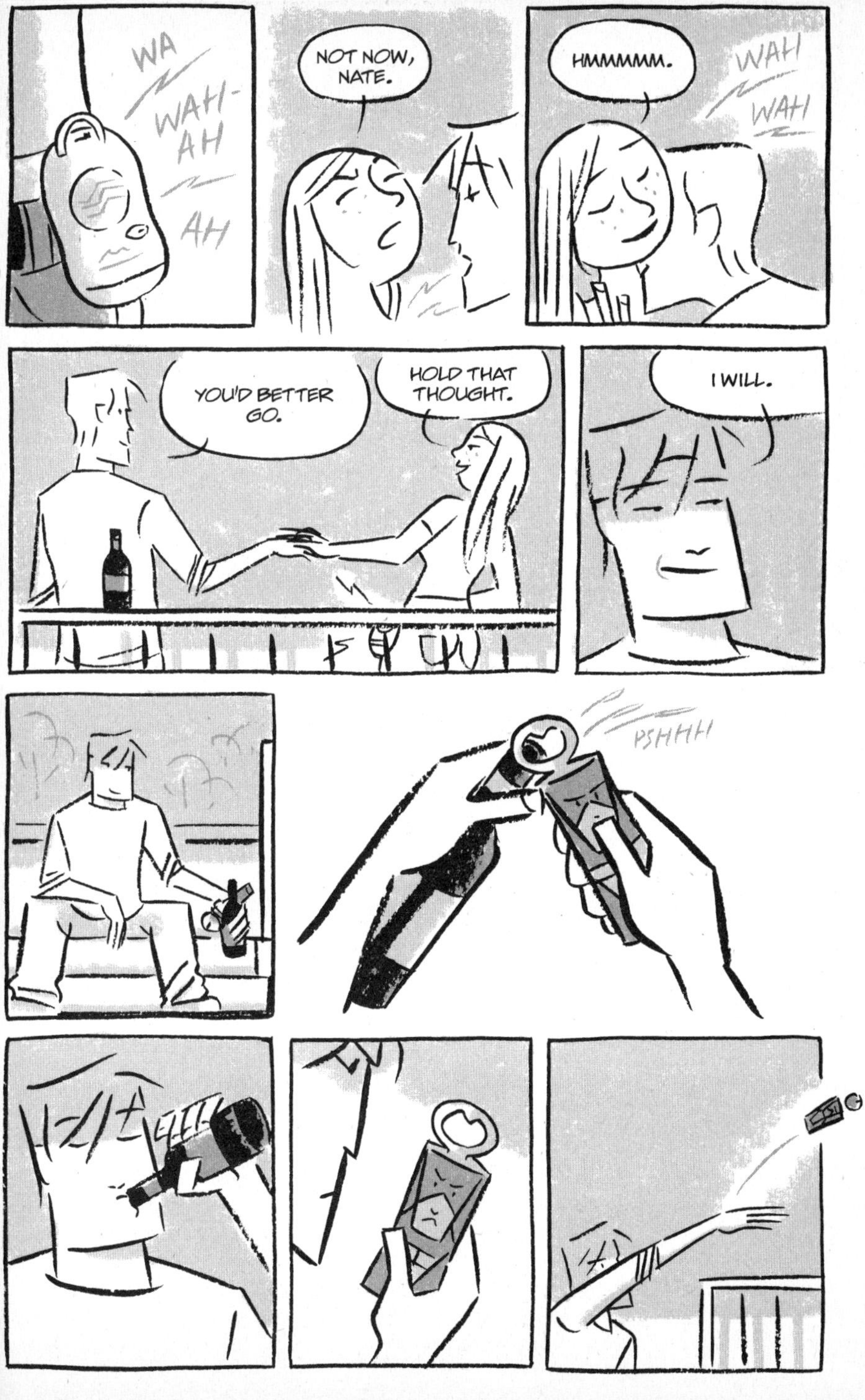
WA
WAH-AH
AH
NOT NOW, NATE.
HMMMMM.
WAH
WAH
YOU'D BETTER GO.
HOLD THAT THOUGHT.
I WILL.
PSHHH

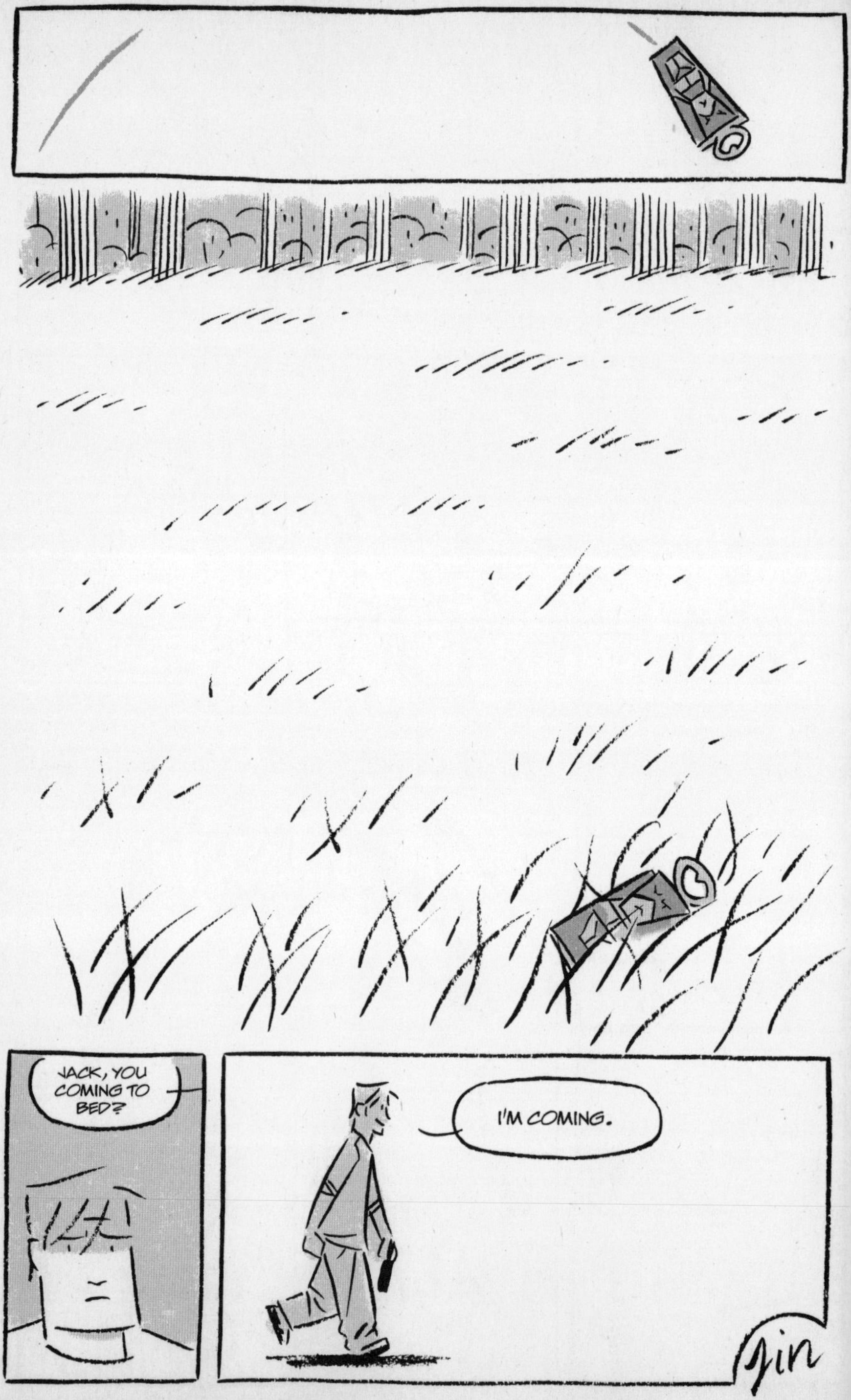
JACK, YOU COMING TO BED?
I'M COMING.
Jin

End.

LOVE FIGHTS

– An Afterword

by
Johanna Draper Carlson

Fandom is the engine driving today's comic industry. Grown men (and it's mostly men) keep reading adolescent-targeted comics for decades because they're fans of this or that superhero character or team or universe. It doesn't matter whether or not they enjoy the stories; they enjoy collecting the books that feature their hero, and completing the set, and knowing all there is to know about a favorite.

Sometime in the last decade, fandom took a turn. A new breed of fan arose, one who instead of following characters followed creators. They looked down on superhero comics, preferring instead to buy everything output from a particular British writer or hunt down obscure small press work by an artist/writer. Online communication drove this fan following, allowing creators to set up their own electronic fan clubs where they could encourage the faithful while their egos basked in the glow of adoration.

A "true fan" is someone who's always loyal to the object of their fascination. They buy everything they can. They're dependable, a solid source of income.

Either way, character or creator, too much devotion is scary. Every character's had bad stories told about her. Every creator has put out a bad comic or an artistic misfire. The more one sees inside the factories in which four-color comics are produced, the easier it is to keep a sense of proportion, to realize that neither the characters or the creators are gods. They're just like the reader, just as flawed, just as petty.

Love Fights is Andi Watson's view inside the sausage factory. His heroes face everyday problems. The Fader is trying to find a place for himself in a world that's passed him by. The Flamer's struggle is more tabloid-y but still relatable: beyond the idea of fathering an unsuspected child, he's trying to keep pleasing a fickle, ever-more-jaded audience.

Andi knows about fandom, about the love/hate relationship that comes from following a character. Nowadays, it even drives creators to work on characters that they don't own because

of a childhood love that can be fulfilled years later. Andi also knows what it's like to be on the other side of that audience, to be working on a character with devoted fans who think everything you do is wrong, to treat creation as a job instead of a drive or desire.

I came back to comics as an adult because of fandom. I was in a graduate popular culture studies program, and I was fascinated by the then-young phenomenon of online comic fandom. The border between "fan" and "professional" was already close in comics, and online communication broke through it altogether. (I also interviewed Andi for the defunct Comicology magazine, my first professional bit of real journalism, online.)

Myself, I'm not a "true fan" of anyone, character or creator. For years, my favorite comic book character was someone who'd only ever appeared in two issues, so I easily knew all there was to know about her. Then they revamped her for the modern era, and I was no longer interested.

In terms of creators, the only person whose work

Love Fights
#8

I've always enjoyed is Andi Watson. Oh, he's done the licensed project here and there I haven't cared for -- scripting *Namor* over then-Marvel head Bill Jemas' "plots", writing some early issues of *Buffy the Vampire Slayer* that were merely ok — but when it comes to his own work, I've never been disappointed. When I first encountered his work, I thought "ah, here are comics for me, not just comics made for someone else that I can enjoy around the edges."

When I first heard of *Love Fights*, I thought, "not another independent creator trying to jump on the superhero bandwagon". After actually reading the story, though, I realized that this was the culmination of everything he's done so far. *Love Fights* has the work and couple worries of *Breakfast After Noon*; *Dumped*'s exploration of the collector's mindset; the fantastic abilities and exploration of the artistic process of *Geisha*; *Slow News Day*'s newspaper setting; and like *Skeleton Key*, the audience watches the characters grow up. (Ok, I left out *Samurai Jam*. I can't figure out how to connect this up with his very early work about skateboarders.)

And all of it's done in his ever-more-refined style, combining the simplicity and easy reading of manga with an advanced design sense. The covers of *Love Fights* were the most eye-catching things on the rack because of their simplicity and symbolism, paring down story milestones to one perfect image every month.

Andi gained success with more personal stories, and for comic fans, superheroes are personal. They've lasted for more than six decades because they're potent symbols. Handled straight, they're forces of justice, allowing put-upon fans to fantasize about a world where might is used for right. Here, they're out-of-touch figures, providing potent contrast with the everyday people just trying to keep a job and find someone to spend time with. Those normal folks can't compete with the attention the jocks and celebrities get, even from those who should know better than to become starstruck.

Character introductions refer visually to older comics, from the Fader's mask resembling Gil Kane's Green Lantern to Future Feline's naming referencing a famous *Dark Knight Returns* cover. Too often, these kinds of allusions boil down to "look, we've all read the same comic books". Andi uses lots of references, but he has something more to say with them.

This is seen most obviously in the references to the Modal Multiverse Conjuncture rewriting the Flamer's memories, analogous to the many times DC and Marvel Comics have taken an eraser to their characters' histories. The explanations provided, about bubble universes and heroic sacrifices and silly story references, are all the more entertaining because they've all been used at one point or another. The more one knows, the more clever it all becomes, without leaving out the unfamiliar reader.

Glimpses of the Flamer's villains show that Andi could do more creative superhero comics than much of what's out there, if he was interested in limiting himself that way. Andi obviously knows the industry as well, with Jack reading the list of Top 300 Comic Sales to find out the book he works on isn't doing well, and the ups and downs of his career as discussed with his editor. The mechanics of comic construction, presented by someone who can do it all, ground the story in realism of the creative process. Along the way, Andi evokes thoughts of how most creators can't avoid dealing with superheroes in today's comic market.

The nature of loyalty is an issue, with Jack's artist team breaking up as the inker wants higher profile work. That also ties back to fandom, where comic buyers often identify themselves as "superhero fans" or "indy (independent) comic readers", rarely crossing lines or willing to see the similarities between the two groups.

It's particularly unfortunate for *Love Fights* that the battle lines are so firmly drawn, because a book like this, a well-done meditation on life that uses superheroes, won't be considered by either group of fans. It's not cool enough for the hardcore alternative types, and it's too realistic for the superhero escapists. The combination, though, of fantastic background with down-to-earth

emotional struggles, is the book's strength.

Jack and Nora have to deal with the mental conflict that stems from letting go of fantasies to live a more imperfect but more real life. Fans can relate to the intermittent feeling of powerlessness, where they love a character but can't control what's done to them, whether they live, die, or go mad.

If you or I lived in a world with superheroes, we'd be a lot more likely to have lives like Jack and Nora's than the Flamer's. That gives me hope, reminding me that the struggles are less colorful but more worthwhile.

Johanna Draper Carlson has been reviewing comics for over ten years at ComicsWorth Reading.com and a variety of other websites. Her short time as DC Comics' webmaster gave her her own look inside the sausage factory and a new appreciation for writers / artists and the small press.

Love Fights
#10